U0108743

From Local to Global and Back

Memoir of a Hongkonger

From Local to Global and Back

Memoir of a Hongkonger

Yue-man Yeung

The Commercial Press (H.K.) Ltd.

From Local to Global and Back: Memoir of a Hongkonger
   By Yue-man Yeung

Published by: The Commercial Press (H.K.) Ltd.
                8/F, Eastern Central Plaza, 3 Yiu Hing Road,
                Shau Kei Wan, Hong Kong
                http://www.commercialpress.com.hk

Distributed by: The SUP Publishing Logistics (H.K.) Ltd.,
                3/F, C & C Building, 36 Ting Lai Road,
                Tai Po, New Territories, Hong Kong

Printed by: C & C Offset Printing Co., Ltd.,
                14/F, C & C Building, 36 Ting Lai Road,
                Tai Po, New Territories, Hong Kong

                © The Commercial Press (H.K.) Ltd.
                First edition, First printing, November 2012

                ISBN 978 962 07 4477 8
                Printed in Hong Kong

To my parents, James Simmons, Norton Ginsburg, Prod Laquian, Rance Lee and Ma Lin, who through their counsel, decisions or actions steered my journey through life

Contents

Abbreviations and Acronyms   vii

1   Growing up in Wanchai   1
2   Home-grown Education   19
3   Beginning a Career   37
4   Graduate Studies Abroad   51
5   Embracing Southeast Asia   69
6   International Development Research Assistance   85
7   Work and Life in Ottawa   107
8   Career Peaks in Hong Kong, 1984-1990   123
9   A Long Career Climax, 1990-2004   143
10   The Twilight of a Career, 2004-2012   165
11   Consultancies   183
12   Research and Publications   199
13   Recognitions and Awards   233
14   Travels   247
15   Forty-six Magic Moments   269

Epilogue   295

Abbreviations and Acronyms

AAG	Association of American Geographers
ACU	Association of Commonwealth Universities
AAPC	Administrative and Planning Committee
ADB	Asian Development Bank
AEO	assistant education officer
ANU	Australian National University
APEC	Asia-Pacific Economic Cooperation
ASAIHL	Association of Southeast Asian Institutions of Higher Learning
ASRO	Asia Singapore Regional Office
BC	British Columbia
CAAS	Centre for Contemporary Asian Studies
CAG	Canadian Association of Geographers
CGB	Commonwealth Geographical Bureau
CPU	Central Planning Unit
CUHK, CU	Chinese University of Hong Kong
CU Press	Chinese University Press
DAP	Divisional Activity Project
ECNU	East China Normal University
EO	executive officer
ERC	Education Commission Report
FF	Ford Foundation
GCSE	General Certificate of Secondary Education
GURI	Global Urban Research Initiative
KGV	King George V
HDB	Housing and Development Board
HKCEE	Hong Kong Certificate of Education Examination
HKEA	Hong Kong Examination Authority

HKIAPS	Hong Kong Institute of Asia-Pacific Studies
HKIC	Hong Kong Ideas Centre
HKTDC	Hong Kong Trade and Development Council
HKU	Hong Kong University
HSBC	Hongkong and Shanghai Banking Corporation
ICAC	Independent Commission Against Corruption
IDRC	International Development Research Centre
IEAS	International Eurasian Academy of Sciences
IGU	International Geographical Union
ISSC	International Social Science Council
ISTAB	International Scientific and Technological Advisory Board
JP	Justice of the Peace
JUPAS	Joint University Programmes Admissions System
IT	information technology
Legco	Legislative Council
NIRA	National Institute for Research Advancement
OBE	Officer in the Most Excellent Order of the British Empire
PECC	Pacific Economic Cooperation Council
PRD	Pearl River Delta
PRC	People's Republic of China
PVC	Pro-Vice-Chancellor
RELC	Regional English Language Centre
SBS	Silver Bauhinia Star
SAR	Special Administrative Region
SARS	severe acute respiratory syndrome
SEADAG	Southeast Asia Development Advisory Group
SHKDI	Shanghai-Hong Kong Development Institute
SOAS	School of Oriental and African Studies
SPUR	Singapore Planning and Urban Research
SSB	State Statistical Bureau
SSD	Social Sciences Division

SSTC	State Scientific Technology Commission
UBC	University of British Columbia
UChicago	University of Chicago
UK	United Kingdom
UMP	Urban Management Programme
UNCHS	United Nations Centre for Human Settlements
UNCRD	United Nations Centre for Regional Development
UNCTAD	United Nations Conference on Trade and Development
UNDP	United Nations Development Programme
UNESCO	United Nations Educational Scientific and Cultural Organization
UNU	United Nations University
USA, US	United States of America
UWO, Western	University of Western Ontario
VC	Vice-Chancellor
WCS	World Conference on Science

WITH ST. BERNARD DOG SCULPTURE, WINTER FESTIVAL, UWO, 1965

NEWLY MARRIED, REPULSE BAY, HONG KONG, 1967

ACROSS THE PACIFIC OCEAN ON PRESIDENT CLEVELAND, 1967

BEFORE FLYING A HELICOPTER FROM ZAMBOANGA TO BASILAN, 1978

MY FAMILY WAS SEEN OFF AT KAI TAK AIRPORT AFTER HOME LEAVE, 1978

AT AN ACADEMIC SEMINAR IN NAIROBI, 1983

AT A CUHK CONGREGATION DINNER, 2001

ANNOUNCING THE LAUNCHING OF THE SHAW PRIZE, 2002

AT CUHK CONGREGATION WHERE CHEN SHUPENG HONOURED WITH AN HONORARY DOCTORATE, 2006

AT A TV APPEARANCE CELEBRATING THE HANDOVER, 2007

WITH TAO-MEI'S FAMILY, AUSTIN, 2007

WITH SZE-MEI'S FAMILY IN VANCOUVER, 2012

FOUR COLLEGE HEADS AT THE 2003 CUHK CONGREGATION

SOME OF MY TENNIS TROPHIES, 2009

FAMILY PORTRAIT WITH GRANDMA, 1957

1 Growing up in Wanchai

I came from a large extended family with many uncles and one aunt, presided over by my grandma. My father was the eldest son in his generation of ten, a position that came with heavy responsibilities. Life for his generation and mine revolved around a tenement flat at 377 Hennessy Road for almost half a century, from the time that it was newly constructed in the 1930s to the 1970s when it was demolished for a new development. This period was one of life and death, war and peace, and happiness and sorrow.

The tenement flat that we lived in could be considered typical tenement housing of the day in this part of Wanchai prior to the Second World War. It consisted of three residential floors, with the ground floor devoted to business. We lived on the first floor, which had a spacious verandah overlooking Hennessy Road and its tram tracks running through the middle. From the verandah one could see Tin Lok Lane, through which trams coming from the Race Course would pass and make a left turn towards Central and beyond (refer to Fig. 1.1 for the locations that are mentioned). Our abode was very well located, as most of the daily needs of life could be obtained within walking distance. The wet market was less than a block to the east on Canal Road West. Across from the market, on the main road, was a public toilet, which still exists. Male members of the family would make daily use of this facility, as the toilet provision in the flat was only of the dry bucket variety. Cooking evolved from the burning of firewood, charcoal to the use of kerosene and liquefied gas with the passage of time.

By the standards of the time when it was new, our flat was a decent place in which to live. The verandah was exceptionally large, offering multiple uses for living, playing, dining, and sleeping, with foldable

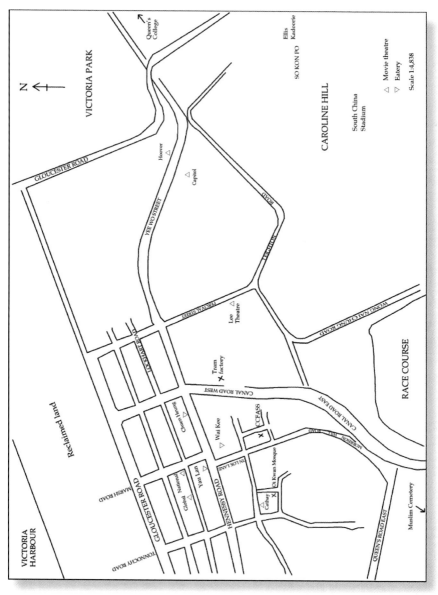

FIGURE 1.1 MY FOOTPRINTS IN WANCHAI, 1940s–1950s

beds being employed at night. In the main flat, the floor space was sufficiently extensive to be partitioned into four bedrooms, with the passageway being used for bed spaces and other uses. At the opposite end of the flat from the verandah were a toilet-cum-bathroom and a large kitchen. A cockloft was later constructed above the toilet for more accommodation. The northernmost bedroom overlooked the open courtyard of the downstairs shop house and offered a view of the National Theatre at the northwestern corner of Lockhart Road and Marsh Road. Prior to the war, when the extended family was still small, the flat had more than adequate space for normal needs. In fact, part of the space next to the verandah was rented to a Muslim Chinese herbalist, Ma Tat Ng 馬達五, who used it for public consultations until the outbreak of the Second World War. One of the bedrooms was rented to a family surnamed Mo 毛, who continued their tenancy even after the war. In the postwar period, when baby boomers added to the size of the extended family, the flat became increasingly crowded. Patience and social skills were tested when as many as thirty people eventually came to occupy the flat. The use of the bathroom and the kitchen called for understanding and give-and-take, especially during peak periods.

From the verandah of our flat, I can still recall scenes that reflected the changing times and changing fortunes of Hong Kong. The Japanese occupation left a deep impression on me of bombing, cruelty, and hunger. Allied bombs intended for the dockyard in Admiralty fell one night near the waterfront, a couple of blocks from our flat. They hit civilian targets, leading to a loss of lives. For us, they created hysteria and fear, especially among the children. I faintly recall scenes of panic, commotion, and cries of helplessness. Another indelible view from the verandah occurred on Hennessy Road itself. Early one morning, trams had to stop midway because corpses or body parts had to be removed from the tracks. They were what remained of people who had been feasted upon by German shepherds deliberately starved and let loose by

Japanese soldiers to prey on homeless street sleepers. Japanese soldiers in Hong Kong committed unspeakable crimes. I saw only some, but heard of many others during and after the war.

However, from the same verandah, there were also scenes of festivity after the war that left me with happy memories. The most impressive one, the procession celebrating the Coronation of Queen Elizabeth II, happened in 1953 and is well etched into my mind. It was an eye-opener for me. The procession was led by a dragon dance, followed for almost an hour by all kinds of trade, organizational, and other floats. Lion dances led prominently by the Luk Chi Fu 陸智夫 group rounded off the procession. The Luk martial arts group occupied the premises directly opposite our flat across Hennessy Road, on the same floor. We occasionally visited them since my cousin from the fourth uncle, Yue-chuck 汝則, had a god-son relationship with the kung fu master. All of the vantage points in our flat and other flats, in addition to streets along the way, were filled with people jostling for a good view to treasure.

In the happier postwar years the verandah bore witness to changing customs and technologies. In those days it was not unusual for people to die in their home. One day, somebody on the top floor of the flat across from us on the other side of the road, died. Elaborate but solid scaffolding was constructed in front of the verandah of that flat from the street level upward. This enabled undertakers to carry the coffin several floors down to the street. The coffin was then placed in a hearse as part of a procession with a live band in front playing funeral music. The procession would eventually have terminated at a cemetery. In contrast to this somber scene, on the second or third day of the Chinese New Year almost every shop of a certain size and importance would light a cascade of firecrackers that would shoot up twenty to thirty feet. It was a noisy and boisterous beginning of another year of thriving business. Or so it was believed, and the custom was respected by most big shops, of which there were at least two or three located across from us. This practice of letting off firecrackers was officially banned in later years for posing a fire hazard and for their harmful side effects. My eldest sister, for instance, died of meningitis developed from fright from the noise of firecrackers on a visit to relatives during the festive period.

Changing customs and technologies also saw the vanishing of some practices that used to bring convenience and fun to residents. In the early morning, daily newspapers duly rolled and tied up would be thrown onto the verandahs of flats on the first and second floors if residents had ordered them. In those early days verandahs had no windows, allowing such a method of delivery to save people the time and trouble of going up the stairs. Also, at least two to three times a week in the early evening before dinner, vendors of various kinds of snacks that could be aerially transported would come along with a flute, playing a tune to attract attention. Dried olives wrapped in paper were a popular snack. After a customer agreed to make a purchase and threw down some coins, the vendor would toss up the goods to the purchaser's floor. Normally, lower floors would not pose any difficulty but the occasional purchase from the top floor might require a couple of throws. It was entertaining to watch this kind of theatrical exchange. As traffic on the streets became heavier and as people came to prefer regular transactions, these early evening shows died a natural death. Changing technologies would render this kind of unorthodox method of purchase redundant.

The verandah could also be used for other purposes. When my sixth uncle, Ka-yin 嘉言, and seventh uncle, Ka-lam 嘉霖, married in the 1950s, their wedding banquets were held in the flat. On both occasions, more than 120 relatives and friends were invited. Two tables of guests in the verandah and another two in the flat itself were simultaneously served with a full meal. The kitchen was a beehive of activity centred on cooking and serving, with many hired hands providing support. As all of the guests could not be entertained at once, many were seated in the next flat, to which a bridge had been built using scaffolding that was erected across from the bathroom. More were seated in the best Muslim restaurant, Yau Lan 友蘭, located just across Marsh Road, only a stone's throw away. Neighbourliness was at its best on such occasions. Everybody, including children, had good food and good fun. Unfortunately, one casualty occurred in our family, arising from an unsupervised game of jumping from the stairs outside our flat. My younger brother, Yue-kuen 汝權, challenged his young friends in his usual competitive spirit:

"I can jump higher than any of you."

So he did jump from high after dinner. But, alas, it was also a jump to the end of a promising and youthful life. He was in kindergarten and two years my junior. He died from appendicitis shortly afterwards, through a misdiagnosis by a well-known paediatrician in Central. Despite my youth, that tragedy shook me to the core. I was henceforth drawn much closer to my elder brother, Yue-goke 汝谷. To this day, I still remember Yue-kuen's burial at the Muslim Cemetery only about 20 minutes' walk from home.

The loss of Yue-kuen brought shock and anguish to our family because it could have been avoided. It revealed the flippant medical practices of the time. His stomach pain lasted a week and the specialist did not even diagnose appendicitis as a problem. With hindsight, perhaps he could not or did not want to perform surgery. Many years later, when I attended secondary school, one of my best friends, Shiu Chi-keung 邵次强, confided to me that he had lost his younger brother in circumstances very similar to mine. His family had also consulted the same paediatrician! Despite his high reputation in the field, he was known to make phone calls to buy stocks or make other investment decisions while attending to patients. In later years, such unprofessional conduct would not be tolerated by the community, as channels of complaint were established.

Life in its full from cradle to grave was played out in our flat. Almost all infants were delivered by a traditional midwife in a facility located a few doors away from our flat. I recall visiting such a facility when my youngest brother, Mosa Yue-wing 汝榮, was born after the war. He was the eighth and last baby for my mother, then underwent a tubal ligation. Death could also come suddenly, as I recall the passing of a younger sister during the war. When cleaning the bedroom after her death, a dead mouse was found. Plague was a deadly disease at some point during the war.

For our extended family, life revolved closely around our belief in Islam. My generation is the eleventh descended from forebears who lived in the present area of Beijing, as detailed in the family genealogy. Our ancestor, born in 1585, was a military officer dispatched by the Imperial Court in the late Ming dynasty to Guangdong, from where he was ordered to quell an ethnic minority rebellion in Guangxi. He and his descendants put down roots in Guangdong. It was my grandfather, Yeung Jan-ting 楊賛庭, who plucked himself up from Guangzhou and moved to Hong Kong early in the twentieth century. Having married my grandmother, Sa Siu-hing 沙少卿, in Hong Kong, he served as a successful chef in a Muslim Indian company. Through grandpa, my father learned some of the Indian culinary skills that were subsequently passed on to my mother. Grandpa's ten children were born in Hong Kong, and father was the eldest. He died at a relatively young age, at about the time that father married in the mid-1930s. With grandpa's passing, my father, Yeung Tat-hing 楊達卿 (also Ka-fat 嘉發), was looked upon to provide leadership to his large family, not only because of his seniority but also by virtue of his academic prowess.

From those early days life for the family centred on the neighbourhood, with Islam clearly in the picture. Indeed, the area where we lived attracted many Muslim migrants from Guangdong. Many came to this area because of the tram factory and terminus located less than two blocks from our home. Times Square, a highly successful commercial project of recent vintage, now stands on the site. The tram factory provided a range of employment opportunities from spray painting and metal work to driving and conducting trams. A community centre (The Chinese Cultural and Fraternal Association)-cum-mosque, established in 1918, was located in Chan Tung Lane. Some decades after the war the facilities were rebuilt on the same site to their present condition. It ran a primary school, which I attended for one year in the late 1940s. The male members of our family dutifully spent every evening praying at the mosque during the month of Ramadan in the 1950s. It was a time when we were instilled with the tenets and essence of the religion. The Muslim cemetery was also close by, next to cemeteries of other religions in the Race Course area of Happy Valley. The mosque on Oi Kwan Road is now the most popular place to pray, eat, and meet these days, but it was opened only in 1981.

The month of Ramadan was a time of abstinence and fasting. For the whole day during daylight hours, we went without food and water. It was a scene to behold when all of the members of our extended family would rise in the middle of the night to have an early full meal. Some twenty members, young and old, would eat with their nuclear families. Our neighbours were at first surprised at this, but later became accustomed to our having meals at such odd hours. It was a time of togetherness and company that resides deep in my memory. The wives in the family would get up even earlier to cook full meals because whatever we ate had to last for a good 14 or more hours before we broke our fast. As far as I can recall, everybody fasted unless illness or other emergencies intervened. My brother Yue-goke and I would occasionally skip sleep after the heavy meal for fasting. We would walk to our school in So Kon Po and began playing ball games before classes began at 8 in the morning. This helped us to develop an early interest in sports. When we continued fasting in my late secondary school days in our public housing flat in North Point, I would take advantage of the time after fasting to recite pieces from the Chinese literary classics. At that time, learning famous Chinese classics by rote was promoted, as these works were required reading for the Hong Kong Certificate of Education Examination.

As the injunction to serve halal food was strictly observed by Muslims, certainly in those days, Muslim restaurants were opened in the Wanchai area. The more successful and popular ones were Yau Lan, Chuen Heung 泉香, and Wai Kee 惠記, the last-mentioned being a tai pai tong (licensed stall) still going strong even now. They all served some specialties that were popular not only with Muslims but with other people as well. Muslim Chinese cooking has certain methods of preparation that have made such food different and tastier than what one might find elsewhere. My mother's culinary skills, for example, were superior to those that could be found in most restaurants. Other Muslim Chinese restaurants opened, offering food with different regional specializations. Over time they came and went, but they were largely within walking distance from our home. The adherence to halal food also explained why my uncles' wedding banquets had to be organized in our flat, as large-scale facilities at Muslim restaurant were not available. Home was the centre of our activities, and many of our relatives and Muslim friends lived within a short distance of us. My mother's family and relatives lived only one block from us.

Life in the extended family and in my nuclear family, especially during the war, was anchored by grandma and mother, Ma Lai-wah 馬禮華, respectively, when father and fourth uncle were seeking work in the mainland. Grandma held everything together in the face of a shortage of food and work. Grandma was illiterate and yet had folk wisdom, a clear mind, and a sweet tongue. She apparently was stern to her children, as fifth uncle, Jun-hing 俊卿 (also Ka-tak 嘉德), a capable and promising young banker at the Chase Manhattan Bank following my father's footsteps, died of an injury incurred by playing the goalie in a soccer game at the Southorn Playground a few blocks from home. For fear of being reprimanded by grandma, he had kept his chest injury to himself until it was too late and he was at his deathbed. Yet grandma was most supportive, encouraging, and sweet with her grandchildren. I had the highest respect and love for her, not only for her most lifting remarks, which were tinged with Islamic flavour, over the years but also for her courage to live in her last years. She was almost blind for much of the last two decades of her life as she had missed the chance to have a cataract operation, which had been vetoed by my uncles when she was in her seventies. She passed away in 1996 at the age of 104, the oldest human being I have ever known. Until her last year she was able to distinguish all her children and grandchildren by voice without any difficulty. This was not a small feat considering the large number of people involved.

My mother, too, had received only a primary education, and yet she was as sweet and wise as a mother could be. Looking after four children with a father who was absent from Hong Kong during the war was a huge challenge. She was always optimistic and resourceful, and I was a good listener. After the war I was especially close to her, as I helped her to attend to my younger siblings before domestic help was hired. Her sweet words of encouragement were sufficient to spur me on academically and to set goals in life. Mother was able to recite from Mencius and her Cantonese folk rhymes left a most favourable impression on me and on our children. Her sudden death in Calgary in 1986 left a wound inside me that has proven difficult to heal.

Although primary schools were readily available in our neighbourhood, for the family the crucial factor with regard to education was the Sir Ellis Kadoorie School, a government school located in So Kon Po, about half an hour's walk from home. Probably because of the Jewish roots of the founder, Muslim students had a priority in being admitted, with the promise of going to Queen's College for secondary education. Father and my relatives went through this route, which was continued in my generation. Muslim Chinese students attending the school had to use Muslim names. My father's Muslim name was Yusuf Shamsuddin, with the family name coming last, Yue-goke's Muslim name is Jacob and mine, Rathman. Yue-goke and I used these Muslim names throughout our time at Ellis Kodoorie, but had them changed to Chinese names soon after we enrolled at

Queen's College. Muslim names proved to be a little too difficult and strange for teachers and students alike. Most other Muslim Chinese students followed this practice.

Father was an outstanding student in the school, winning scholarships year after year. This made him famous among Muslim Chinese families. An indication of his academic abilities was the fact that his Urdu was reputed to be on a par with that of Indian students. He was such a successful student that he won a three-year government scholarship to Queen's College, an exceptional honour and feat in those days. Unfortunately, he was only able to study half a year at the prestigious school as family circumstances required him to cut short his education to begin his career at the Chase Manhattan Bank, one of the leading banks in Hong Kong at that time. Father was an avid learner and since he did not learn Chinese at school, he decided to learn it at night school. While working, he went through this route and learned to be quite proficient in the language, as evidenced by his very respectable handwriting. This less formal education in Chinese gave him the needed skills to be appointed as an interpreter in the US Army, a job that he served with distinction in Guiyang during the war. Given this backdrop, my four-year tenure (1954-1958) at Queen's College was of the utmost importance, as I indicated in the following lines written for The Yellow Dragon (1992), the annual publication of the school:

> For me, attending Queen's carried a special meaning and a family purpose. My father, brother, cousin and many relatives and friends followed the same educational ladder of finishing at Ellis Kadoorie before entering Queen's. There was therefore a family, almost community, expectation for one to do well in this school. Soon after being a student at Queen's, the long tradition and reputation of the school was reinforced on me. I felt a sense of pride in being a member of this school and this was translated into hard work and a desire to do well

in school work and other activities.

As the unofficial head of the extended family, father instilled upon his own children from a young age the importance of love, unity, and honesty within the family. As the scholar of his generation, he was looked upon for advice and major decisions affecting the welfare of the whole family. He would show his devotion to Islam in many ways and encouraged all family members to do the same. Despite his responsibilities at work and in the family, he found time to further educational and religious causes by assuming the vice-chairmanship of the Chinese Cultural and Fraternal Association and even acted as the vice-principal of the primary school for some years. My seventh uncle told me that the latter appointment would even entail occasionally correcting the class work of pupils. His earlier success as the top student among the Muslim Chinese community made it incumbent on him to help the Muslim community. He had a keen sense of responsibility to extend help, particularly towards the family and religious causes.

With his return to Hong Kong after the war, father returned to work for the Chase Manhattan Bank in Central. Later, he changed jobs and went to work for Dairy Farm Co., Ltd. when the Bank withdrew from Hong Kong in the face of political uncertainties arising from the outbreak of the Korean War. With the savings he had brought back after working for the US Army in China during the war, father had the wherewithal to think beyond his regular job for the extended family.

As fourth uncle, Ka-fok 嘉福 had been working as a taxi driver for some years, it dawned on father to run a taxi business. That plan drew sixth uncle to the trade, with him taking the day shift and fourth uncle taking the night shift. This was well orchestrated and planned but the problem lay in obtaining taxi licenses, which in those days could not be formally transacted. Father as the buyer had to go through an informal process whereby the total amount of the purchase changed hands, with no formal papers going into his hands. This was risky and highly unsatisfactory from our point of view, but there was nothing father could do about it. I still remember that every year during the Christmas season father would prepare a box of lavish gifts, such as 24 tins of abalone, bottles of cognac, and other costly items, to be delivered to the de jure owner of the taxi. He lived only two blocks to the west of us on the same road. It was almost like a ransom payable at least once a year. This invidious relationship lasted for years. What a way to buy into the taxi business! Many years later, when taxi licenses could be purchased through a public bidding process, father succeeded in buying another taxi license. The taxi business thus became part of the extended family's economic mainstay. The licenses were sold off when my uncles retired, before their market value soared.

In partnership with some Muslim friends, father also opened a shop named Standard opposite Global Theatre on Lockhart Road. It sold paint and dry goods, including cigarettes. This was where father got into trouble, as he did not know that one needed a license to sell cigarettes. Seventh uncle was tending the shop one day when it was visited by two government inspectors. They lectured on him on the need to procure a license to sell cigarettes. Instead of paying a stiff fine for violating the law, we were offered the option of paying the inspectors off so they would turn a blind eye. A certain amount of dollars changed hands. Father settled the matter, but it was a case of blatant corruption, which was rampant before the establishment of the Independent Commission Against Corruption (ICAC) in the 1970s. While the taxi license impasse penalized de facto owners, as my father had experienced, bribing government officials was the only way to get things done. Corruption seeped into almost every aspect of life, from traffic offences, health inspections, the installation of a telephone line, and applying for a driver's license. With regard to that last activity, the worst example was told to me by a colleague of mine when I began working. Her father, a Western oil painter of some repute, had a continuing nightmare because he would not pay bribes as a matter of principle. He needed a driving license badly, as his on-site painting required him to be on sites at odd hours. He took the driving test ten times and failed. I did not follow the matter to its conclusion but it proved the folly of the system. As ordinary citizens we could do nothing about the social injustices that we encountered but to accept them.

When we lived in Wanchai a vast majority of our daily activities were carried out on foot. Schooling in Ellis Kadoorie and Queen's College entailed walking half an hour in either direction from home. I saw many changes over the years while en route to the schools. These included the levelling of Lee Yuan Hill close to Lee Theatre, which belonged to the Lee family. The work of flattening the hill using dynamite was a daily routine that took place shortly after noon, when traffic along Hennessy Road would be cordoned off. The project took a couple of years to complete. Residential and commercial developments, including the Japanese department store, Mitsukoshi, were located in the area where the hill once stood. In 2012 the whole area was redeveloped into a modern shopping complex named Hysan

AT A FAMILY OUTING IN THE NEW TERRITORIES, 1964

Place. Another large-scale project was the reclamation of part of the Victoria Harbour to build Victoria Park. Certainly with the latter, Yuegoke and I stood to benefit from the soccer pitches and other facilities, especially during our time at Queen's College.

Going to movies was a favourite pastime for me and Yuegoke, with many movie theatres offering a wide choice of Chinese and English movies. At least ten movie theatres were within walking distance of our home. The ones that we patronized most were National, Global, Oriental, and Capitol. Hoover and Lee Theatre were also our favourites, as the former offered first-run English and Chinese movies and the latter distinguished itself by having the best stage in Hong Kong designed for Cantonese operas and other large-scale performances. Only on special occasions would father take us to see a first-run English movie at King's and Queen's Theatres in Central. The time when we went to Princess Theatre (now a shopping centre owned by the Miramar Group) on Nathan Road to watch "The Greatest Show on Earth" in 1953 left a deep impression on me. That was considered an excursion, as we rarely ventured across the harbour.

Going to watch soccer matches at Caroline Hill and later at the Hong Kong Stadium in So Kon Po was a weekend family outing involving father, Yue-goke, myself, and an uncle or some combination, which carried on even to my university days. Father was a soccer fan who was a staunch supporter of South China, with the other side usually featuring the Kowloon Motor Bus team in finals. Yue-goke and I also loved the annual athletic meets or other events held in both stadiums. We tracked Hong Kong records in some athletic events. As well, we followed with keen interest basketball and ping-pong matches held in the Southorn Playground. Hong Kong ping-pong players were at the top of world rankings and mesmerized us. I followed the ascendance of Chinese ping-pong players in world championships. Yong Kwok-tuen (Rong Guotuan) 容國團, the first Chinese ping-pong player to win a world championship, in 1953, was actually from Hong Kong. Chinese ping-pong players continue to dominate world championships to this day, with Zhuang Zedong 莊則棟 winning three world championships in a row in the early 1960s.

At the risk of crossing the "political divide", I never missed the related ping-pong movies screened at Cathay Theatre. In its showings, Cathay Theatre was widely viewed, certainly by the colonial government, as oriented towards the new China. Rumour had it that the theatre had been "blacklisted". It was said that anybody watching movies there risked having their applications for government jobs rejected. This was not substantiated, but was a popular belief that did not die. The prevalence of movie theatres was a reflection of the times in Hong Kong. Seeing a movie was the main form of entertainment at a time when radio was a weak form of competition and television had not yet come on the scene. All of the movie theatres mentioned above and more in Wanchai and elsewhere have since been demolished in favour of more lucrative residential and commercial developments.

The ambit of normal life for most members of the family was clearly within the Wanchai area, involving less than half an hour of walking in three directions except to the north. Gloucester Road marked the boundary of the waterfront before reclamation in the 1970s opened up more land for road construction and other development. There was a small public pier at Tonnochy Road, where the sewage outlet emptied into the harbour, which attracted many people to engage in fishing. The middle sections of Gloucester Road and Lockhart Road were devoted to free parking on a first-come-first-served basis at a time when automobile ownership was far from common.

Father owned a Morris Minor, and on some weekends would take the family to the New Territories. A trip around the New Territories would take the greater part of a day. Such occasions usually involved a relatively large number of family members, or father's colleagues on special occasions. He would need to mobilize other vehicles for these trips. Mother would spend a couple of days preparing the food for such parties, and the specialty that everybody looked forward to the most was curry chicken. Such occasions further cemented the relationships among members of the family and father's colleagues. It gave me valuable opportunities to learn more about the more sprawling parts of rural Hong Kong. They were relatively inaccessible to most people in Hong Kong before the development of public transport infrastructure that reached different parts of the New Territories.

In the postwar period, our nuclear family had increased by three, with the birth of two brothers (David Yue-wood 汝活 and Mosa Yue-wing) and sister Farita Suk-yin 淑賢 . I am the third child in the family, and my name Yue-man 汝萬 has Muslim roots. My generational name is Yue, but Man is adopted from my Muslim name, Osman (also Rathman), given to me by an imam after my birth. Through their pronunciation, Muslim Chinese names can often be traced to religious links. We had become a family of seven. Father observed that living conditions in the flat were not conducive to studying and doing homework. By the early 1950s, Yue-goke and I had entered Queen's College and had much homework to do. Father rented a small cubicle in a flat across the road, which became our haven for study and concentration at night and at other times when we needed peace and quiet. This went on for a while until father succeeded in his application for a new public housing flat in Healthy Village at 664 King's Road in North Point in a project of the Hong Kong Housing Society.

Momentously, my family moved to live in North Point in 1956 and began our life in a setting quite different from that of Wanchai. We would begin to live in a new high-rise flat with an independent kitchen and toilet for the family, a far cry from our familiar flat in Wanchai. Socially, it was a move away from the extended family environment, although there were many occasions that would still bring us together. It was also the beginning of the progressive expansion of my activities, vision, and participation in ways far beyond the area that my feet would take me. I was leaving the familiar for a better living environment that was to open up for me many new opportunities and new chapters in my life.

WITH MY CABINET AT MAY HALL, HKU, 1962

2 Home-grown Education

Immediately after the Second World War, I began my formal education in barely adequate circumstances. Life for most people at that time could be described as materially wanting but emotionally fulfilling. After three years and eight months of Japanese occupation, the British colonial government of Hong Kong only began to pick up the pieces after Japan's unconditional surrender on 2 September 1945. As in other war-torn areas in Europe and Asia, materials of every kind were in short supply. Life was lacking in material comfort but the idea of being free and having the chance to go to school were more spiritually satisfying than anything else.

Many children missed years of education because of the war and had difficulty fitting in or catching up. These children ended up not receiving a good education and had to pursue their careers without the benefit of a normal education. I was fortunate enough to be of the right age to begin my schooling. I was enrolled, like my brother Yue-goke, in Tuen Ching Primary School, a private institution, located in tenement flats on Lockhart Road, less than a block from home. Prior to that, I had attended a year or so of kindergarten, also in the neighbourhood. It was purely Chinese education, in which the rudiments of reading and writing were taught. Apart from classrooms, administrative offices, and teachers' offices, the facilities were extremely limited. In the latter years of my enrolment in this school, I recall having to troop off in line to go to the Southorn Playground for the physical education class that was held once a week. That was the only chance that we had all week to go outdoors during school hours. Tuen Ching was, in fact, a rather good school, as some of my classmates in secondary school that I later got to know also studied in that school.

Most schools in Hong Kong at the primary level were purely

Chinese in their medium of instruction. However, English was held at a premium in the colonial administration and in the job market. Switching to an Anglo-Chinese school would come normally at the end of the primary stage or thereabouts. Anglo-Chinese schools constituted the mainstream, with all subjects taught in English apart from the Chinese language and Chinese history, which were taught in Chinese (Cantonese). Although Anglo-Chinese schools were preferred by parents and students, some families still insisted on their children being schooled in a Chinese-medium school. This led to a division of schools into two types by their language of instruction. Anglo-Chinese and Chinese schools have been operating for decades, down to this day. In my family's case, the target was the Ellis Kadoorie School, which had a policy of giving Muslim students preference in admission. As mentioned in the previous chapter, this school, followed by Queen's College, was the ladder of education favoured by Muslim Chinese in Hong Kong.

Yue-goke successfully switched from Chinese to Anglo-Chinese education in 1948, and was two years ahead of me in entering the Ellis Kadoorie School. I sat for the entrance examination in 1949 and failed to enter Class 8. This allowed me a year to study Primary 4 at the primary school run by the Chinese Cultural and Fraternity Association at Chan Tung Lane. Our class master was Mr Ma Tao-kin 馬道堅, who taught us, among other things, to recite some Chinese literary pieces. It was a good beginning but, looking back, I wish he had been more systematic, by exposing us to more works and requiring us to recite more. That year I also found the opportunity to learn some basic parts of the Koran by heart.

In the autumn of 1950, I succeeded in entering the Ellis Kadoorie School by enrolling myself in Class 9. This was my first exposure to Anglo-Chinese teaching, which was much to my liking. I did well in every subject and came third in a class of 40. One day after the examination results were released, my class master Mr Lee Wan-fei 李雲飛 spoke to me privately.

"Yue-man, you have done well in the final examination and you should skip Class 8 and go on to Class 7."

"I am not sure if I can do it," I timidly replied.

"Silly boy, if you could not succeed I would not have suggested it."

With the confidence that Mr Lee had given me, I followed what he had suggested. Mr Lee was right, because in the first term examinations in Class 7, I came fourth in the whole class. Skipping Class 8 helped me to catch up with my age group. From then on, I was about the same age as my classmates, as entering Class 9 had been an ultra-conservative move. It meant, in effect, repeating a year. My father made sure that I would not fail the second time I entered the school.

As we entered Class 6, a new education system came into practice, and our class became Form 1. However, Form 2 was far more important to me because it was to be concluded with a School Leaving and Joint Examination for government schools. Fortunately for me, our class master in Form 2 was Mr Wong Bing-leung 王炳良, a young graduate of Northcote College of Education. His way of teaching, particularly the subject of Geography, was refreshing to me. It was in his class that I developed my early interest in the subject and in drawing maps.

Ellis Kadoorie School was located in So Kon Po near the Tung Wah Hospital, in a rather quiet part of town. It was a boys' school with about eight classrooms, divided into morning and afternoon sessions. The school was special in many ways. First, the students came from diverse backgrounds, mainly from lower middle-class families. Different from most other schools, a small proportion of students originated from India, Pakistan, and the Middle East, providing an ambience for speaking English not otherwise found in most other schools in Hong Kong. Second, the school was well endowed with a large sports ground, namely two football pitches and a basketball court, with a teaching and office building in the middle. At the bottom of a hilly area, the minor staff of the school lived in a modest house with a large garden for growing vegetables. The hills behind the school were a favourite area for the braver students to explore and to collect insects and plants. There were also several large trees in the school compound, providing shade and space for students to play in. We felt close to nature. Third, being a government school Ellis Kadoorie was run on a pattern no different from that of other government schools with good teachers and facilities. It had a history going back to the pre-war years, and had links to other government primary and secondary schools. Finally, both teachers and students in the school left a deep impression on me, and I remain friends with some of them to this day. I felt a close affinity to the teachers, including the principal, Mr Tong Chong-chung 唐宗聰, who was the master of my father's class when he studied there before the war. It was an unusual and intimate kind of historical link.

The Form 2 Joint Examinations to proceed to Form 3 were organized for government school students in Ellis Kadoorie, Wan Chai, and Yaumatei. As these were all boys' schools, those who passed the examinations were admitted to Queen's College, King's College, or the newly opened Queen Elizabeth School. I was admitted to Queen's College and began a new chapter of my school life in Form 3D. There were eight classes in Form 3, with the A and B classes being reserved for students promoted from within the school. All outside students were admitted to the six classes of C to H.

I entered Queen's College in the autumn of 1954. Studying at Queen's College was a dream come true. I continued the family tradition. Father studied there on a scholarship for less than a year before the war, but had to cut short his studies to work. Yue-goke was in Form 4 when I entered Form 3. Two years later, my cousin, Yue-chuck, was also admitted. In addition, many of our Muslim Chinese friends went through the Ellis Kadoorie route to Queen's College.

A reputable school that was much bigger in size than my previous school, Queen's College provided an excellent environment for me to learn and grow up. Everything was a new experience. For example, we had morning assembly in the school once a week in the school hall. The school song, which was well composed and written, lifted our spirits every time we sang it. We had to wear a school uniform, which was not required in Ellis Kadoorie. This was one way to instill in us a sense of rules and proper behaviour as students. There was a prefect system, where higher-form students were picked to be prefects. The Head Prefect was normally a student in the Upper 6 Class, who was well versed academically and in other ways. Teachers, prefects, and students in upper forms could use the main door, whereas all other students would use the side doors to enter and exit the school. Students violating the privileged access rule would be punished by detention at the end of school hours on Fridays. Another unforgettable daily routine was the morning rounds to the classrooms made by the Principal, Mr Williamson. He was a typical English gentleman who exuded an air of importance and seriousness. All of the students, and some teachers, were awed by his presence and paid him the highest respect.

As might be expected, the deepest impression I gained from my days at Queen's College revolved around some teachers and students. Some teachers were impressive and had a strong influence on me and my learning habits, including Mr Wong Ying-ming 黃應銘 (mathematics), Mr Cross (English), E. P. Chen (English), Mr Clarke (English) and Mr Salisbury (History). Mr Wong and Mr Chen, graduates of the famous St John's University in Shanghai, spoke immaculate English and reflected the high standard of English taught at this exclusive university. For the first time, we had native speakers who taught us English as well as other subjects. Some of the teachers were very learned and prepared for higher degrees while they taught. One was Liu Chuen-ren 柳存仁, a teacher of Chinese who had come from Beijing. He later obtained his PhD from the University of London through the external route. He proceeded to make his name in

Chinese studies over many years at the Australian National University. Joseph Whitney, a Cambridge graduate, was another teacher who had a good reputation in teaching Geography. I did not study Geography under him in my four years at Queen's, which I considered a personal loss. Nevertheless, many years later the wheel of fortune brought us together far from Hong Kong. I was associated with him as we both undertook our doctoral studies under Professor Norton Ginsburg at the University of Chicago. We then became friends, rather than teacher and student. Life is never short of surprises, and people can be connected in ways beyond imagination.

What is clear from the above is that at Queen's College we had some of the best teachers, who came from China, Britain, and Hong Kong. Among the teachers from Hong Kong, the most unforgettable was Raymond Huang, the elder brother of Professor Rayson Huang, who later became the Vice-Chancellor of Hong Kong University (HKU). Mr Huang taught English and History, but what he taught did not matter because at least once a year he found an excuse to bring his violin to class. He taught us intonation in English, using his violin to produce notes as demonstration. That was his unique way of teaching oral English, which I still remember vividly after so many years.

Strange as it may sound, I did not learn much from my teachers in Geography at Queen's College. Mak Cheuk-hon 麥卓漢 was my Geography teacher for three years in a row from Form 3 and he was hardly an inspiring teacher. Our Form 6LA master, also a Geography teacher, was Mr Halliwell, who had a reputation for having an unpredictable temper and for talking off-subject in class. However, I compared notes with good friends, especially those in the same form but not in the same class, not only in Geography but in English as well. I found this to be a more effective way to learn. Self-learning began early for me when teachers did not help as much as I would have liked, at least in certain subjects.

There were many things at Queen's College that I appreciated. One that probably made the school highly successful in training generations of good students was that the atmosphere for learning was incomparable. There was a motivation to learn and to be competitive. Report cards at the end of term twice a year carried marks in every subject with one's position in class and comments by the subject teacher. The class master would make more extensive remarks on one's general progress and conduct. Good students would compare examination results, which provided the incentive to work hard and to improve. Another incentive to work hard was the fact that prizes would be awarded in every major subject in every form, in addition to scholarships for those who achieved the overall top positions. These would be presented at the annual speech day. This was an annual special and solemn occasion attended by all teachers and students of the school, with a Guest of Honour delivering a speech. I became a prize-winner in my upper years.

For a school of the size of Queen's College, with 24 classes at that time, sports facilities were woefully inadequate. There were only four basketball courts and a very small pitch used for playing football. The school hall had two badminton courts and several table-tennis tables, hardly sufficient to meet the demand. The facilities were almost always oversubscribed, but Queen's College had been traditionally good at these disciplines, winning many inter-school championships. The school also excelled in other inter-school competitions, such as in Chinese drama performances, for which the school had the advantage of having scripts written by Mr Liu Chuen-ren. Of course, there were and still are plenty of sports facilities, including swimming pools and football pitches, in Victoria Park across from the school.

One of the reasons why students had to work very hard at Queen's College in those days was the fact that the school followed a system of the survival of the fittest. A student was allowed to fail once in any one year, with a second failure resulting in expulsion from the school. The selection process was especially harsh in Form 3 – in our year only five of the eight classes were promoted to Form 4. In the upper forms the system still produced results that were pyramidal in nature, although the selection process was guided more by subjects in the science or arts stream. Form 3 was the main grade for filtering out students. This process of harsh elimination meant that many good students lost their opportunity to move on within the same school. They would find places in private schools, move on to other pursuits, and have other experiences in life. Many students in Hong Kong, not finding the schools that they wanted to attend in Hong Kong, went abroad to study and found success in another environment.

At the Hong Kong Certificate of Education Examination (HKCEE), the exit point of Form 5, Queen's College students normally performed well. Leung Song Shan 梁嵩山, who was one year my senior at Queen's College, did exceptionally well. He was the top student in Hong Kong, scoring six distinctions and four credits in 1956, providing a benchmark for academic excellence at the HKCEE. Apart from his outstanding academic ability, Leung was highly skilled in reciting English poems and won top prizes year after year at the Hong Kong School Music Festival. While studying at HKU, Leung spent a year as an exchange student in Europe. This allowed us to be in the same Diploma of Education class at HKU in 1962-63. Fortune again brought us together many years later after I returned to work in Hong Kong in 1984. As a senior education officer with the Education Department, he served in the British Commonwealth Scholarship Selection Committee to select the best Hong Kong students to study abroad. I happened to be a member of the Committee and after serving for two years was informally invited by him to serve as Chairman. As a University Registrar at that time, I had to turn down the invitation as there would be a conflict of interest were I to serve in that capacity. That was the last I heard from Leung, who soon afterwards emigrated to Australia ahead of the 1997 political jitters.

After our HKCEE in 1957, only a small class of about 20 remained to read arts subjects in Form 6LA at Queen's College. At the end of that year, only seven students qualified to move on to the Upper 6. It was obviously an unviable task to organize a class of this small size. The same situation arose in King's College and Belilios Public School. Necessity was the mother of invention. The way forward for these three government schools was for all arts students to be pooled as Form Upper 6 at Belilios. In addition, there were several students who joined from the Special Class of the Chinese schools. With students concentrated from four schools, the result was quite a sizeable class of arts students at Belilios.

For me and other boys as well, studying at Belilios in the Upper 6 was a completely new and challenging experience. As in the previous eight years I had studied in boys' schools, suddenly being thrust in the environment of a girls' school in Sheung Wan required a great deal of adjustment on my part. Moreover, travelling to and from the new school took much more time than previously. In any event, I detected a different kind of teacher-student relationship at Belilios, characterized by more interaction and attention. For me, the quality of teaching there was very good, especially in Geography, where we had three teachers that year. After all of the uncertainties and lack of continuity from the change of teachers, the last Geography teacher was a wonderful surprise. She was Mrs Yau, a Malaysian Chinese married to a Professor of Surgery at HKU. I was inspired by her, and she became a positive force in improving my interest in and understanding of the subject.

Our class did very well at the HKU Matriculation Examination in 1959. My distinction in Geography earned me a Hong Kong Government Scholarship as well as Teaching Bursaries tenable at HKU. Chau Wah-ching 鄒華正, also originally from Queen's College, shone as the top arts student in Hong Kong that year, having scored three distinctions that earned him the Shell Scholarship. Most of our class was admitted to the Arts Faculty at HKU, a creditable performance considering the fact that less than one per cent of our age cohort managed to enter HKU. The fact spoke clearly and loudly that the pooling of arts students at Belilios was a highly successful effort.

It continued for another four years before Queen's had enough arts students to start having its own arts class at the Upper 6. Our studies at Belilios marked the beginning of several years of cooperation among secondary public schools to meet the need to prepare arts students to enter HKU.

Admission to HKU in 1959 began a new and last chapter of my home-grown education. For me, it was an all-round education that provided me with the opportunity to discover and prepare myself for later stages in education and life. My time at HKU began with hostel life at May Hall, a hall of residence known for its scholastic orientation, as many scholarship students were attracted to it over the years, dating to before the Second World War. As a government scholar, I was offered a place to stay in May Hall. But to be able to actually make the move involved a personal and family struggle.

As a Muslim, my family and I were aware of the inconvenience that dietary restrictions would impose on me if I stayed at a hostel. We tried to explore with the Education Department the possibility of my staying at home. We were told that, in that case, the scholarship would be provided to the standard amount of $1,000 a year, without the payment of a living allowance (bursaries), the rationale being that hostel living and other expenses would no longer need to be paid. That was reason enough for us to choose the option of staying in residence. That decision was of the utmost importance, because I benefitted so much by learning in so many ways and by making many life-long friends. That experience has fully convinced me that university life is incomplete without staying in a hostel. The community life there would provide opportunities for learning and self-discovery not otherwise possible if one were to stay outside or at home.

In the end, I was awarded a full scholarship plus a bursary package of $3,800 per year for three years, an award that was most generous, making me quite independent financially. The highest possible award from a government scholarship plus living allowance was $4,200. Every year 20 Government Scholarships tenable at HKU were awarded for its five faculties at the first year. In those days, information about all awards, including the list of Government Scholarship awardees and the amount awarded, was publicized in the leading local newspapers. In fact, the results of the HKU Matriculation Examination and HKCEE were announced in the local newspapers in full, with the names of individual students along with their examination results and school taking up many pages. There was usually much community interest in the results, followed by theme reports and interviews. It was probably the result of a greater awareness of the importance of personal privacy and the increasingly large number of schools and students involved that this practice of freely disseminating public examination results was dropped in Hong Kong after some years.

During the time that I entered May Hall, there was a new push to change its traditional image from one of bookishness to one of all-around achievement. More specifically, efforts were made to encourage students to excel in sports and leadership. Sure enough, the year of my entry and several subsequent years saw the admission of some outstanding sportsmen. The achievements of May Hall soon created a stir in the hostel/hall community because its occupants won many inter-hall competitions. Students of May Hall garnered the most championships in the disciplines on offer to become the overall champion among all hostels in 1960-61, a feat repeated in the following two to three years. The sudden emergence of May Hall in inter-hall competitions owed much to some of the talented sportsmen who excelled in track-and-field and ball games, notably Thomas Wong, Cheung Kung-wor 張恭和, and Pang Chung 彭沖. Thomas was especially outstanding as he excelled in multiple disciplines. He and I became good friends, a connection we cherish to this day even though we live in different parts of the world. Under the able Chairmanship of Chow Wai-yin 周威炎, a brilliant physics student who was the Head Prefect in my senior year at Queen's College, we perpetuated the new atmosphere in May Hall. I served as the Honorary Secretary of the Hostel Committee under Wai-yin, 1960-61. I continued on to serve as Chairman when I was in my final year, immediately after Wai-yin completed his term. I followed his pattern of serving as Chairman when he was in his final year of study. Combining the tasks of servicing the hostel and preparing for my final examinations taught me critical ways of managing time, a habit I found extremely useful in my later career.

Serving as the leader in the hostel life of 78 students was a challenge and a most valuable opportunity that had literally been thrust upon me. I did not have the ambition to take on the role, but the person who was planning to run for the Chairmanship of May Hall was also a Geography student of my year and of the sporty type. He was an outstanding football player. He was not popular with many students and, after much persuasion by students from the other camp and following many mental struggles with myself, I acquiesced to running against him. When the election was held, I narrowly won by two votes. The result clearly showed, though, where the hearts of the electorate lay, as I had only had two weeks to prepare for the election while my opponent had been doing so for almost two years. Having taken up the challenge and won the election opened my eyes to what leadership meant and required. Apart from the issue of time management alluded to earlier, I learned to work with colleagues as a team, took initiatives where required, sharpened my public speaking ability, learned social etiquette, and learned the importance of planning ahead. All of these skills were most helpful in my pursuits later in life.

Geography was a strong and popular discipline at HKU at the time that I was enrolled there. Three of the five Government Scholarships in the Arts Faculty in my year were held by Geography students, and there were many good students in that discipline. As the only male government scholar in Geography, I was elected the Class Representative, a position I have continued to hold since my return to Hong Kong in 1984, with the responsibility of organizing class reunion activities. The many field trips that were organized by the department helped to cement friendships among students in Geography. Some were of a social nature (launch picnics), but most opened our eyes to the physical and economic geography of Hong Kong. The trips to Cape D'Aguilar (to study coastal erosion), the Pat Sin Range (geomorphology and geology), and the Shek O Golf Country Club (to measure the ground, under the direction of Mr Shepherd) ranked among the most unforgettable. For our graduate exercise, an independent field study would normally be undertaken under the supervision of a lecturer. In the year before us, plagiarism was found to be a serious problem; thus, we were assigned something different as a graduation requirement. In our graduate exercise of 1962, we were assigned the task of conducting and writing up field surveys, with the assistance of the Planning Department. Vivian Yuen and I were assigned as a team to carry out a field study in Shatin/Tai Wai. Our write-up on this endeavour was acquired by the HKU library, constituting the first of the many publications in my career.

In those years, Geography majors at HKU were also required to study geology. Geology entailed the examination in one written paper and one practical paper. Essentially, to graduate in the discipline of Geography involved examination in a total of ten papers. I spent an unusually large amount of time preparing myself for the Geology paper, because we faced a new method of examination. Dr Reiley, a new Geology lecturer from Canada, taught us with a new emphasis on the practical identification of rocks and minerals. He adopted a refreshingly new way of approaching the subject, forsaking the previous emphasis on the microscopic examination of rocks and minerals. We had plenty of room to put into practice what we learned in the classroom, given the diversified and rich geological make-up of Hong Kong. We went often to the Tolo Harbour area, as many parts of it offered what may be viewed as ready-made laboratories for study. This is the location of Hong Kong Geopark, one of 26 global geoparks in China recently designated by UNESCO. In the Geography

Department our teachers were mostly expatriates, as locals who qualified to teach were just coming on stream. The quality of teaching at HKU was uneven, but as in many subjects at this level, self-learning was something we had to do. Life-long learning began seriously at the undergraduate level.

Serving as the Chairman of May Hall made me *ipso facto* a member of the HKU Student Union Council. It provided another opportunity for me to know other student leaders at the university. On important occasions, such as the visit of a British dignitary in December 1961, namely Miss Barbara Black, I was in the receiving party of student leaders. When the Council received an invitation from the Hong Kong Federation of Students to send representatives from Hong Kong to attend the Ninth International Students' Conference held in Japan in the summer of 1962, I was elected the chief student representative from HKU. That was my first foreign trip to Japan, with a secondary trip to Taiwan, creating an interest in me to do more of the same in later years. It was my first international exposure.

The trip to Japan to attend the student conference lasted for more than a month, with ten days devoted to formal meetings and visits in Tokyo and the immediate area. In addition to Japanese students, there was a good mix of students from as far away as the USA and many countries in Asia. After the first exposure to Japan and its people in Tokyo, the students were divided into two groups to visit other parts of Honshu. One group was sent to the north, to the area in and around Sendai, and the other to Matsue and its environs in the south. I was assigned to the southern group. This division into two groups allowed us to see more parts of Japan, with the assumption that we would exchange and compare our experiences afterwards. The Hong Kong delegation consisted of a total of seven persons, with three from HKU and four from Chung Chi College, which was not yet part of the Chinese University of Hong Kong, newly established in 1963. The Hong Kong delegates got along very well with the student representatives from Taiwan, in part because of our common Chinese language and cultural background. Consequently, arrangements were made to invite us to visit Taiwan for a week on our way back to Hong Kong. We therefore left Japan from Nagasaki on a cargo liner bound for Jilong. We had a fruitful and educational visit, although our arrival was interrupted by a typhoon that struck Taipei. What started as a trip to understand Japan was extended to the beautiful island of Taiwan.

This initial trip to Japan opened my mind to the beautiful country and its people. As one who suffered so much during the Japanese occupation of Hong Kong during the war, I harboured certain antagonistic feelings towards the Japanese. The trip had the intended purpose of acquiring and deepening understanding among young people from different countries. After getting to know many young Japanese students, including a visit and overnight stay with a Japanese family in Tokyo, my ingrained hostility to the Japanese gave way to a more sympathetic understanding of the Japanese people. The young Japanese students we met and lived with were certainly peace loving, perhaps more so than their counterparts in other countries. The young Japanese saw and felt the bitter fruit of aggression. I certainly opened up my mind towards Japan and its people after the trip. I also had much to learn and admire from the Japanese society in terms of the way it was organized and in its advanced technology. Its civic-mindedness was something that really impressed me, in sharp contrast to what I understood of Chinese communities, and I regarded that as a model for many countries to learn from. As a Muslim, I also remember how uncomfortable I was when many of the meals I was served had only pork in it. It was not unusual for me to go to meals without eating meat. I began a vegetarian early!

After graduating in Geography with an honours degree, I continued to do my Diploma of Education at HKU, a contractual commitment that I had made with the Hong Kong government by accepting the offer a teaching bursary. There was the additional need to complete two years of teaching at a secondary school to satisfy the contractual requirement. After completing this diploma, my formal education in Hong Kong was complete. I was ready to enter the workforce.

The trajectory of my home-grown education from kindergarten to university occurred at a time when Hong Kong was in transition and undergoing rapid change. I began with a Chinese education at a level organized by private institutions but at a time when almost anything beneficial to pupils was welcomed. In the postwar period, families and parents welcomed anything for their children. My conversion to the Anglo-Chinese stream was smooth, with a change of designation from class to form. This change was related to the shortening of one year of studies at the university from four years to three; linked to this, secondary education was extended from six years to seven. When I entered HKU, it was clearly elitist in orientation, with only a tiny proportion of students able to enter the university. I graduated in 1962, one year before founding of The Chinese University of Hong Kong. I was thankful that the war had ended at a time when I was due to begin my formal education. I consider myself extremely fortunate to have gone through the stages of formal education smoothly, attending some of the best institutions and learning from some of the best teachers and friends.

OPENING CEREMONY OF CONFUCIAN TAI SHING SCHOOL, 1964

3 Beginning a Career

As the first person in my family to have received a university education, it was my ambition to become a secondary school teacher, with the idea of joining government service as an assistant education officer (AEO). This was almost a collective choice of the family, as father was mindful of my younger siblings, who would logically follow in my footsteps in receiving a university education.

With this career ambition set, I was quite frank to teachers and friends alike at HKU when asked about my future career plans. I had an excellent academic record, creditable experience as a student leader, and a record of active participation in academic and other activities. On what I judged to be objective criteria, I stood a good chance of being appointed to the AEO post. How wrong-headed and presumptuous I was! My application for the AEO post dragged on, as if indefinitely, without any news. I had an anxious and uneasy summer in 1963 after completing my course of studies for my Dip. Ed. I waited in vain for a positive response to my AEO application. Only much later, when waiting further for a call for an interview would not serve any purpose, did I look elsewhere. A caring former classmate from Belilios who had been admitted to be an AEO, reminded me that a new school had just opened and was looking for teachers. Luckily for me, I was admitted to Confucian Tai Shing Secondary School, a brand-new subsidized school that had opened in the Wong Tai Sin area near Kai Tak Airport. What really attracted me to this school was its Principal, Dr Irene Cheng, a retired Senior Education Officer and the fourth daughter of Sir Robert Ho Tung, a legendary figure and head of a prominent family in Hong Kong. Consequently, I began my career teaching English and Geography, with principles of educational theories and practice learned over the past year fresh in my mind. I was ready to put into practice what I had learned.

The first year of teaching and my career was very enjoyable. We had teachers of more or less the same age group, with a few who had more experience in the profession. Dr Cheng was a warm-hearted individual to her colleagues as well as pupils. Born and raised in one of the most famous families in Hong Kong, she received her university education at HKU as the first female student to graduate before the war, and her PhD in education at the University of London. She thus had impeccable family and professional credentials for us to look up to. She was able to create a culture-bound and purposeful atmosphere in the new school. She was a source of information, knowledge, and advice, and we all learned from her life experiences, scholarship, and family background. We worked hard and for a common purpose as a team under her able leadership. The school was located next to a resettlement estate, which meant that the pupils came largely from the lower strata of society. Among the teachers, a close relationship was forged no matter where we had come from, as we had all started together in this new school. I was especially close to a few teachers who began teaching at the same time, namely Ng Wing-shui 吳詠絮, Elaine Lee 李碧華, and Helen Ng 伍杏元. I saw much of Helen in the next two years, as we both left for graduate studies in Canada in 1964. She was in Toronto while I was in London, Ontario, and we had many opportunities to get together. We were in the same group of friends from HKU pursuing graduate studies in universities in southern Ontario.

During the year that I was engaged in my Dip. Ed. studies, I was attracted by a scholarship offered by the newly established East-West Center in Honolulu, tenable at the University of Hawaii. It was a scholarship that provided for a Master's degree, extendable upon good results to a doctoral programme in a choice of American universities. My chosen field of studies was volcanology – the study of volcanoes – to which I was attracted given the volcanic environment in which the Hawaiian Islands are located. Given that I had taken physical geography and geology at HKU, specializing in volcanoes as a field of studies was not beyond reach. The idea of studying volcanoes did not resonate with my father, who saw it as irrelevant to our life and family history in Hong Kong. More to the point, getting another Master's degree from an American university would not improve my chances of getting an AEO job, a target clearly in father's mind. In retrospect, father was absolutely right in advising me not to be tempted by the scholarship offer. It would have been the beginning of studies that would be fraught with too many uncertainties, not the least of which were related to my relationship with my family and my own future. The East-West Center Scholarship was offered to begin studies in September 1963, but instead of going to Hawaii, I began to teach at Confucian Tai Shing School.

With the study of physical geography not being feasible, in 1963, in the year that I began to teach, I applied for a Commonwealth Scholarship, this time with a focus on urban geography. In due time I was informed by the officer-in-charge in the Education Department, Mr Fong Nai-ching 方乃正, that of all students in different fields applying for such scholarships in Australia and Canada, I was at the top of the list. To be fair to all concerned, I was asked to pick one of two countries, so that more students would have a better chance of success. I chose Canada, as it is next to the United States and therefore would be laden with other opportunities. Indeed, events turned out as expected and I was offered a Canadian Government Scholarship to pursue a Master's degree in Geography at the University of Western Ontario (UWO) in London, Ontario. The idea of studying abroad arose from two considerations. It was a way for me to test the waters for graduate studies and to gain another qualification to strengthen my application for the AEO post. In this way, I reasoned with myself, my career could develop in either direction.

In the year that I began to teach, I came to be acquainted with a Muslim girl, Ameda, at a Muslim youth social function. She became close not only to me, but to my family and colleagues at the Confucian

Tai Shing School. We had many occasions in which to pursue common activities and interests. After close to a year of knowing Ameda and before I left for London, Ontario, to pursue graduate studies, my father made sure that we were engaged to be married. This act was viewed as a natural and formal expression of our love, which had the blessing of both families. Furthermore, from the family's point of view, this would be another guarantee that I would return to Hong Kong after my studies, although the Commonwealth Scholarship had already made that a condition.

During the first year of my career, I was juggling many things after work. Apart from dating Ameda, I was learning how to drive, taking lessons in French, taking an extra-mural course on the techniques of photography and of the darkroom, teaching at a night school a course on Advanced Level Geography for the HKU Matriculation Examination, and was applying to pursue graduate studies abroad. I was able to use my time to the full, having learned time management from my undergraduate days. It was the beginning of a life and career in which I always undertook multiple tasks and interests during the time at my disposal.

As good results in public examinations in Hong Kong were so important to determining whether a student would be able to proceed further up the academic ladder, it was common for students to enrol in night schools and seek private tuition to improve academically. During my undergraduate days at HKU, many students took private tuition or night school jobs to supplement their income and to gain experience. For many students, this was a way of supporting their university education, as scholarships were scarce and student loans had not yet been made available. Large and well-advertised tuition schools, common these days in every part of Hong Kong, were unknown in the 1960s. During my undergraduate years, I took on private tuition jobs only sparingly, as they would compete with my other commitments. Similarly, I taught in Geography in night schools on a selective and limited basis. Making choices in life was something I had to learn early.

In the autumn of 1964 I was very warmly seen off at Kai Tak Airport by a large crowd made up of members of Ameda's family and my family, and friends. I was on the same flight to Vancouver as Nae Ismail (Ma Ka-on 馬家安), my bosom Muslim friend at Queen's College, who that summer had completed his first degree in Engineering at McGill University. After a visit home to Hong Kong over the summer, he took the same flight as me back to Canada to begin his Master's degree course at the University of New Brunswick. In Vancouver, we were warmly hosted by the student office of the University of British Columbia (UBC). We stayed at the home of a UBC mathematics professor. I was highly impressed with UBC's campus and visited the Department of Geography. I recall being warmly greeted by Professor Lewis Robinson, Chairman of the Geography Department, himself a Geography graduate of UWO. We got to meet each other many times afterwards, especially in the 1990s when my daughter, Sze-mei, was studying law at UBC. Professor Robinson told me that he was an ardent ice hockey player even in his advanced years, playing in a league that included games held outside of Canada. In our first visit to Vancouver, we saw some tourist attractions and were left with very favourable memories of BC hospitality and the province's natural beauty. Then, Nae and I went our separate ways, although we both headed in the same direction eastwards to begin the next stage of our education. We indeed had much in common. We had been together from Ellis Kadoorie School to Queen's College. Life would bring us together again many years later in Ottawa, where we pursued our respective careers. We both came from devout Muslim Chinese families in Hong Kong, and our families were well acquainted with one another.

My graduate studies in Canada went very well, a subject that will be focused upon in the next chapter. During my graduate studies in London, Ontario, I did not forget my AEO ambition. When I was close to completing my Master's studies, I again applied for the

AEO post in Hong Kong, this time from overseas. After some time, I was informed that I had not succeeded in obtaining an AEO post. Moreover, the teaching post that I had left at the Confucian school was still being occupied by the incumbent. For these reasons, I had to cut short my European tour in the summer of 1966 and rush back to Hong Kong to look for a job for that autumn and beyond.

Given the little lead time that I had had in the late summer of 1966, I was only able to find a teaching position in a private school, the Tai Tung Middle School in the Mong Kok area, located in a high-rise building owned by the school. I was assigned to teach Geography and English to students in the higher forms. I found teaching English to Form 6 students rather challenging, but I took this as an opportunity to improve my English. The atmosphere among the teachers and students at this school was very different from the congeniality and warmth that I had encountered at the Confucian school, but in any event I made the best of it. The post was purely a teaching job, with few opportunities to get together with colleagues and students after working hours. Nevertheless, Edmund Fung 馮兆基 and Lee Kai-ming 李介明, teachers of History and English, respectively, later met up with me in Singapore and Hong Kong when we worked for the same university.

Being twice disappointed in not being able to penetrate the AEO barrier, I sought assistance from a senior education officer to find out what had gone wrong with my applications. He spent some time on the matter and after a few weeks invited me to his home at Tin Hau Temple Road. In the verandah of his flat, he came straight to the point:

"Yue-man, I have carried out some investigations and this is what I have found out. Apparently, the Political Branch of the government has some minor objection to your taking up a teaching job."

"What exactly did it object to? What have I done wrong?" I was impatient to find out.

"This was all I could find out, with no more details or explanations, I'm afraid," my friend concluded. This was not too enlightening, but at least it shed some light on why I had been banging my head against the wall for the past few years.

To me, the response was most unexpected because to this day I remain puzzled about what I had done that was considered politically incorrect. As I surmised, I could have been judged to be politically incorrect in going to watch ping-pong movies at Cathay Theatre. Alternatively, attending activities organized by the Chinese Literary Society at HKU might also have been seen as politically incorrect as they were organized by "leftist" students. On the other hand, my trip to Taiwan in 1962 might conceivably be branded as leaning to the right. Visiting Taiwan could also be considered as politically sensitive in those days. I am not any the wiser after all these years about why I was labelled politically problematic by the Political Branch. After all, I had a clean record before being awarded the government scholarship several years earlier. That finding was decisive in settling my career ambition once and for all. I would complete this second year of teaching to fulfil the last contractual commitment of the teaching bursaries I had accepted at HKU. I would then be free of any more binding obligation to the Hong Kong government. This also meant that the way was open for me to pursue doctoral studies as soon as possible.

Although the reason for my failure in getting an AEO post was known, I was disgruntled and felt that an injustice had been done to me. As if to test myself and the government, I applied for the post of Executive Officer (EO). I sat the written examination at, incidentally, Queen's College school hall with many applicants. The next stage was going through interviews at the government offices. At the end of the process, I was offered a job – an offer to which I did not respond for some time. I received repeated phone calls to take up the job. For me, the test of the system revealed that the only political objection was to my teaching in a government school. The offer of the EO post showed that I was still appointable in the civil service, which I had no interest whatsoever of joining after the AEO experience. I had set my mind on academic work as my career.

Indeed, when I did my Master's degree at UWO, my supervisor, Professor James Simmons, repeatedly urged me to continue my doctoral work at the University of Chicago under his former professor, Brian J. L. Berry. Professor Berry was a pioneer and leader in the Quantitative Revolution in Geography and was a prolific writer. He was one of the most famous scholars in the discipline. Only the requirement of the Commonwealth Scholarship for a holder to return to his/her place of origin and my continuing interest in the AEO job caused me to return to Hong Kong. Of course, there were also the marital vows that I had to honour. In retrospect, being denied a career of teaching in a secondary school, a career that my family and I had wanted, forced me to pursue further studies. The decision was made for me, and certainly a future in academia looked more promising and inviting than teaching in a secondary school. This is a clear case of the aptness of the Chinese saying based on the story of an old man who had lost his horse but thereby escaped calamity: a setback turns out to be a blessing in disguise. Throughout my life, I would later encounter several similar setbacks. The silver lining in the cloud would shine all the more brightly afterwards.

Although luck was not on my side in the pursuit of an AEO career, I was a lot more fortunate in applying for graduate studies. In the autumn of 1966, when my father was aware of my ambition to begin a doctoral programme at the University of Chicago, his initial reaction was lukewarm. However, knowing now that any attempt at landing an AEO post would be futile, he began to soften. His indecision later turned into a green light when the Cultural Revolution began to spill over to Macao, with serious disturbances occurring in the Taipa area. Father was highly perceptive about what might happen next to Hong Kong, and encouraged me to apply for admission to graduate schools in the United States and Canada. This timely clearance from father for me to apply to graduate schools ranks first among the most critical junctures in my life journey. I have to give the highest respect to father for clearly seeing that Hong Kong was soon likely to be rocked by political turmoil. The ensuing summer, marked by violent and long-drawn riots and confrontations, spoke eloquently of the correctness of my father's decision. Having barely sufficient time to meet the deadlines for submission, I applied to three universities. In the spring of 1967, I received offers of scholarships and/or assistantships from all three. There was no hesitation on my part to choose the University of Chicago, given its laudable reputation and all the encouragement I had received earlier to enrol there. I was offered a full University Endowment Fellowship to pursue a doctoral programme, only one of two such awards for the in-coming class of 32 students.

In the 1960s, apart from the Star Ferry riot in 1966 and the politically motivated riots in 1967, Hong Kong was faced with several critical challenges. The resolution of these ushered in a phase of development in Hong Kong that contributed to its subsequent rapid change and modernization. First, the rapid increase in the population, accelerated by an influx of illegal immigrants from the mainland due to a relaxation of border controls in the summer of 1962, had caused the water supply situation in the colony to go from bad to worse. In the summer of 1963, water rationing reached a peak of four hours every four days. Ensuring sufficient water for everybody's daily needs was a societal, family, and personal concern. In the face of this escalating water supply crisis, the government mounted an ambitious engineering project to construct a large reservoir by building a huge dam across a bay in Tolo Harbour. This involved damming a bay and emptying its sea water to form the second-largest fresh water reservoir in Hong Kong. Named Plover Cove Reservoir, it is located in the proximity of The Chinese University of Hong Kong in Shatin. Construction began in 1963 and the reservoir was completed in 1973. Indeed, the centralization of the three colleges of the university in its present site owed much to the availability of two large platforms created by flattening them to provide stones to build the gigantic dam.

The second important decision for Hong Kong was the establishment of The Chinese University of Hong Kong in 1963, to respond to the rapidly increasing demand for higher education. It was established as a university based on a federal model of three colleges, with the decision to make Chinese the medium of instruction generally regarded as bold and forward-looking.

The third epoch-making event in the 1960s was the inauguration in 1967 of TVB (Television Broadcast Group) as a free-to-air commercial broadcast station. This marked the beginning of a new medium of free-of-charge mass entertainment, which had a revolutionary impact on the quality of life and the subsequent successful development of the Hong Kong movie industry on the world stage.

The decade of the 1960s has been seen as one that prepared Hong Kong for its later rapid development. Important headway was made in developing public housing for social and economic needs, vastly expanding the education system, and rapidly developing Hong Kong's manufacturing industries. Although measured in per capita GDP Hong Kong was comparable to Peru, South Africa, and Greece, its GDP was about half of Argentina's and a third of Venezuela's. Nevertheless, Hong Kong was building itself up in many ways to prepare for its economic transformation in the following decades. The foundation for its emergence as a major economic centre began to be laid in finance, transport, manufacturing, and services. Standards of living were rising and the workforce was diligent and resourceful.

In 1964 the government signed a contract to purchase water from China's East River, an arrangement that has lasted to the present day. This essentially solved Hong Kong's water supply problem once and for all, eliminating the need to build more reservoirs. For passengers as well as vehicles, transport between Hong Kong Island and Kowloon was dependent entirely on ferries. A better link between these two main parts of the city was clearly needed. Again in the late 1960s Hong Kong prepared for a breakthrough, and the cross-harbor tunnel was opened in 1972. All in all, steady but critical developments across many spheres prepared Hong Kong for the impressive economic development that in subsequent decades earned it the sobriquet of being one of Asia's Four Little Dragons, along with Singapore, Taiwan, and South Korea.

With my admission to the University of Chicago, suddenly it was as if the world had turned around for me. Having completed two years of secondary school teaching and having discharged all of my obligations relating to the teaching bursaries, I was on the threshold of doctoral studies in one of the best universities in the world. This time when I crossed the Pacific Ocean, I was to be accompanied by my new wife, Ameda.

The summer of 1967 was a tumultuous period in Hong Kong, when the spillover from the Cultural Revolution brought societal tensions to the boiling point. There was plenty of armed conflict between leftists and the police, dragging over many months, with mounting casualties on both sides. Hardly a weekend went by without a curfew being imposed somewhere. Ameda and I were fortunate in having picked the weekend of 13 and 14 May for our wedding. The wedding banquets were held in two successive nights for Muslim and non-Muslim guests at different restaurants and locations, and our chosen weekend turned out to be the only one in that long hot summer that was free from curfews. We reasoned that we had to have been blessed by the Almighty for starting our married life without any unnecessary hassles.

Once the wedding was behind us, we prepared for our trip to Chicago. As newlyweds and with the idea of settling down somewhere in North America after my studies, we were loaded with luggage on our way to North America. Flying or taking the steamer would normally have cost approximately the same. However, considering the fact that we had thirteen pieces of luggage, we decided to take the voyage across the Pacific Ocean on the President Cleveland, as under those circumstances it would have been prohibitively expensive to travel by air. In addition, the attraction of travelling by boat was that one could see places en route and would be fed for many days. For me, it was the second time to travel on the President Cleveland, since my first foreign trip to Japan in 1962 had also been on the same steamer.

The trip from Hong Kong to San Francisco via Kobe and Honolulu took eighteen days. I left Hong Kong with a sinking feeling when our boat left via Lei Yue Mun to the east of the Victoria Harbour. I looked at Hong Kong from the harbour with a feeling that I had not had before. We did not know when we would be returning, given that we were psychologically prepared to work and live in North America after my studies. The voyage across the Pacific was exceptionally peaceful, with hardly any of the rough spells on the ocean that had put many of us on a tailspin in my earlier but shorter trip to Japan. It was for us a restful and memorable trip, with many on board also on their way to begin college studies in the United States.

The long voyage across the Pacific is still fresh in our mind. We loved the immensity of the ocean, over which we saw the sun rise and set as we had never seen it before. Meals were provided at many times of the day, and they were good. The fire drill early on in the trip brought all passengers to the top desk wearing their lifejackets. It was a sight to behold and to register in one's memory. The stopovers in Kobe and Honolulu gave me a chance to revisit Kobe, albeit only briefly. The day-stop in Honolulu enabled us to visit the Sea Life Park, with the killer whale jumping up from the water giving us a sharp sensation. Leaving the pier from Honolulu with countless strips of coloured soft paper connecting the steamer to the shore still reminds me of how different and exceptional it was to say goodbye when travelling by steamer. The old-fashioned way certainly resides deeper in one's memory.

On arriving in San Francisco for the first time, we were met by members of the Hui family, who had been known to Ameda for years as she went to school in Hong Kong with the eldest daughter of the family, Wong Hui Man-kay 黃許文琪. We were given an excellent and warm introduction to this beautiful city with the largest concentration of people of Chinese origin in the United States. Most of our luggage was put aside to be transported separately to Chicago via the Greyhound bus, which Ameda and I took after a short stay in the city by the bay. We saw the major highlights for visitors and were impressed with the hospitality extended to us.

The trip across from the west coast to Chicago went smoothly. What we passed through and saw was new and memorable to us. The bus stopped briefly in Reno, Nevada, before heading towards Salt Lake City. We had an overnight stop there to break the long trip. We did some sightseeing in that city and also viewed the nearby sights, including the Great Salt Lake. We then continued with our journey, which was unbroken except for a short stop in Omaha City. We arrived safely in Chicago the next morning, after a most enjoyable and educational trip across half of the continent, during which I had seen some special geographical landforms that were of interest to me as a geographer. We were met by Dr. Chan Sai-kit 陳世傑, my former hostel mate in May Hall, HKU and a brilliant physicist working at the University of Chicago. He took us to our apartment near the university pre-arranged by another former classmate from Hong Kong. Sai-kit lived in the same apartment building and became our closest friend in Chicago. Having arrived at our destination, we were ready to meet the challenges ahead.

ON CAMPUS AT U CHICAGO WITH AMEDA, 1968

4 Graduate Studies Abroad

After the longest flight I had ever taken, from Hong Kong to Tokyo, Vancouver, Winnipeg, and Toronto, I arrived in London, Ontario, in the fall of 1964. I was met by Ho Hon-hing 何漢興, my former classmate at Queen's College and an alumnus of HKU. It was the beginning of a period of a growing friendship and companionship over the next 20 months.

I moved into Sydenham Hall, a large residential hall for men located on the main campus, only a stone's throw from the main gate of the university on Richmond Street. The hall was divided into several blocks, each housing about 40 students. These blocks were the organizing units of the daily life of the resident students. Three meals a day were served in the cafeteria, buffet style with free seating. This was where socializing took place on a daily basis, as the students came from many parts of the world although the majority were from Ontario and other parts of Canada. I ate quite often with friends in our block but on many occasions I would eat with students from other blocks and other parts of the world. The food was generally good, and I made it a habit to drink two glasses of milk with every meal. Milk, I soon discovered, was one of the best and most affordable drinks in Canada.

The University of Western Ontario (for short, Western or UWO) truly has one of the most beautiful campuses in Canada. Its attractive buildings are constructed of sandstone and set in a wooded environment traversed by a section of the Thames River. The British influence in London, Ontario, can be seen in the many streets and geographical features with British names. Walking around the campus was never boring, with the changing seasons and their attractions and unfolding student activities fully able to enchant passersby. I was especially thrilled by the colourful maple leaves of the fall season and by scenes of freshly fallen snow, both of which provided much scope for my photographic interests.

Western is traditionally famous for its football team, the Mustangs, which regularly won inter-university competitions. During the two autumns that I spent at Western, I never allowed myself to miss the opportunity of watching the Mustangs compete on campus. The atmosphere at the football field was always electric. During the school year, large-scale and grand cultural performances were held that attracted large audiences. I still remember the live performance given by the Brothers Four, an American folk song group highly popular in those days when they were in their prime. Many years later in Hong Kong in the late 1990s I attended their concert held at the Hong Kong Convention and Exhibition Centre and listened to many of the same songs. The songs had not changed, but we all had aged. Another performance by students at Western featured Oh! Oklahoma, which left an indelible image in my mind. I was henceforth introduced to the works of Roger and Hammerstein and have seen many of their plays on stage or in movies. It was general education by example, and most enjoyable at that.

However, it was the academic exposure to the North American way of conducting graduate studies that opened my eyes. The approach was different from the one that I went through at HKU. Many field excursions were held within driving distance from London to observe different kinds of geographical phenomena, with an emphasis on physical geography. Some of these were compulsory for both undergraduate and graduate students. The first field study that I participated in, led by Professor Robert Packer and held in the late fall of 1964, was to the Bruce Peninsula, part of the Niagara Escarpment in the Georgian Bay area next to Huron Bay. After waking up in the first morning, I saw snow for the first time. It was an exhilarating and beautiful scene. The landscape was dominated by evidence of glacial erosion on limestone formations, with disappearing streams, glacial grooves, and limestone caverns. We had studied these features in textbooks in Hong Kong, but here they were living land forms for us to examine and learn about. They could be touched and were out there for us to explore.

In my remaining period at Western, similar field trips were organized to the Beaver Valley in the fall season, to Pelee Island – the southernmost point in Canada, to various urban areas in Ontario, and so on. Conducting land use and household surveys in sub-zero temperatures in small towns in Ontario was a test of endurance. I also wrote a term paper based on a field investigation into land use in the Chemical Valley between Sarnia and Port Huron near Windsor, Ontario, straddling the Canada-US border. During my stay in London, Ontario, I took full advantage of my spare time to travel to different towns and cities within driving distance, often in the company of friends who had a means of transport. These places included Owen Sound, Kitchener, Stratford, Toronto, Montreal, Quebec City, Ottawa, Hamilton, Niagara Falls, Sudbury, Windsor, Detroit, and Ann Arbor.

The graduate programme in Geography had a large enrolment and a healthy mixture of nationalities. In addition to myself from Hong Kong, students came from England, Wales, Germany, India, East Pakistan (later Bangladesh), the United States, and, two years before my arrival, from Singapore. Canadian students constituted the mainstream. The Chairman of the Department was Professor Edward Plever, an eloquent American who had been teaching Geography at Western for many years. He was especially kind to foreign students who were a long way from home. More than 20 students were enrolled in the doctoral and master's programmes.

The curriculum of the geography graduate studies programme was balanced and up-to-date. The subjects taught included statistics, urban geography, and political geography – subjects that were not taught at HKU. Foreign students had to adjust to a new physical and academic environment. I was able to embrace the academic challenges well and had Professor James Simmons as my dissertation supervisor. Also under him in a doctoral programme was my fellow

Commonwealth Scholar from Pakistan, Nazrul Islam. He found the challenges not so easy to overcome and encountered difficulties in adjusting. We worked closely together for two years, notwithstanding our varied experience and academic objectives. We had many good friends who offered to help us immerse ourselves in the Canadian way of life. The friendships we developed with Ron Welch and Wolfgang Feiguth were especially warm and lasting. After graduation, Ron had a career as cartographer at the University of Windsor. I met him there when I toured southern Ontario again in 1972 to scout for a job. Many years later, in December 2004, I hosted a lunch for Ron in the company of our wives at the Vancouver Hotel in downtown Vancouver. Again, the wheel of fortune brought us together there because our daughters were married and working in Vancouver. I also met Wolfgang again in 1981 when on International Development Research Centre (IDRC) business I visited the Department of Geography at the University of Alberta in Edmonton where he was working. It was an unexpected joy to be re-united with these old friends after many years.

My academic target was modest and focused, which was to obtain a Master's degree and return to Hong Kong to begin what I hoped would be an AEO professional career. When I was close to completing my Master's dissertation, Professor Simmons spoke privately to me one day.

"You have worked with me, Yue-man, for more than a year on your thesis, and you should be thinking about what to do next. I think you should continue with a doctoral programme under my former teacher, Professor Brian Berry, at the University of Chicago," Professor Simmons went straight to the point.

Taken slightly by surprise, I politely said, "It is very kind of you to think so positively of me and to point the way forward. But I am bound by contractual agreement to the government of Hong Kong and by marriage vows to my fiancée."

"Should you not look further than your present? You should continue your doctoral studies when you are ready and young."

Fearing that my reply to such a kind suggestion might be misinterpreted, I hastened to say: "I do very much appreciate your kind suggestion, but if circumstances change in Hong Kong after my return, I will get in touch with you." Given the situation that I was in, that was the best I could say to leave an option open for the future.

To put things in perspective, the University of Chicago was one the best universities in North America. Its Geography Department was the first one to be established on that continent, in 1903. Often rated as the best Geography Department in North America, it had on its faculty some of the shining lights in the discipline, including Brian Berry. The suggestion for me to study there was tempting, but I was not moved, having set my modest career goal and having a fiancée waiting for me in Hong Kong.

In the short term, my goal was to learn as much as possible of the North American way of life and to visit as many places as possible. During the summer of 1965, Ho Hon-hing and I decided to take two weeks off to tour the Northeastern Seaboard, ending up in New York, where New York World's Fair was to be held in Flushing Meadows Park. This site has since been redeveloped and deployed to host one of the four Grand Slam events in tennis, the US Open, every August/ September. We left London, Ontario, on 30 June and returned on 14 July. We went through the Niagara Falls area to reach New York, where we stayed for eight days. Our hosts were Chow Wai-yin 周威炎, an old and dear friend from May Hall, HKU, and his roommates, Lam Tsit-yuen 林節玄 and Wong Sheung-kai 王襄佳, who were living in an apartment close to Columbia University, where they were enrolled in doctoral programmes. Tsit-yuen and Sheung-kai also hailed from May Hall, HKU, and hence were old friends of mine. With both I was to further consolidate our friendships years later in Chicago, Berkeley, and Hong Kong during our academic and professional careers.

We visited most of the tourist sights and found New York World's Fair a completely new experience in our two days there. Some of the exhibits, like that by General Electric, were moved to Disneyland in Anaheim, California, where I visited in June 1969. We also spent two days in Washington, D.C., and were impressed with its urban planning. The presence of government and political power was keenly felt, with clusters of US government buildings and UN organizations in the heart of the city. We returned via Cleveland, Ohio, where we spent a night to break the long drive. To me, it was a most educational trip in every way. It was my first experience with long-distance driving on expressways and toll ways, a task that I shared with Hon-hing. Only a few months ago, I obtained my first driving license, practicing for a few hours before the test in Hon-hing's Volkswagen Beetle. I had already learned the basic skills of driving in Hong Kong before I left.

As the focus of my study was modest and as I had other interests at Western, I found time to pursue them. One convenience was that I was able to write my thesis in two months, leaving me with time on my hands to draft all of my maps in long hand with the right tools, often at night in the Department of Geography. I taught myself cartography, a skill that proved to be useful when, two years later at the University of Chicago, where cartography was one of five diagnostic tests in geography, I passed upon entering its graduate programme. As it turned out, my thesis entitled "The Commercial Structure of London, Ontario" was most popular with students who appreciated my base maps of the city. When I returned to Western in 1972, I was told that my thesis had been rebound three times in six years. Not a bad indication of its popularity! The other thing I did after completing the writing of my thesis was to obtain employment as a research assistant to Professor Alan K. Philbrick, a former faculty member in geography at the University of Chicago. This was a job related to his field surveys in Michigan, when he was a faculty member of geography at Eastern Michigan University in Ypsilanti before coming to Western to teach. We visited his former university in his car after a field reconnaissance in Michigan. Through this and other jobs, I earned extra dollars beyond my Canadian Commonwealth Scholarship in preparation for my grand European tour immediately after leaving London, Ontario, in May 1966.

In order to gain a wider range of living experiences, I moved out of the university residence in my second year and found a rented room in a house owned by a high school English teacher called Paul, who had originally trained as a dentist at the University of Toronto. He did not like the life of a dentist, and gave up after one year of practice. Dentistry was not his love, but he took up the professional training at his father's insistence. It was a lesson of what a parent should not do – forcibly herd a child into a university programme chosen more for its professional appeal than out of consideration of the child's interest. The house was at 249 Huron Street, only half a block from the main gate of the university. Apart from the landlord, there was an undergraduate student, Eric Boyd, another boarder from Toronto and an athlete runner. The three of us had the run of the house, and I learned the Canadian ways of life at close range not otherwise experienced in a university dormitory environment. I have fond memories of the house, its people, and its grounds frequented by squirrels in the snow-free periods. After two years, I became well used to the Canadian way of life and its approach to scholarship.

For me, studying at the University of Chicago on a full scholarship and only at the urging of my professor at Western was a God-send opportunity. The initial lukewarm but later positive support from home was another critical factor. I arrived in Chicago in mid-September of 1967 with Ameda after a long but most enjoyable trip by steamer and Greyhound coach across half the globe from Hong Kong. Once we had settled into our apartment in a mid-rise building on Kenwood Avenue between 55th and 56th Streets, I only had a few days to prepare myself to participate in a field camp at Chesterton, Indiana.

The field camp was organized for the period 21-29 September by the Department of Geography for the in-coming batch of 32 graduate students. It was an excellent way to plunge right into work and to get to know each other, with a succession of professors at hand to address us on their specialties. The students were also required to complete tasks and academic exercises in the field and to be tested on their resourcefulness. The camp was headed by Professor Gilbert White, a leading geographer in the field of resource management. The spirit at the university was one of almost zero distance between professors and students, and the professors preferred to be addressed as "Mr" regardless of their fame in their field of scholarship. What an academic environment!

The Geography Department at Chicago was at its peak when I enrolled. Established in 1903 as a separate discipline from geology, it was the first geography department in North America. Its establishment almost coincided with the inaugural meeting of the founding of the Association of American Geographers (AAG) in 1904, held in Philadelphia under the initiative of William Morris Davis. Over the years, the department had trained generations of geographers, who had established themselves academically and set up their own departments in different parts of the country and beyond. The department also had a string of distinguished geographers who did much to advance the academic status of the discipline. The following are but a few of the early illustrious geographers at UChicago who were influential and left their mark: Derwent S. Whittlesey, Charles C. Colby, and Robert S. Platt. Although the Chicago School of Thought was largely associated with urban sociology through the publications and thoughts of Ernest Burgess and Robert Park, geography at UChicago rapidly established itself with its distinctive brand of scholarship. The emphasis on field investigations was characteristic of Robert Platt's contributions, a tradition that was followed to the time that I was a graduate student there. The spread of the Chicago influence in geography was typified by the Berkeley School of Cultural Geography through the seminal work of Carl Sauer, a UChicago graduate. From day one, it was impressed on new graduate students that we had a mission to accomplish – that of carrying the torch of excellence in geography at UChicago forward.

The status of geography at UChicago and in the latest national and international settings was systematically reviewed and interrogated in two compulsory graduate courses, Geography 300/301. All faculty members of the department would take turns introducing and speaking about their sub-field. At my time in UChicago, the geography faculty could simply be depicted as a who's who in the discipline. Each professor was arguably the best, or among the best, in their field. Notable among the faculty were Chauncy Harris (Chair, urban, Soviet), Gilbert White (resources, hazards), Brian J. L. Berry (urban, quantitative), Harold Mayer (urban planning), Norton Ginsburg (Asia, atlas), Karl Butzer (physical, paleo-geography), Marvin Mikesell (cultural), Wesley Calef (geographical thought), and William Pattison (education). Peter Goheen (urban, Canada) joined in my second year. Paul Wheatley, an eminent geographer of British origin, was also appointed, but he was affiliated more with sociology than geography.

The university was run on a quarter system, meaning that there were four quarters in the academic year, with ten weeks in each quarter. High standards were set throughout the faculties. As our in-coming class was large, there was a continuous process of sorting out students who were not of the right material and encouraging them to move on. The field camp, 300/301, diagnostic examinations, and other requirements in part served this purpose. The last mentioned consisted of five tests that all new graduate students had to take to ensure that they met certain requirements in geography, as they might have come from different disciplines. The five tests included cartography, climatology, and physical, cultural, and economic geography. I passed in all five, but was advised to take economic geography, which was taught by Brian Berry, a young and popular faculty member of rising eminence.

Being spared the need to take courses in geography meant that I could take full advantage of UChicago's strengths in the social sciences. I took courses in Statistics, Sociology, Political Science, Economics, and Anthropology. They opened my eyes to the relevance and importance of the cognate disciplines to geography and greatly assisted my work in later years, after I left academia to become involved in international development work for some years.

The campus of the university was located in Hyde Park, next to the black neighbourhood of Woodlawn to the south, separated by a wide stretch of rolling fields called the Midway, a part of the site of the Chicago Exposition held in 1893. For this reason, the neighbourhood in which the university was located was not at all safe, especially after dark. During our stay in Chicago, a couple of graduate students a year were mugged and killed in the neighbourhood on their way home after dark. We were careful when, usually for social reasons, we had to leave home at night. However, our apartment was very conveniently located, only a short distance from campus and the lakeshore, where a train would take us right to downtown Chicago. The neighbourhood was architecturally delightful and well served with the necessities of life.

Chicago, the second largest American city and the transport hub of the continent, offered much for geographers to learn and analyze. We went on many field trips in and around Chicago led by the faculty, especially Harold Mayer, who appeared to be encyclopedic in his knowledge and details of the geographical evolution of the city. He had worked for a decade as an urban planner in Chicago before joining the geography faculty in the late 1940s. His field excursions in central Chicago and the metropolitan waters still rank with me as models of excellence that defy replication. The "Windy City", a name associated with Chicago, had much to offer as a city. It was a pioneer in high-rise architecture, boasted a lakeshore development as picturesque as it was functional, the nation's largest commodity exchange, the largest American convention and exhibition facility at McCommick Place, a downtown characterized by the loop of the overhead train and many cultural symbols, and a Navy Pier that bears witness to the enduring visions of the brilliant Chicago architect, Daniel Burnham. Chicago as a thriving and multi-dimensional city had much to offer to the tourist and visitor, with its range of museums, art galleries, an orchestra, cultural and theatrical shows, and hotels and restaurants.

Consequently, during our short stay in Chicago we were very often visited by friends and relatives. We took them around the tourist sites – downtown, the Planetarium, the Aquarium, Meigs Field, the Lakeshore, museums, Chinatown (including the Bihai temple in Evanston), and Northwestern University. We had our favourite restaurants in Chinatown and in the old town. In addition, our social circle gradually extended from our fellow graduate students and their spouses in geography to people in other disciplines. Within geography, our close contacts in our class included David and Judy Meyer, Joshua and Hannah Cohen, Geoff and Didas Cliff-Phillips, and Rud and Connie Platt. The best friends that we had in Chicago had to include those coming from Hong Kong and Taiwan, namely Chan Sai-kit 陳世傑, Peter and Grace Lam 林煜明, Marian Ming 閔錫慶, Bosco Ngai 倪嘉陵, and Lam Tsit-yuen 林節玄. Marian, who studied law and was of Muslim and Taiwanese origin, was our link to the Muslim community. We became and remain close life-long friends, especially after her marriage to Kung Chin-man 龔展民, a specialist doctor of Hong Kong origin. She has been running a most successful law practice in downtown Chicago since her graduation.

Life at Chicago was for us a good balance between work and social networks. There was never a dull moment and we enjoyed life to the full, with so much to learn and to look forward to. Apart from the tight networks formed by friends and colleagues, the faculty had the habit of inviting students to their homes for socializing. I can still recall social functions held in the homes of Gilbert White, Chauncy Harris, and Harold Mayer. Years later, I was a repeat guest of Norton Ginsburg in his well-appointed apartment, which had an elegant Asian ambience. Even Lloyd Rudolph, with his wife Susan, entertained his class in political science, which I took for credit. They hosted us in their spacious and comfortable home at the end of the quarter after the examinations. Maintaining a close professor-student relationship was a tradition at UChicago.

Although our stay in Chicago was relatively short, I tried to maximize every opportunity to learn beyond my immediate graduate programme. Keenly aware of the importance of reading more speedily, especially in view of the arduous reading requirements in every course, I took and completed a speed-reading course over several weekends at the Reading Dynamics Institute located downtown. The course fee was high, but I at least learned the rudiments of speed reading. Beyond what I could learn in the graduate programme, I also worked for two months in the summer of 1968 as Brian Berry's research assistant at the Center for Urban Studies in his project on the City Classification Handbook. I was responsible for handling his data analysis in that project, devoting 20 hours a week on it. It was a practical way of learning how research was undertaken and improving my quantitative skills.

Married life with Ameda was off to a good start. I was on a full scholarship but supporting a spouse without any other income was hard on the budget. We explored job opportunities for her at the university, several of which looked promising, including working in the university's Far Eastern Library, headed by Professor Qian Zhuanxun 錢傳訓. However, she would be required to apply for a J1 visa, tenable for only 18 months, after which she would have to leave the country. We did not want Ameda to take this option of no return. However, in April 1968 Ameda managed to find a job with the Center for Research Libraries, an independent national institution but located almost within campus. This provided her with an opportunity to expand her experience and understanding of American life. It also helped us with our finances, allowing us to participate fully in social activities of diverse kinds. During our 2009 official visit to the UChicago campus after many years, our itinerary included a visit to the new and impressive premises of the Center for Research Libraries in the vicinity of the Law School. Nostalgic thoughts of her days at the Center came back to Ameda during our visit.

One of our most unforgettable experiences was of the six-day summer break that we took with Peter and Grace Lam in a fishing-cum-sightseeing trip to Wisconsin-Michigan. Peter and I shared the task of driving his car. Our trip focused on the Wisconsin Dells and the Tahquamenon Falls, and we visited many small towns in the area, including Preshtigo, Escanaba, Newburg, Clare, and Ludington. It was August 1968 when we took this trip away from Chicago, the scene of the stormy Democratic Convention that saw Hubert Humphrey emerge as the Democratic Party's candidate for US president. We saw on the TV in our motel room in Michigan evidence of police brutality associated with student demonstrations in downtown Chicago. Senator Humphrey eventually lost the presidential bid to Richard Nixon. The year 1968 was a politically turbulent one for the United States. Both Dr Martin Luther King, Jr and presidential candidate Robert Kennedy were assassinated in April and July, respectively, of that year. The political unease spilled over into the New Year. Even the Administrative Building of the University of Chicago was taken over by radical students for two weeks from 30 January to 14 February 1969. The trigger for this student activism was the university's decision not to rehire Marlene Dixon, an assistant professor in sociology. Only patience and efforts from many sides finally led the students to see reason and withdraw. I can still remember a scene in which the world-renowned and eloquent economics professor, Milton Friedman, spoke to students via a TV interview in the lobby of Rosenwald Hall where the Department of Geography was located. All of these incidents provided real and close-up examples of American politics that left a deep impression on us.

As all this political turmoil swirled around the campus and the country, I was determined to complete my studies as soon as I could. I went to UChicago fully prepared mentally to pursue doctoral studies on Chinese cities. However, after one year of course work and interacting with professors like Tsou Tang 鄒讜, Ho Ping Ti 何炳棣 and others, in addition to Norton Ginsburg, the conclusion was obvious. After taking a course in the spring of 1968 on Advanced Reading on China with Norton Ginsburg held for me and another graduate student, Norton had a private session with me one day when the quarter session was about to conclude.

"Yue-man, you have been here for about a year and have taken courses in this and other Departments under very knowledgeable professors. The prospect of undertaking a doctoral study on Chinese cities is dim. What is your thinking by now?"

I was taken aback by this line of questioning, but realized that sooner or later some hard decisions would have to be made. Choosing a dissertation topic was uppermost in the mind of every new graduate student.

"Indeed, I have taken courses or had discussions with China experts in the faculty. I even prepared a term paper on Chinese cities for Professor Tsou Tang in the course that I took with him. But what you have said to me before is true. Without the opportunity to undertake field work in China, any study of contemporary Chinese cities is out of the question," I explained.

"As long as the Cultural Revolution is still affecting large parts of the country, any kind of social science research on contemporary China is next to impossible," Professor Ginsburg insisted.

He went on, "Perhaps you should take a course on Southeast Asia with me this summer. It will open your mind to another part of Asia, and who knows, perhaps something will come out of it."

This change of direction for my doctoral work took a while to sink in. It was at first disappointing but, in retrospect, it was a tactical move for the best. After taking the summer course on Southeast Asia and avariciously soaking up the literature on Southeast Asia in the university's excellent library, I was ready to move on. With the new quarter that started in the fall of 1968, a happy turn of events occurred. Norton Ginsburg through his friend, Hamzah Sendut, Professor and Chairman of the Department of Geography at the University of Malaya in Kuala Lumpur, secured for me a teaching position in his department. I was delighted and quickly prepared a dissertation proposal on the Ecology of Malaysian Cities. The target was in sight and I was working towards it.

However, the offer of a university teaching job in Kuala Lumpur soon evaporated when Professor Sendut had to leave Kuala Lumpur for Penang to take up the position of the founding Vice-Chancellor of Universiti Sains Malaysia. I had to accept this sudden turn of events as something that I could not do anything about. On a trip soon afterwards to Singapore, Norton Ginsburg visited the University of Singapore. Professor Ooi Jin Bee 黃仁美, Professor and Chair of Geography, asked Ginsburg if he might have a student ready to take up a teaching position in economic geography. After the exchange of a few letters, I was offered a job as assistant lecturer in February 1969. The next priority was for me to prepare still another dissertation proposal on Singapore. I prepared one focused on public housing and the marketing system in Singapore. I defended it successfully in an informal oral examination held in the evening at the Eagle, a favourite place that we geography students used for the oral defense of doctoral proposals among peers. It was a ritual I had attended several times before my turn came. It was a mock oral examination that was found to be very effective and helpful to graduate students. The other place for a similar but less formal get-together was a pub called Jimmy's.

The next hurdle I had to scale was to take the Field Problem. This was a requirement that was dreaded by some graduate students on their way to completing the doctoral requirements in geography. When one was ready, the student had to inform the department. On an agreed Monday morning at 9:00 a.m., a field problem was picked up at the Chairman's office. Two weeks later at the same time, the completed field problem report had to be handed in. In my case, I took my field problem in April 1969, and the topic I was given was The Decline of Central Michigan City, a city located about two hours' drive from Chicago in Michigan. It was indeed a challenging problem; first, logistically, I did not own a car and, second, it happened to snow heavily when I did my field work in that city. In any event, I did research at the university library before I left and did some more at the public library after I arrived in Michigan City. I rented a room in the central city area, arranged my appointments, and carried out a sample survey with a prepared questionnaire. When the field report of almost 70 pages was completed and examined, I was told that I had passed without any problem. I breathed a sigh of relief and was ready to leave the university with all requirements for the doctoral degree fulfilled except for the dissertation.

As I reflect on my days at UChicago, I counted my blessings in joining a university that had the philosophy of not holding any student back in his or her doctoral programme by some stringent time requirements. The minimum requirement that could not be changed was six quarters in residence. Certainly in Geography, when one was considered ready for graduation after meeting all assessments and requirements, the department would expedite one's completion of studies to graduate. In my case, I completed all requirements within seven quarters, including the summer quarter between two academic years. The length of study was something grounded by a philosophy and so was the doctoral dissertation. We were encouraged to think from day one that the doctoral dissertation is a test of independent research, not something you would do only once in a lifetime and then forget about it. Reference was made to some students who regarded their doctoral dissertation as their most important and only study in life. After pouring all of their energies and efforts in it, they would be deterred from doing more and, indeed, became disinterested in research. We were cautioned to develop the right attitude towards a doctoral dissertation. It is but an academic exercise, but of course one to which high requirements and standards are attached. It should be the beginning of a process of research that will last the whole of one's life and career.

Ameda and I left Chicago on 30 May 1969 and were seen off at O'Hare by Chan Sai-kit, Peter and Grace Lam, as well as my brother David, who came all the way from Wisconsin. That was the last time we saw Peter and Grace, and that remains our biggest social regret as we were truly close friends when we were in Chicago. All attempts to reach them since have drawn a blank. We stopped by Los Angles to visit Disneyland for the first time. It was another welcome dimension of the west coast after a visit to San Francisco two years earlier. After another stop in Tokyo to revisit old friends, we returned home to Hong Kong and were delighted to meet our families. Our parents arranged a tour to Macao with us, as a gesture of congratulations to me for having completed my doctoral studies so speedily. It was an achievement of which my parents were immensely proud.

Indeed, the twenty months each that I spent at Western and UChicago were the best investment I have ever made in my life to prepare myself for my future career. I met some of the best professors and students at both universities, who would later become life-long and caring friends. My supervisors, James Simmons and Norton Ginsburg, helpfully and thoughtfully steered my study trajectory towards a timely completion. Studying at two different universities in two countries enabled me to learn more about North America and widened my horizons in many ways. I had to thank my lucky star for having to start my teaching career at the tertiary level in Singapore instead of Kuala Lumpur. My career could have unfolded very differently had I started at the latter. That I was to start teaching in Singapore rather than Kuala Lumpur was one of the most important turning points in my career and life. As has happened several times in my career, an initial disappointment was succeeded by much better things than I could have anticipated. The dramatic turn of events made me believe that the Almighty had to have helped me to begin my university career in the best possible way.

A YOUNG FAMILY AT THE UNIVERSITY RESIDENCE IN
LINDEN DRIVE, SINGAPORE, 1973

5 Embracing Southeast Asia

Prior to arriving in Singapore on 9 June 1969 to begin a new career in university teaching, my only exposure to Southeast Asia was a brief stopover in Bangkok in 1966 after a grand European tour on my way back to Hong Kong. Beginning a career at the University of Singapore (renamed the National University of Singapore in 1980 after merging with Nanyang University) was infinitely superior to doing so in Kuala Lumpur, in terms of what I would have been able to accomplish at the start. Less than a month earlier, on 13 May 1969, Kuala Lumpur had been convulsed by an unprecedented and calamitous racial riot leading to horrendous casualties and followed by the implementation of radical policies. Had I started working at the university in Kuala Lumpur, I would have had to learn Bahasa Malaysia to teach and to undertake field work for my doctoral dissertation, and possibly confronted insurmountable obstacles. I could only thank my lucky star for this turn of events.

Ameda and I were warmly met at the Paya Lebar Airport by Dr Lee Yong Leng 李永能, Chairman of the Department of Geography at the university, and settled in the university mess hall near its south gate. My first lecture on Economic Geography, I was told, was to be given a week later. We were to stay in our temporary accommodations for 13 days until our flat in Linden Drive was ready for us to move in. The staff accommodation in Linden Drive was brand new, most comfortable and spacious, and was located off Dunean Road about half a mile from the university campus on Bukit Timah Road. We were allotted a flat on the first floor, in the first of four low-rise blocks. It would be our proud home for the next six years, with many happy memories for us to treasure.

We hardly encountered any problems in settling down, assisted as we were by Chia Lin Sien 謝麟先, my geography colleague. Singapore was a city with inhabitants of largely Chinese extraction. It was very easy for us to find our footing and feel at home, in terms of food, customs, language, and institutions. After all, Hong Kong and Singapore have both benefitted much from British rule over these places as colonies for many years. I found English being used and spoken much more than in Hong Kong, and the multi-lingual and multi-racial environment as the background to enriching our lives. Certainly for us, having as we did ancient Muslim roots, the religious environment was to our advantage. We would regularly pray at the small mosque near the university and at the Sultan Mosque on Hari Raya and other important Islamic occasions. We soon purchased a Volkswagen Beetle, which provided us with the needed mobility for the next 11 years. It was a most reliable car, and it helped me to familiarize myself with Singapore and Peninsular Malaysia. Strange as it may sound, because of a policy adopted in later years by the Singapore government to take older vehicles off the road for environmental reasons, I made a small profit when selling my car in 1980, after having used it for all those years before leaving for Ottawa.

The university at Bukit Timah was built around a ring road, with different buildings nestled around the extensive central lawn. Geography occupied House 4 and the Economic Research Centre and the Institute of Southeast Asian Studies, House 1, where I was a frequent visitor. Dr Lee Yong Leng was Chair of Geography when Professor Ooi Jin Bee 黃仁美 was on leave during my first year. Some of my other colleagues were Warwick Neville, Bernard Swan, Ron Hill, Chia Lin Sien, Teo Siew Eng 張秀英, and Lee Wah 李華. Wong Poh Poh 王寶寶 returned with his PhD from McGill University the following year. The department had many former staff members who later made their names in the discipline, namely Paul Wheatley, Dick Hodder, and others. During the period that I was with the Department, there was an almost constant stream of geographers and other scholars visiting our department. Some names that come to mind are Charles Fisher, Robert Steel, Harold Brookfield, J. E. Spencer, Gerald Ward, John Nystuen, Ronald Ng 吳卓堯, and others. Tea time in the department at mid-morning was not only an occasion for the daily exchange of news among the staff, but also for visitors to mingle with us. The fact that the geography departments in Singapore and Kuala Lumpur once belonged to the same university meant that cooperation between the two persisted to the time that I was there. Later, the *Journal of Tropical Geography* that they had once jointly published, was split into two, each under the name of their respective country. As a member of staff, I along with other colleagues contributed to the running of the journal in various ways. I contributed a couple of pieces, but mostly helped by reviewing in-coming manuscripts. It was a way of gaining some hands-on experience in research publications through the actual work associated with producing a respectable journal.

During the first three years of my affiliation with the department, my academic goal was specific and open-ended. My specific objective was to carry out the field investigation and writing related to my doctoral dissertation. I completed this task by mid-1972, coinciding with the end of my contract. However, before I set my mind on my thesis, I was to be engaged in other research tasks and writing. One immediate offer that I received was to write a piece on Kwangtung (later Guangdong) for the *Encyclopedia Britannica* within six weeks. This was an arrangement made by Norton Ginsburg, who was on the advisory board of the prestigious publication. Given this tight time constraint and the difficulty of gaining access to references and even basic information on China in Singapore at that time, I invited Chang Chen-tung 張振東, my fellow graduate student in sociology at the University of Chicago who had also recently joined the staff at the university, to be a co-author. With his Taiwanese background, he had access to some intelligence information and critical data for our piece. An idea of how difficult it was to obtain access to any material and information about China can be illustrated by what must now be viewed as a ludicrous episode. At the university library I tried to read *China Reconstructs*, a popular magazine with many pictures and some very general information. On borrowing this magazine, I had to read it outside the office of the university librarian in a chair specially provided! In any event, we were able to complete that piece of writing on time by November 1970. This piece on Kwangtung became an entry in the 1974 edition of the Britannica, and was subsequently updated for one more edition. Then it was only available on the Internet edition. The printed version of the heavy volumes has now been discontinued. Before I was able to begin writing my doctoral dissertation, I had already written several articles by early 1971. With the field investigation completed with the help of my students, I completed writing my dissertation within six months in early 1972. My students assisted me in collecting data on public housing and night markets, both fascinating socio-economic phenomena against the backdrop of rapid change in the new island country.

As a young lecturer I was close to my students, especially a handful who helped me in my dissertation field surveys. The relationship between teachers and students was generally cordial and productive, as the regular departmental field trips shortened the social distance. However, within the social circles of my peers, there was a feeling that Hong Kong people were somewhat different, and were viewed initially as outsiders. Academics with a Hong Kong background had to prove their worth and ability. This we-they attitude was not surprising, since Singapore was a new nation and nation building had to start from scratch. What I could not and did not appreciate was the top-down approach to the making of some academic decisions within the university.

At the end of my first year of teaching, two students whose bachelor's theses I had supervised wanted to go on to do a master's degree under me. They were interested in undertaking two studies on urban transport in Singapore. I was ready to take them on board, but the Vice-Chancellor, Toh Chin Chye 杜進才, personally vetoed their topics, which were to be undertaken by them as students of geography. They should be studied, according to him, by engineers! I was flabbergasted that such mundane matters would involve the highest decision-maker at the university. In any event, one of the students in question went to study at the University of California at Berkeley. He completed his doctoral degree and returned to teach geography at the National University of Singapore and flourished in his career. The episode, in fact, had worked in his favour. The refusal to allow him to take a master's degree at home was, for him, a blessing in disguise.

An important factor in my being able to tackle my tasks efficiently and to complete them on time was the fact that I had arrived in Singapore well prepared. I read widely to prepare my dissertation proposal. More importantly, Norton Ginsburg provided many key contacts, which opened doors for me in acquiring information and securing cooperation. These contacts included Howe Yoon Chong 侯永昌, Stephen (Steve) Yeh 葉華國, Tan Jake Hooi, You Poh Seng, among others. Mr Howe, who played a key role in developing public housing in Singapore, was certainly of much value to me in gaining the access that I needed to the Housing and Development Board (HDB). Steve Yeh at the Economic Research Centre was a vital link in my research on housing as well as in other personal and professional endeavours.

Norton Ginsburg came to Singapore several times during my initial few years with the university and more or less guided me by example. He was actively involved in research on Southeast Asia through his leadership in SEADAG (the Southeast Asia Development Advisory Group), a group funded by USAID. Together with Clifton Pannell and Jim Osborn, my fellow graduate students at UChicago who were pursuing field research in the region, I attended meetings related to SEADAG held in Manila in December 1969 and in Penang in September 1970. The latter, which focused on Research Priorities in Urban Roles in National Development, was hosted by Hamzah Sendut. During these meetings, I had the opportunity to get to know Ambassador Bernie Zagorin (Ginsburg's room-mate when they studied at the University of Chicago and whose former wife, Ruth, I would later work under in Ottawa), Arch Dotson, Henry Tunne, Mortan Kaplan, and Kim MacGovern, many of whom visited me in Singapore during my tenure there.

Indeed, a continual stream of friends and relatives visited us for varying durations of stay. These included my mother and sister Farita, my brother Yue-goke and his wife, and Ameda's parents and sister Mable, all in 1971. Farita later returned in 1974 when she married a Singaporean banker, Christopher Yip. They fell in love in Hong Kong, where he had been sent by the Singapore office of HSBC for training as part of a rising career path. She settled in Singapore and went on to raise a family there.

The Hong Kong connection was prominent during our Singapore days. I was the first among my peers to join the University of Singapore in 1969. In the following two years, I saw John and Anna Kwan-Terry join the English Department after completing their doctoral studies at Cambridge, and John and Aline Wong 黃朝翰, 簡麗中 join the Economics and Sociology Departments, respectively. Edward Ho 何司能 (music, chair, and my geography classmate at HKU) and his wife Maria joined at about the same time. Thus, it was just a coincidence that from different directions and graduate schools, the two Johns, Aline, Edward, and I all converged at the same university in Singapore after our graduation from the same Arts Faculty at HKU in 1962. We became close friends as a result. To broaden myself in general education, I took, along with Tommy Koh 許通美, Dean of Law, a course on Western music appreciation given by Edward over several weeks of lunch hours. There was another link to Tommy – we both lived in adjacent blocks in the Linden Drive staff quarters and we had children of similar ages. Tong and Anne Wu 伍宗唐 (urban planning), Allan and Mary Lee 李慶麟 (geography), Edmond and Lucia Fung 馮兆基 (history), and others also joined a little later. A close network of friendships was woven among these friends of Hong Kong background and their families. There were also other academics of Hong Kong background teaching at Nanyang

University, such as Ho Man-chue 何文柱 (physics, my May Hall hostel mate at HKU) and wife Cheung Yung 張容 (biology), Wong Hong-hin 黃康顯 (history), and so on. Not all of these scholars of Hong Kong origin have stayed in Singapore to pursue their careers, but almost all of them have flourished professionally.

Beyond the Hong Kong and geography connections, I developed strong friendships with Peter and Didas Weldon (sociology), our downstairs neighbours at Linden Drive Ragbi and Joan Bathal (physics), Chang Chen-tung (sociology), and William (Willy) and Lena Lim 林少偉 (architecture). The New Year's Eve parties hosted year after year by Willy and Lena attracted dozens of guests, and were later held at their posh penthouse in the Golden Mile Building, offering unparalleled panoramic views of the city. Willy Lim was an enterprising and successful practising architect with scholastic flair and boundless energy. With his colleagues at Design Partnership, Ltd., he addressed many critical issues of urban development under a professional cluster called Singapore Planning and Urban Research (SPUR), of which I was an active member. It was the only professional group that dared to challenge the government on urban development matters. Its initial high-profile portrayal of alternative paths to development was not always welcomed by the authorities, hence the group gradually withered into inaction.

Although I started my career in Singapore, I never forgot the preparations that I had made for a dissertation proposal on urban Malaysia when I was at UChicago. At the conclusion of my first academic year in March 1970, I made the somewhat bold decision to undertake a driving trip to Peninsular Malaysia from 20 to 30 March. It was bold because Ameda was six months pregnant with our first baby. More details on this trip are given in a later chapter, but it was an unforgettable and most fruitful trip in every way. The baby was born smoothly on 16 June. I named him Tao-ming 道銘 and an imam gave him the name Anwarudin (Anwar, for short), meaning glory to religion.

Soon after our arrival in Singapore, Ameda had the idea of developing herself professionally and personally. She discovered and advanced her interests in flower making and flower arrangement. She attended professional courses on these subjects, quickly acquired qualifications in them, and began to teach at the university's extramural department. She also gave demonstrations in some leading department stores. As well, she developed her interests in singing Cantonese operatic songs. She developed a rapport with Joanna Wong, our downstairs neighbour in Linden Drive and a leading artist in the field in Singapore. Joanna later became Registrar of the university and I was her counterpart at the Chinese University of Hong Kong with some overlapping years.

Despite the many demands on my time during my first appointment as lecturer, I found the time to undertake a consultancy report, in collaboration with Peter Weldon of the Department of Sociology, on a study of shops and shoppers in People's Park Complex, funded by Design Partnership, Ltd. The survey was carried out on 2-8 December 1971, resulting in a great deal of data to help us prepare our consultancy report of about 50 pages containing a similar number of tables. More details will be provided about this consultancy in a later chapter.

With my doctoral dissertation written and approved by Norton Ginsburg by early 1972, I now had to defend it orally by presenting myself at UChicago. It was also my intention to test the waters in looking for a tenure-track teaching position in Canada. Thus, after settling Ameda and Tao-ming in Hong Kong, I set out on 18 March 1972 on a marathon trip with multiple purposes. I travelled from Singapore to London, England (visiting SOAS), Montreal (McGill), Ottawa (Ottawa University, Carleton), Kingston (Queen's), Toronto (Toronto, York), Oakville, London (Western), Windsor, Chicago, Detroit, Toronto, and London, England. I gave lectures at Carleton, Queen's, Western, Windsor, and UChicago. The preparation from lecturing so many times greatly helped my smooth doctoral defense at UChicago. I returned to London, England, for a rendezvous with Ameda before beginning our two-week tour of Europe from 30 April to 13 May with Global Tours, followed by a trip on our own to Amsterdam and other parts of Holland. We returned to London, England, where Ronald and Vera Ng again played host to us, as they would do several times during our sojourns in London over some years. Again, more details on our European tour later.

We returned to Hong Kong and picked up Tao-ming from Ameda's family. After a warm get-together with family and friends, we returned to Singapore on 25 June, ready to begin another contract with the university and to meet whatever challenges and opportunities lay ahead for me and my family.

By the time I started my second term of service with the university, my family and I had wholly embraced Southeast Asia, with Singapore as our home. At academic meetings abroad, it was customary for me to represent Singapore. Little did I know that I was to enter a phase of my career in which I would have to balance competing priorities and make some hard choices.

The year 1972 was crucial to me in two ways. First, that year saw the founding of the International Development Research Centre (IDRC) as a Canadian crown corporation, following the passing of the IDRC Act in 1970. It was an expression of Canada's commitment to assist the Third World, arising from a new philosophy embodied in a new UN publication, *Partners in Development*. The editor of this book and the chairman of a related UN commission was Lester B. Pearson, Canada's Prime Minister. The IDRC had a global vision of assisting developing countries, with a network of regional offices to further its cause. The regional office in Asia was to be established in Singapore. Second, not only did I obtain my doctoral degree from the University of Chicago in 1972, but I had also chosen to study public housing and the marketing system in Singapore. These were the subjects that the newly founded IDRC had decided to investigate in two separate multi-country research projects on low-cost housing, and hawkers and vendors in Southeast Asia.

I was invited by the coordinators of both projects to play a role. Steve Yeh was the coordinator of the low-cost housing project that would examine eight countries. He invited me to assist him in the Singapore component of the project. At the same time, Terry McGee, of the Department of Geography and Geology at HKU, invited me to assist him in coordinating the three-country, six-city project on hawkers and vendors. These were timely opportunities, considering the fact that I had just completed the relevant studies for my doctoral dissertation. With McGee, it was the beginning of a career-long close collaboration and lasting friendship. Through Norton Ginsburg's advice, I had gotten in touch with him after completing my studies at UChicago.

My participation in these regional research network projects greatly increased my understanding of the region and enabled me to get acquainted with researchers and professionals from different countries. However, these demands on my time had to be balanced against my basic responsibilities of teaching and research as a lecturer. I had a heavy teaching load in addition to supervising undergraduate and graduate students on their theses. I was also involved in a research project with Patrick Low on the Kra Canal organized by Kernial Sandhu, Director of the Institute of Southeast Asian Studies.

In terms of family life, our daughter, Sze-mei 詩媚, was born on 21 February 1973. I gave her the Chinese name and an imam gave her a Muslim name, Jamila. With two children and a large flat to take care of, we had the luxury of having at least one and a maximum of three maids, for various tasks at different times. Domestic help was necessary, as my regional research projects as well as other invitations frequently took me away from Singapore. We had both Malay and Chinese maids, and were able to learn some basic Bahasa from them. We hardly learned any Hokkien during our years in Singapore, through lack of practice and the right social environment.

Singapore food was something we truly loved for its variety and cultural diversity. We had our favourite restaurants and hawker centres to which to take friends and visitors. I was able to associate different types of food by our favourite shops and localities. By the end of my second term with the university, I had developed an excellent sense of the geography of Singapore. Every year, official duties would have required me to take students for field trips to different parts of the island and the offshore islands. I developed a walking tour of Central Singapore, with a focus on Chinatown, beginning and ending at the Maxwell Market. During this period rapid urban development occurred in many parts of the island, especially in the Orchard Road area and the city centre. The Chinatown area was at the point of having its traditional shop houses demolished in favour of modern structures. Only when alternative views on urban development were put forward by groups such as SPUR and others did the authorities change course. For this reason, the Chinatown area retains many of its traditional building patterns and structures to this day. Basic infrastructure projects were implemented, such as the prevention of floods that used to plague even the city centre when I first arrived. Urban flooding in Singapore then became a thing of the past.

The two IDRC-supported regional research projects provided opportunities for me to visit cities and institutions in Southeast Asia. Between October 1972 and January 1975, in relation to the low-cost housing project I attended project meetings and went on trips to Singapore, Bali, Penang, and Manila; and to the hawkers and vendors project I visited Hong Kong, Jakarta, Kuala Lumpur, Manila, and Baguio. It was a speedy and privileged way to get to know the countries, cities, researchers, and politicians of Southeast Asia.

An idea of the special treatment experienced in some of these trips can be gained by the fact that after attending the low-cost housing meeting in Bali in April 1973, Albert Katarhardja, Director of the Regional Housing Centre in Bandung, invited the participants for a reconnaissance visit of Bandung via Yogyakarta. From Bali we flew to Yogyakarta, where after a two-night stop, we got up at 4 a.m. on 21 April 1973 to take a 6:00 a.m. train to Bandung. Albert had arranged an air-conditioned train wagon with 26 seats for only nine of us, whereas the other four ordinary wagons were overloaded with passengers to the point of overflowing. After a nine-hour train journey over a distance of 403 km, we arrived at 3 p.m. in Bandung. To me, going by land was the best way to see densely populated Java, with changing human and physical landscapes unfolding every minute. The image of hundreds of farmers harvesting their rice crop in the same field still recurs in my mind. It was intensive agriculture in Java at its height, with more people in the field than anywhere else I have visited, including many parts of China. Since Chandra Soysa, a Sri Lankan participant, and I had business to follow up in Jakarta, Albert arranged for a large American car to take both of us there via the Puncak Pass and Bogor, where we even managed to visit the botanical gardens.

Other special treatment accorded us on our research meetings included a meeting with the Mayor of Jakarta. Similarly, President Marcos and the First Lady Imelda received us in their Malacañang Palace in Manila. Another indelible memory derived from one of these trips is something that occurred on Saturday, 1 June 1974. After the conclusion of our hawker research meeting in Manila, Terry McGee was informed by Australian Embassy representatives who came to the Hyatt Hotel where we were staying, that his wife had died of a heart attack in Canberra the day before. I tried my best to be in Terry's company without saying anything, which was what he asked of me. We walked over long distances along Roxas Boulevard. He left that evening for Canberra, where he had moved from HKU a couple of years earlier. One of the objectives of these multi-country research projects was to build networks of cooperation and friendship that should last beyond the duration of the projects. On this trip I gained first-hand experience of the value and effectiveness of such networks.

As my participation in these research projects continued, Dr Aprodicio (Prod) Laquian, Associate Director of the Social Sciences Division of the IDRC in Ottawa, became interested in me and my work. Through a feeler via Steve Yeh, I was approached about the prospect of joining the IDRC as its regional representative in the social sciences in the newly opened regional office in Singapore (ASRO, Asia Singapore Regional Office). At the low-cost housing meeting held in April 1973 in the government holiday bungalow complex along a private beach in Bali, Indonesia, I met Dr Laquian for the first time. After the conclusion of the second day's proceedings, Dr Laquian met me privately on the sandy beach for a private and fruitful discussion under a moonlit sky.

"It is good to have you here for this meeting in such wonderful surroundings. I trust you have learned from Steve Yeh that the IDRC is looking for someone to represent its Social Sciences Division in its Asia Singapore Regional Office. Are you interested?" Dr Laquian went straight to the business he had in mind.

"Sure, I am highly interested in the research projects on low-cost housing and hawkers and vendors that the IDRC has been funding. But to work for it as a full-time job is a different matter. It means that I will have to resign from my university job," I quickly spelled out my position.

"Of course, it is a major career move. But the IDRC job has many things to offer. It will broaden your views on international development, build up your professional contacts, and you will visit places and institutions on a regular basis. Also, it pays well and will allow you to enjoy special tax-free status in Singapore," Dr Laquian was quick to point out the positive aspects of the job.

"At this point, I am interested in the job in principle. But we have to see how I can leave my university job as I am bound by contract," I hastened to explain.

That was where we concluded on my prospects of joining the IDRC. There were many uncertainties surrounding the move, but the IDRC was urgently looking for someone who could represent its Social Sciences Division in Asia. Negotiations with the university began in early 1973 and did not go far, as I was bound by contract to serve until mid-1975. Discussions were protracted, with different options being explored and involving Ooi Jin Bee and the Vice-Chancellor, Dr Toh Chin Chye. Nihal Kappagoda and John Friesen of ASRO represented the IDRC and facilitated the discussion. In the end, it was agreed that I would serve to the end of my contract before joining the staff of the IDRC in ASRO. Meanwhile, Dr Jacques Amyot was appointed the Social Sciences Representative in ASRO. I was offered a contract as a consultant to the IDRC to undertake two trips to Indonesia, and Malaysia and Thailand on specific assignments.

Taking a job with the IDRC was a struggle for me and my family. It meant that I would have to call a halt to my academic career, which appeared to have started as well as one could anticipate. Promotion to senior lectureship was within sight. On the other hand, the IDRC job was a very special one, as it had come through a selective process and had not been advertised. It would open up opportunities of another kind and enable me to gain world perspectives on development. The job also entailed a considerable amount of travel and frequent absences from home. As the job meant only relocation within Singapore, I considered the challenges to be manageable. The job offered other attractions, with its better remuneration package and tax-free status in Singapore. I also reasoned with myself that, as long as I kept publishing there would be opportunities for me to return to academia, a scenario that was my ultimate objective. I would only be adding value to myself with the kind of international experience I would be getting into.

Having made up my mind, Ameda and the children were sent to Hong Kong in February 1975 to stay with my in-laws before I told Ooi Jin Bee of my career plan. I lived by myself in the university quarters for several months, which gave me the space I needed to complete some writing commitments and get ready for a new career move. I had our household goods stored before leaving the university and our living quarters, as the family would not be settled for a few months. I moved out of my office at the university in June and began to work in ASRO, located on the 7th floor of RELC (the Regional English Language Centre) on Orange Grove Road next to the Shangri-la Hotel.

The arrangement with the IDRC was that I would work in ASRO for a month before being posted to the IDRC Head Office in Ottawa for three months from 15 July to 15 October 1975. I would bring my whole family to Ottawa for a complete orientation to my job as Senior Programme Officer in the Social Sciences Division (SSD). Then, we would return to Singapore for me to work with Jacques Amyot to represent the Social Sciences Division in Asia, covering from Turkey to the South Pacific, and from Indonesia to South Korea. There would be more than enough work to keep both of us busy.

With this career change, I completed six years of university service in circumstances that were satisfying academically, socially, professionally, and from the viewpoint of the family. I felt that I had laid a good foundation as an academic, with a fair record of publications and growing links to many universities. I was leaving academia with an uneasy feeling, with the full expectation I would return one day. I subscribe to the age-old dictum: Nothing ventured, nothing gained.

AT A POLICY CONFERENCE IN KATHMANDU, NEPAL, 1979

6 International Development Research Assistance

Leaving academia and devoting myself to the work in international development research assistance meant that I had to effect a wide-ranging and basic change in my working habits, cope with the need to travel constantly away from home, meet old and new friends all the time in different places, struggle to find the time to read and write, and adjust to being part of a large organization spread over different regions of the world. The past few years of working and living as an academic in the vibrant and new nation of Singapore gave me an advantage when working in ASRO (Asia Singapore Regional Office), the IDRC's regional office in Singapore. Having already built up my personal contacts at many levels, I could tactically use Singapore as a base from which to better understand the region and its development. The superior remuneration package with the IDRC included almost unlimited travel support, excellent logistical assistance in terms of relocation within and from Singapore, tax-free status in Singapore, and annual paid home leave with my family.

After leaving university service and moving to work out of ASRO in RELC, I underwent a long period of orientation. It began in mid-June 1975, when I was in ASRO for a month, during which I also stayed in RELC as my family had already left for Hong Kong. Thanks to the logistical support from ASRO, all of our household effects were to be stored for several months until our return from Canada.

In July 1975, I met up with my family in Hong Kong and began our long trip to Ottawa via Vancouver and Calgary. We arrived in Ottawa on 22 July and settled into the Juliana Apartments on Bronson Avenue on the edge of the downtown area. Helping us to settle in was Nae Ismail and his large family. We were to spend a great deal of time socially with his family not only during the next few months, but also over several years after we relocated to Ottawa in 1980 to live and work.

Working in the head office of the IDRC on 60 Queen Street in downtown Ottawa allowed me to get acquainted with my colleagues in the Social Sciences Division and beyond. Ruth Zagorin, the Director of the Division, had a sharp mind and provided well-considered directions for its development. My immediate superior was Prod Laquian, who had become a good friend of mine through our earlier projects in low-cost housing and hawkers and vendors. I also developed good working relationships with Tom Walsh, Rafique Rahman, Larry Hannah, Alan Simmons, Shirley Seward, and others within the Division. It was the only way to get a thorough understanding of the philosophy and approach to international development research assistance as championed by the IDRC. I liked the professional and working environment in the IDRC and the living conditions in Ottawa.

During the period of our stay in Ottawa, I made a trip in August 1975 to Vancouver to attend the 13th Pacific Science Congress and presented a paper. It was also an occasion to meet many old and new friends, including Norton Ginsburg, Terry McGee, Charles Fisher, Charles Grant, Robert H. T. Smith, Ron Hill, Rance Lee, and others. I was much encouraged by the IDRC's policy of supporting its professional staff to attend academic meetings, especially if one had a paper to present or an important role to play. I had time to spend with Norton Ginsburg, who was accompanied by his wife, Diana. This was the first time that we had met since I had left my university teaching position in Singapore. He had been a source of good advice to me professionally since I had left UChicago, and our cordial relationship continued for many more years. With a conference held in Vancouver, it was expected that many would make a side trip to Victoria on Vancouver Island. I did so with several participants of the conference and updated myself on the place since my earlier visit in 1964.

In September 1975, I also undertook a duty trip all the way to

Kuala Lumpur and back. A policy dissemination conference on the Hawkers and Vendors Project was held at the Regent Hotel on the 24th of that month. Prod Laquian, Terry McGee, and other researchers from the project, as well as Jacques Amyot and Peter Weldon, were all present. The mayor of Kuala Lumpur featured prominently at the meeting, which drew some critical comments from the media. We were taken to task for holding a hawkers and vendors project final meeting in the most expensive hotel in the city. The adverse publicity aside, the conference was most successful, as it brought to a conclusion several years of hard work and pioneering research in all of the countries in question on a common socio-economic phenomenon, to which scant policy attention had been devoted to date. It was multi-country research collaboration at its best and spoke highly of the funding agency that had made it possible. Consequently, the book that took stock of the research findings and their policy implications, co-authored by Terry McGee and me, was eagerly awaited. When it was finally released in 1977, it was in great demand and ran out in no time. It has remained a classic in the field and has withstood the test of time.

In the course of our short-term stay in Ottawa, we had already developed social networks. In addition to colleagues in the IDRC, I had reconnected with Dr Geoffrey Tse 謝鄂韡 and Agatha (with Geoffrey hailing back to Queen's College and HKU days) and had become close to Dr Brian Luke and Mei. We also re-established contact with Mi-ki Kan 靳美琪 and Susan, from Oakville, where we went on a weekend trip. During the coming few years, Mi-ki and his family became close to us, as they were within easy driving distance from Toronto. Mi-ki was my geography classmate at HKU.

As we were in Ottawa during the summer period, we rented cars during weekends, whenever the weather permitted, to visit places within driving distance. Over several weekends, we drove to visit Gatineau Park (Ottawa), Montreal, Quebec City (after Expo Quebec), Gananoque, Upper Canada Village, and other places. These trips deepened our understanding of the beauty and variety of Canadian scenery and life. The fall season, typified by maple leaves in full-coloured splendor in Gatineau Park, still ranks as one of the most picturesque scenes of natural beauty that I love about Canada. Some years later, when we lived in Ottawa, I would always make it a point to revisit the park whenever I had the opportunity to take my family or visitors to it. We were proud to showcase one of the best and most enchanting scenes of Canada. Montreal and Quebec City charmed me and my family with their French tradition and history. I still remember arriving in Quebec City in a rented car and encountering difficulties in finding accommodation. Normal accommodation was difficult to find at a time when the city was hosting a large annual social event. Upper Canada Village intrigued us with its depictions of the early settlement patterns and ways of life of early settlers. Conservation efforts by the government ensured that the historical heritage was well preserved for educational and other purposes.

The staff meeting of the Social Sciences Division (SSD) was held in Ottawa from 7 October 1975. This was my first opportunity to meet many staff members coming from the regional offices in Nairobi, Dakar, Cairo, Bogota, and Sussex (UK). From their presentations, I formed favourable impressions of Francisco Sagasti, Geoff Oldham, and Don Simpson. During this meeting, Dr David Hopper, President of the IDRC, who was married to Ruth Zagorin, hosted an after-dinner party for Ottawa and field staff of the SSD at their posh penthouse in a high-rise building, which offered a panoramic view of the Rideau Canal and beyond. Dr Hopper, visionary in perspective and powerfully persuasive, was a pioneer and unparalleled leader of a new funding agency in Canada. He established the foundations and traditions upon which the IDRC would grow and on which it has prospered to this day. I met Dr Hopper a few times, all too briefly. My regret is not to have had a chance to become more closely acquainted with the great man. When he passed away in 2011, the outpouring of grief and sorrow among his former colleagues and friends at the IDRC was spontaneous and overwhelming.

After my last day of work at the IDRC head office on 10 October, we left the next day via Los Angeles (Disneyland), Tokyo, and Hong Kong. The Hong Kong stop, as usual, provided an opportunity for me to update myself on the low-cost housing situation there by visiting Fung Tung, Ms Sersale, Bernard Williams, and E. G. Pryor. It was a way to gain an understanding of the rapid policy changes in the sector that needed to be followed up from time to time. We returned to Singapore on 19 October.

Upon our return to Singapore in my new capacity as an employee of the IDRC, we were put up at Orchid Inn. We began hunting for an apartment, a process that took a few weeks. Finally, on 16 November we moved into 70E Phoenix Court on Kiliny Road, just off River Valley Road but one long block from the busy Orchard Road area in the opposite direction. Tao-ming was soon settled into Dover Court Preparatory School. Our household effects, which had been in storage for five months, were delivered to our new residence. My sister, Farita, and her husband Chris helped us to settle in. We now had a close relative and her family living in Singapore. Over the next few years, we would get together many times and help each other.

My job as Senior Programme Officer of the SSD at the IDRC based in ASRO necessitated some division of labour within the Division. As Jacques Amyot was the regional representative of the Division, my main responsibility was to assist the SSD in monitoring existing projects and developing new ones in the region. I was to work primarily for the Rural Urban Dynamics Programme headed by Prod Laquian, and secondarily for the Public Policy Programme headed by Rafique Rahman.

Over the period I was at ASRO, I had many social science projects to look after on the spot, so to speak. Some of these projects included Bureaucratic Behaviour (specifically, graft and corruption), Public Enterprises, Low-cost Transport, Resettlement and Transmigration, the Trans-Sarawak Highway, Cooperative Regional Development,

Small Manufacturing Enterprises, the Economic Impact of Tourism, and so on. My job was to be helpful to the researchers of these often multi-country projects, trouble shooting and attending their project meetings. Consequently, my work involved a great deal of travelling within the Asian region and beyond. It was not uncommon for me to travel on one-day return trips to Penang, Kuala Lumpur, and Manila on matters related to project management. I covered the region quite thoroughly, with repeated trips to Jakarta, Yogyakarta, Manila, Los Baños, Penang, Kuala Lumpur, Bangkok, Pattaya, Chiang Mai, Hong Kong, Taipei, Tokyo, Nagoya, Seoul, Kathmandu, and other places.

Travelling in those days was not as comfortable or convenient as it is nowadays. Delays in flight departures were very common, often for many hours. Telephone calls, especially long-distance calls, were very difficult and/or expensive to make in those days before the arrival of the information age spearheaded by the use of optical fibre. Jakarta, Manila, and Cairo were notorious for the difficulty of arranging telephone conversations, even within the city. I recall that in the Cairo regional office, which I visited several times, local phone calls were never made or attempted. Messages and letters were delivered by the official car. In addition, long-distance trips took a long time because the planes in those days were limited in range and had to refuel often. Travelling between Singapore and Ottawa would normally involve two or three stops en route. I did cover the distance between Ottawa and Hong Kong without an overnight stop a couple of times. It is hard to believe now that it took me more than 33 hours to complete each of those trips. Lastly, to add to the inconvenience, all confirmed flights had to be revalidated, at least a day or more before departure. This was an onerous burden when local and long-distance phone calls were difficult to make. This practice of having to revalidate air tickets, in fact, continued for some years. For instance, even as late as in May 1984 during the IDRC "road show" to several major cities in China, our last business stop was in Nanjing. To ensure that our delegation would be able to leave on time from Shanghai several days later, arrangements had to be made for somebody to travel all the way to and from Shanghai to have our tickets revalidated. It was a full-day's work, as China at the time did not have the high-speed trains that it has now to cover the 267 km distance between the two cities.

A major part of my travel as an IDRC employee was to attend two SSD staff meetings in Ottawa every year, once in the spring and once in the fall. The only exception was in November 1979, when ASRO hosted the SSD staff meeting in Singapore. My usual itinerary was to fly via the Pacific, with stopovers en route as required to attend to business. Where the trip could serve special purposes, I took the round-the-world route, such as in March 1978, when I stopped in Bombay, Nairobi (where an IDRC meeting was held), and London (met academics at SOAS), before proceeding on to Paris, Montreal, and Ottawa. On that trip I bade farewell to Ruth Zagorin, who was leaving the IDRC, where she had served as the founding Director of the SSD. I returned to Singapore on that trip via Vancouver, Honolulu, Tokyo, Seoul, and Hong Kong. On another trip to Ottawa to attend the SSD staff meeting in September 1977, it was announced that the Rural Urban Dynamics Programme was to be disbanded, with Prod Laquian to be posted to Nairobi to take charge of a new "circuit rider" project. The objective of sending a senior colleague to Nairobi was to explore ways to accelerate social science development and assistance in the African region. That change provided at least an additional incentive for me to travel to East Africa to develop projects. I was naturally affected, as I had mainly been hired to serve in that programme. In still another SSD staff meeting held in April 1980, my posting from Singapore to Ottawa was confirmed. It is clear that major decisions were often made and announced at the SSD staff meetings held once every six months.

During the course of my posting in Singapore, I did undertake a number of medium to long trips for various purposes. Between 30 March and 6 April 1976, I travelled with Niew Shong Tong 饒尚東,

the main investigator of the Trans-Sarawak Highway Project, as well as with his colleague in Singapore, after they had completed the study. We visited government officials in Kuching and elsewhere, travelling the whole distance of the just completed highway. We went from Kuching to Sibu, Bintulu, and Miri, over a distance of 513 km close to the border with Brunei. We covered, in fact, most of the distance of that state in East Malaysia. Covering some of the pristine equatorial landscapes of that state was one of the highlights of the trip.

Two stops on this trip are particularly hard for me to forget. One was an overnight stop at Niah, a small town of fewer than 40 houses, close to Miri. When we arrived at about noon, we checked into the only hotel in town, which had only one room with two beds available for our party of three men. Facilities in the town and hotel could be described as very basic, almost primitive. The town stopped the supply of electricity after 9 in the evening. I did not always stay in five-star hotels on IDRC trips. I remember staying in similar primitive hotel conditions during a field visit to the third-largest city in Nepal on another IDRC trip. The attraction of stopping in Niah was to pay a visit to the Niah Cave, which took 40 minutes to walk to, passing through some really dense and lush equatorial vegetation. When we reached it, the cave greatly surprised us by its size. It was bigger than one football field in area, with very high ceilings. All kinds of wooden frames, hangings, and ladders were constructed for people to use in climbing up to collect bird's nests. The nests would be processed afterwards as an expensive delicacy priced for its nutritional, even medicinal, value. The second special stop was in a little town called Bintulu, almost mid-way along the new highway. Our hotel was just beside the little runway at the airport next to us. From our room, we could easily see planes taking off and landing, despite seeing only scant air traffic during our brief stopover.

Another duty trip, to Australasia and the South Pacific, involved more than a month of travel, from 1 August to 3 September 1977, mainly to touch base with some academics specializing in tourism research and to scout for possible researchers in the South Pacific to participate in a multi-country study on the economic impact of tourism. This long trip took me to Port Moresby, Brisbane, Sydney, Canberra, Christchurch, Auckland, Papeete, Nadi, Suva, Apia, and Noumea. It was my first exposure to this geographically extensive region, including the South Pacific, which was within the geographical purview of the SSD. It opened my eyes to life in this sprawling region of the world and to studies about this area. It was my first visit to Australia and New Zealand, which allowed me to meet old friends and make new ones. All of the five stopovers in these two countries were purposeful and helpful in their own ways, paving the way for later professional cooperation and collaboration. The swing around the island countries in the South Pacific provided me with a new understanding of the life there, which was led at a more leisurely pace, with obvious cultural differences among the various places. Apart from the University of the South Pacific in Sava, Fiji, and the University of Papua New Guinea in Port Moresby, indigenous research capacity was by and large at a low level. The highlight of the visit came in Papeete, Tahiti, and will be reported in Chapter 14.

Still another duty trip, in May 1978, took me to both Java and Kalimantan, two major islands of Indonesia. It was a trip that began in Jakarta, to visit government officials. What followed was something that we had not done before. Researchers from the various countries networked in the project went on a reconnaissance trip to Banjarmasin in Kalimantan to visit a transmigration site. We attempted to understand the life of new transmigrants in the receiving area. We spent time speaking to them in their paddy fields and in their homes. We all took our shoes off and walked into the paddy fields. We not only got our hands, but our feet, dirty! These pre-conference visits were succeeded by the final project meeting for the Resettlement and Transmigration Project, held in Yogyakarta, Java, from where most of the transmigrants had come. The researchers would have appreciated the contrast in the living conditions in the two places. The final project meeting provided an occasion for policymakers and researchers from Indonesia, the Philippines, Malaysia, and Nepal to share the main findings of the project. Holding a final meeting during which researchers would present their major findings after many months/years of labour was the usual way to conclude a multi-country research project.

My first duty trip to Africa took place in July 1978, when I travelled to Zaria from Kano. I had flown from Cairo to Kano, after arriving in Cairo earlier, via aircraft transfer in Bangkok from my starting point in Singapore. The purpose of the trip was to attend a Population Commission Meeting held in Zaria in northern Nigeria under the IGU Inter-Congress rubric. With Alan Simmons heading the Population Programme at the IDRC, financial assistance was extended to a handful of researchers from both Anglophone and Francophone African countries. After an overnight stop in Kano, I travelled by taxi to cover the 163-km distance between Kano and Zaria, where the Inter-Congress meeting was held. What followed the meeting was an exciting, hair-raising, and ever-changing transect on a chartered mini-bus of a part of Nigeria hitherto unknown to me. Led by Leszek Kosinski of the University of Alberta, and John Clarke of Durham University, there were about 15 geographers on our bus. Apart from the colourful market towns, which we passed and visited in our two-day trip, what was most unforgettable about the 698-km transect from Zaria to Lagos was the large number of auto wrecks littering the entire route. Noticing the large number of auto wrecks after a short drive, we soon took a statistical sampling, which indicated that we had encountered approximately one auto wreck every 0.45 km. Apparently, as we were later told, this prominent display of auto accidents was due to the fact that drivers had the habit of drinking a local alcoholic brew before taking to the wheels. Most of us had never been more scared in our lives than when we were completing this frightful journey across a large part of Nigeria. Travelling in a foreign country with unknown local conditions can be hazardous, and we truly appreciated the truth of this statement.

The main IGU Inter-Congress was held in Lagos, which struck me as a large city without the kind of infrastructure to make it function well. Leaving the country after the meeting could also pose problems of a different kind. With the airport in Lagos being very crowded most of the time, getting your seat with a confirmed ticket was not always easy. Asking for bribes to facilitate the issue of tickets was common. One Canadian professor was stranded at the airport for a long time because he refused to pay any bribes. More space is needed in a later chapter to tell stories about the return trip to Singapore from Lagos via Mombasa and Seychelles. Because I was stranded in Seychelles due to a British Airlines strike, all of my appointments in my next stop – Colombo in Sri Lanka – had to be missed. This was far from being a smooth way of getting to know that charming island country on my initial visit. Travel uncertainties were something we had to live with, especially when travelling was so much a part of my job.

My last but one duty trip while based in Singapore was undertaken in September 1978 at the invitation of the Director of Resettlement in the Philippines, Romeo Castaneda, with whom I became acquainted at the final meeting on Resettlement and Transmigration held in Yogyakarta a few months earlier. In the company of Excy Ramos and her colleagues from De La Salle University in Manila, Director Castaneda and his colleagues flew with us from Manila to Davao, then to Zamboanga. From this southwestern corner of Mindanao, two military helicopters escorted us to Basilan, a sensitive site on an island housing a sizeable community of resettled migrants. The views from the helicopter when crossing the strait from Mindanao to Basilan on a sunny morning were magnificent. One helicopter had soldiers manning machine guns to give us protection. Little did I know until after the trip that day that, only two weeks before our visit, a Japanese tourist had been kidnapped on Basilan. It was therefore a very sensitive area by any standard. Our reception on the island at a resettlement site was warm and well attended by many villagers. Since the weather had changed for the worse, with a threatening rainstorm, we cut short our stay for security reasons. We did not even attend the welcome lunch that had been laid out for our party. This official introduction was a direct way of understanding a little of the life of migrants in the southern Philippines. From the whole episode, I was able to feel sharply elements of sensitivity, official precaution, and the settlers' warmth. It was a privileged exposure to a dimension of resettlement not normally accessible to researchers.

My last duty trip in June 1980 was to cover both Colombo and several cities in India. By that time, my trip to India had the support of the newly opened IDRC regional office in Delhi. I went to Bangalore, Mysore, and Lucknow for the purpose of meeting some prospective project researchers, followed by an update on the Indian situation in the regional office. Mysore and Lucknow impressed me with their unique regional character and beautiful indigenous architecture, especially the latter city, which had played a key role in history during the Indian Mutiny. Bangalore, by contrast, was a regional city that did not give me any hint of its later emergence as the centre of the IT revolution in India in providing related IT communication services. What was so special about this trip was that it was my last duty trip before being posted to the head office in Ottawa. I therefore made arrangements after completing my official duties to meet Ameda in Delhi. We then began another personal trip to this ancient land, highlighted by visits to attractions in Delhi, Agra, and Kashmir. We also visited Kathmandu in Nepal. Again, more on this part of our Indian trip will be found in Chapter 14.

As the terms of my remuneration with the IDRC in ASRO included travel with the family once a year, we did take advantage of this provision to expand our understanding of the region. Our first family trip was in August 1976 to Taiwan and Manila, with an excursion to the Pagsanjan Falls in the Philippines. In the next summer, the family visited Jakarta, Bali, Yogyakarta, and Borobudur. I picked the places and introduced them to the family, as I had been there several times before on official travel. At that stage of our family life, I viewed family travel as a critical component of our family's well-being, not only to gain new common experiences away from home, but also to spend time together to make up for my frequent absences from home on official travel. It was a way of giving the children a general education and inculcating in them certain cultural and educational values that I did not have time to do often enough at home.

In the summer of 1978, the family trip was extended to more places and was divided into two phases. First, on the way to Hong Kong, we stopped in Penang, Phuket, and Bangkok. Phuket was especially delightful, being at the time relatively quiet and having an almost pristine beauty with its karst topography in a sea of islands. I recall the boat we were in sailing past James Bond Island, soon after the release of the theme movie that made the island famous. After arriving in Hong Kong, we left Tao-ming and Sze-mei with Ameda's family. Then, Ameda and I made a momentous trip to Guangdong by joining a guided tour organized by a Hong Kong Muslim group. We visited Guangzhou, Zhaoqing, Conghua, and Foshan. It was a timely and important trip for me that I had eagerly waited for years to be able to make, as China had just shown signs of opening up. Except for a sojourn in Guangzhou during the Second World War, I had never set foot on China, as the country had essentially sealed itself from the outside world for the past three decades. This trip has formed the baseline against which I measure the vast economic and social progress that China has since made. Indeed, I made detailed notes on what I observed and felt, and published a couple of articles. A detailed paper that I wrote about the trip was translated and published in Chinese in Hong Kong.

In our last home leave in June 1979, we made the same arrangement as the year before by leaving our children with Ameda's family. We joined a guided tour to the eastern and northern parts of China. In 16 days of that month, we gained a more comprehensive experience of a just-awakened China by riding overnight trains, visiting tourist sites, and sampling daily life in different cities. Much was in evidence of the socialist organization of daily life, as food and major commodities were still rationed. After crossing the border in Shenzhen, we travelled by train to Guangzhou, Hangzhou, Shanghai, Wuxi, Nanjing, and Beijing, from whence we flew back to Hong Kong. We were astounded at the very basic facilities at the Beijing airport, at both its size and backwardness, which compared unfavourably with most airports in the region outside China at that time. Again, this trip provided the basis for me to compare China's subsequent development in my research. In all of the cities that we visited, even Hong Kong visitors like us never failed to attract attention, distinguishable as we were by our clothing and mannerisms. This was especially the case in rural Guangdong, which we visited briefly. I will never forget the stares aimed at us when we were in central Nanjing near the Bell Tower. From what we saw, life was regimented and people wore drab clothing. In all of the cities that we visited, people got around largely by bicycle, with the few motor cars of Chinese make being strictly for the use of officials. In spite of groups of visitors like us, the move towards openness in China was tentative and its continuity was uncertain. However, a crucial start towards a new life had been made and, as the country's later spectacular development has testified, this was the beginning of new page in its history.

This period also saw our family life expand in many ways. Both Tao-ming and Sze-mei started their education by attending kindergartens at international schools before switching to local schools. This route was chosen in the belief that local schools would ensure their bilingual education early in English and Chinese. Despite my constant travels away from home, I made sure to help them to develop their reading interests and habits. Early on, I enrolled them with the National Library in Singapore, where we would spend our Saturday afternoons whenever I was in town. Sze-mei developed into an avid reader, a habit she continued in Ottawa and beyond. They also started piano lessons, with Tao-ming having shown an early ability in swimming as well. He was awarded a certificate for swimming unaided for a mile when he was about nine years old. However, their lessons in drawing were abandoned early, as were lessons in ballet for Sze-mei.

My mother visited us again in November 1978, when Farita had her first baby. We took a three-day tour of Malaysia, with the last stop at the Genting Highlands. On the last day before leaving the hotel, Sze-mei fell from a playset in the garden and broke her right arm. After consulting local doctors, we rushed her back to Singapore. She was admitted to the General Hospital in the wee hours of 18 November and remained there for five weeks. Fortunately, her healing programme was perfect under the supervision of competent doctors. The quality of medical care was high, as the surgeons attending her came from the university. She fully recovered from her injury and has not been hampered in her life by this frightful accident. It also taught her to be more cautious, and to refrain from taking unnecessary risks.

Our social networks built around friends from the university over the past years continued to thrive, as did my connections to the extended family in Hong Kong. Frequent trips through Hong Kong allowed me to keep contact with my parents, relatives, and friends. In a couple of years I was in Hong Kong in most months of the year, thus witnessing most of the major events in the British crown colony. During one of these trips, my father broached the topic of buying property in Hong Kong with assistance from me. It has remained a lifelong regret of mine as a filial son that I was not able to respond positively, as our life had not settled to any long-term pattern and my savings were rather modest. This turn of events sped up their emigration to Calgary in 1981 to live with their youngest son, Mosa, and his wife, Patsy. One positive aspect of this decision was that my parents were spared the uncertainties and worries of the handover syndrome over the next few years. A Canadian way of life would open their eyes to a world that they had hitherto not experienced.

Life as a professional in a large organization with a global mandate meant new opportunities and some drawbacks. One of the most attractive aspects of the job, for any person with an academic bent, was to be fully supported in attending conferences and such activities. The justification was to present a paper or play an important role. I was thus supported in attending academic conferences in Hong Kong, Bangkok, Manila, Kuala Lumpur, Baltimore, Vancouver, Toronto, Canberra, and other places. Of these trips, the International Conference on the Survival of Humankind held in Manila in September 1976 was special in many ways, as will be touched on further in a later chapter. Often, I was able to combine IDRC travel with additional personal interests. It was the only way to keep up academically and force myself to write.

As soon as I settled down on the job, I discovered that it involved a great deal of writing, but of a different kind than the sort that I had been accustomed to, and that I was expected to turn out written documents with great frequency. In the head office, project documents had to be prepared for the Board for approval, along with other shorter documents seeking financial assistance for grantees. Whatever the location of one's posting, all programme staff had to write trip reports. These reports were detailed, indicating the purposes of each trip and actions, relevance to programmes, people met, budget implications, and follow-up actions by concerned colleagues. In 1976, for instance, I wrote 12 trip reports, averaging one a month. That was an exceptional year in terms of number of trips, as a normal year involved six to eight trips. In the long Australasia and South Pacific trip, the report went to 36 pages. There was also a never-ending stream of letters and memos to write. During my almost decade-long career with the IDRC, I wrote a total of 76 trip reports.

Given this requirement for the kind of rapid output mentioned, I quickly taught myself how to dictate letters, telexes, memos, and trip reports. I could dictate a dozen letters in one stretch and, in most cases, completed dictating my trip report on a dicta phone before returning home from trips. Such work was carried out in hotel rooms wherever they might be. The ability to work almost anywhere, any time, and to dictate greatly helped me to subsequently complete my consultancy projects swiftly and to undertake a key university administrative job in Hong Kong years later.

As I learned further on the job and interacted with my colleagues in Ottawa, it became apparent that the IDRC professional jobs, such as those related to programmes, were never intended as career posts. They were essentially positions that would allow a person to revolve between academia and the IDRC, and back. That was the case for me, at least. With this mindset and particularly when the Rural Urban Dynamics Programme was to be discontinued, it was incumbent on me to explore other job possibilities. One was to return to academia in Singapore or Hong Kong, and the other was to get posted to Ottawa. The last-mentioned possibility was proposed as early as May 1977, when Terry McGee turned down an appointment to join the head office.

When my position became known, several possibilities came my way. First, I was kindly approached and sounded out by Liu Thai Ker 劉太格 and earlier via Steve Yeh on whether I would be interested in joining the Housing and Development Board in Singapore as a research director. Then, a post as senior researcher at the Institute of Southeast Asian Studies was suggested by Director Kernial Sandhu. Finally, the prospect of assuming the position of Chair Professor in Geography at Universiti Sains Malaysia in Penang was floated by Pro-VC Kamal Salih. Furthermore, Teo Siew Eng, a close friend and former colleague, also wanted me to rejoin the Department of Geography. However, with the merging of the two universities in Singapore as the National University of Singapore, there was no opening in geography. I also applied for the position of the Chair of Geography at The Chinese University of Hong Kong in late 1978, but was unsuccessful on account of my yet-to-be-fully-developed credentials. It was, frankly, only an attempt to test the waters and to register my interest in the job, a frame of mind that several years later yielded fruit.

My greatest hope at that time was to get appointed as a Reader in Urban Studies in the newly established Centre for Urban Planning and Urban Studies at the University of Hong Kong (HKU), with the advertisement inviting applications to both disciplines. I was flown to Hong Kong as a guest of the university and stayed at the Lee Gardens Hotel. On the next day, on 21 November 1979, I presented myself at HKU for an interview with a panel. Except for a couple of questions that I could have answered better, I thought I did well.

After dinner at the hotel that evening, I received unexpectedly a phone call from Charles Grant, Chair Professor in Geography and a member of the interviewing panel, and he went straight to the point:

"Yue-man, how do you feel after today's interview?"

"I am quite happy with what I said, except that my reply to Professor Murray Groves' question could have been better," I replied without hesitation.

"I thought you did well on the whole. The external assessment about you was also very positive. In my view, there is a 99.9 per cent chance of the university offering you an appointment," Professor Grant continued in a most confident tone.

"Is it really that good? I shall be delighted if I do receive an offer," I only half believed what he said.

"I'll call you before you leave tomorrow, so that you may carry a positive feeling back to Singapore," was how he concluded our conversation.

Despite Charles Grant's most encouraging remarks, the slim chance of my not being offered an appointment turned real. What happened was that the other candidate for the Urban Planning slot had been interviewed two weeks after me. He claimed to have expertise in both fields – urban planning and urban studies. Sure enough, the university advised me soon afterwards that I was not successful in my application.

Not to be joining the new centre at HKU was indeed a big disappointment at the time. In retrospect, it was probably the best thing that could have happened to me and my family. Some of my good friends at HKU had already warned me of the difficulties surrounding the job in the new centre. Moreover, had I returned to Hong Kong in early 1980, we would have been put in the awkward position of facing the uncertainties of the handover and the family's future. As it turned out, that period up to the signing of the Sino-British Joint Declaration in September 1984 was the most unnerving time for Hong Kong people. It was period when large numbers of people emigrated from Hong Kong, and the untimely return to Hong Kong of me and my family would be fraught with all kinds of uncertainties. The Almighty again helped me and my family in ways that turned out to be much better than what we wished for at the time, as later events were to show.

When alternatives were explored and did not turn out to my satisfaction, I made up my mind to get myself posted to Ottawa. There were uncertainties, to be sure, as my tentative urban statement in a meeting in ASRO earlier on was not well received. In truth, this was not surprising because I was pushing myself to design a global urban programme when I did not have anybody to interact or work with. I was determined to give myself a chance to prove myself. After all, emigration to Canada had been a long-time dream of mine after my studies at Western.

In early August 1980, my family and I were preparing to leave Singapore after eleven most productive and enjoyable years. We bade farewell to Farita and her family, and many good friends. We left with the intention of staying in Canada for the long haul. For this reason, we took advantage of the IDRC's relocation policy to pack many belongings, many newly acquired, in 265 boxes and pieces, enough to fill one and a half long containers. With additional furniture that we bought and shipped from Hong Kong, we had enough stuff to fill more than a full house. After staying briefly at Goodwood Park Hotel, I left with the family on 8 August for Hong Kong, Vancouver, Calgary, and Ottawa. It was a move to the known and familiar, because the family had already stayed in Ottawa for a few months in the summer of 1975. I had also visited Ottawa many times over the past few years to attend SSD staff meetings. Nonetheless, it was an important trip for the family to travel to Canada as new immigrants to start life afresh. We looked forward positively to our new challenges and opportunities. We were excited and full of hope about entering another chapter of our lives.

IN FRONT OF OUR HOUSE IN OTTAWA, 1982

7 Work and Life in Ottawa

Moving from Singapore to work and live in Ottawa was a momentous decision for me professionally and for my family. We had to make major adjustments, as we would be living in the capital of a large country adjacent to the United States. The adjustment in weather was huge. In our first Christmas in Ottawa in 1980, the temperature plunged to -32 °C, almost the other extreme of equatorial Singapore, where the temperatures are often in the thirties in the opposite direction. The challenge of driving in harsh winter conditions was something I had to prepare for and learn. The formal education in Ottawa is bilingual, but in English and French. This was good for Tao-ming and Sze-mei, who would learn French as a new language. They would later continue in this combination when they attended King George V School in Hong Kong. We were prepared to tackle new challenges and opportunities as new immigrants in Canada.

We left Singapore on 8 August 1980 and after stopovers in Hong Kong, Tokyo, Nagoya (IDRC work), Vancouver, and Calgary, arrived in Ottawa on the 31st. We were met and warmly greeted by David Steedman, Director of the SSD at the IDRC, and his son Eric. We were settled into Park Lane, where we stayed for one month until we found our own accommodation. Nae Ismail and his family, as well as other friends, helped us a great deal in settling down. We went house hunting, but soon restricted ourselves to the Alta Vista area because we wanted our children to attend the Alta Vista School. We were attracted to 2050 Palmer Place, a lovely bungalow with a big lawn in front and the back located on a quiet and short side street one long block from and parallel to Alta Vista Drive, a major north-south artery of the city. We moved into the house on 1 October, coinciding with my 42nd birthday. We bought a brand-new blue Pontiac Phoenix one week after our arrival. It was an America car with four-wheel drive, prompted by the assumption that such a car would be better able to withstand the cold weather in Ottawa. I was soon to be proven wrong in the first winter, as after a few hours outside in the extreme cold, I often would have problems restarting that car. The situation improved after one winter after the car had fully run in.

The house we owned in Ottawa signalled a new stage in our life. It was the first house that we had ever owned, since in Singapore the most comfortable flats we lived in were those provided by my employers. For me, home ownership was a challenge, both in terms of the skill and time required to look after not only the house itself but the spacious grounds on which it stood. The house was solidly built and 18 years of age. My work in the house related to wood work, electric and household appliances, heating and air-conditioning, and roof maintenance and upkeep. Soon after we moved in, I had to climb up on the roof to fix a leak. I was thrilled that I was able to fix it after learning what was needed from a self-help manual. There was also a great deal of work at different times of the year, what with the need to take care of the lawn by cutting the grass and raking the leaves, and to shovel snow from the driveway. We had two Dutch elm trees in the front and two maple trees in the back, along with other smaller trees, enough to keep us busy during the snow-free seasons. I considered the work of keeping the house and grounds in order to be a kind of exercise and a way of plunging into the Canadian way of life. Occasionally, I sought advice from neighbours, who had to go through these household drills themselves. As we settled in more, I farmed out the work of cutting grass and shovelling snow to neighbourhood youngsters who needed pocket money. All in all, it was a form of living close to nature, and our daily activities were keenly felt to be under the dictates of weather conditions. Still fresh in my mind are the experiences of a heavy overnight snowfall making the driveway impassable until it was dug clear of snow, of prolonged and heavy rain causing flooding in our basement, and of freezing rain immobilizing our car and making it impossible to negotiate slippery roads. We had to face different consequences from all of these weather hazards, calling for different kinds of action.

With our prior experience of living in Canada, we quickly found our footing in Ottawa and loved the clear change of seasons, the many attractions of the city, and our social networks. As the Chinese community was very conscious of the need for the young to be knowledgeable in the Chinese language, Chinese education up to Grade 6 was provided. Both Tao-ming and Sze-mei were thus enrolled soon after our arrival in Ottawa. While they attended Chinese lessons at the High School of Commerce every Saturday, it was also time for me and Ameda to engage ourselves in ping pong, badminton, and other activities at the same school. In fact, for me ping pong became an important physical pastime and a channel through which to meet other Chinese and other friends. I even joined a B-grade city league in playing ping pong during the winter months, in which players from many parts of the world participated. Unfortunately, the city league in ping pong came to an end in my third winter. We used to rent facilities in high schools for the weekly play, using membership dues and accumulated savings. To our astonishment, in the absence of a system of checks and balances, the honorary treasurer embezzled the funds. Tennis was also another pastime, but since I was only beginning to master the game and was away on trips too often, I did not consider it worth my while to join the Ottawa Athletic Club to play indoor tennis because of its high membership fee. However, I played occasionally in its indoor courts through invitations from my Chinese friends or IDRC colleagues. I was also improving my game and played in public courts.

Ameda was active in her own ways, being in demand for demonstrating flower making, flower arrangement, and Japanese doll making in community centres and occasionally on television. She also developed her keen interest in singing Cantonese operatic songs. She played host to her friends in practising singing these songs together in our basement. Her group gave occasional performances in Ottawa, and even once in Montreal. The downtown public library was a popular place for Tao-ming and Sze-mei on some Saturday afternoons. Sze-mei took pride in having read all of the fairy tale books by country in the library's collection. I was delighted, as was her teacher, to read her well-composed and imaginative essay written in class based on some of the readings she had done on fairy tales. To meet the cold winter head on, the family had a collective project soon after our arrival of learning how to skate. After mastering the basic skills, we ventured occasionally onto the Rideau Canal, which without fail froze during the winter months to provide a large natural skating rink for the public. Skating along the Canal gave me and my family members the identity of being citizens of Ottawa, something we would never forget and of which we will always be proud. The feeling of skating in the open against the backdrop of the city is different from skating in an indoor rink. The Winterlude on Dow's Lake was an annual winter festival and a popular destination for the family and visiting friends. We enjoyed the ice sculptures, which had a different theme every year. The festival attracted Ottawans as well as people and families from near and far, who came for the exhibition and atmosphere. During the summer, we found it equally enjoyable to make trips within driving distance to pick strawberries and apples. We learned recipes for freezing strawberries, which would last the family the whole winter. We had a huge freezer in our basement to store meat, fruits, and other food. We often hosted dinners at home for relatives and friends in Ottawa or from afar. On these occasions, to enliven such gatherings, I would often show my latest colour slides taken on recent trips. Photography, my life-long hobby, has served me well, academically and socially, wherever we lived. Frequent travel and photography were, for me, mutually reinforcing.

Nae Ismail (surnamed Ma) and his large extended family had strong roots in Ottawa, and very often got together with us, especially during weekends. Nae and I went back to our common school days in Hong Kong, with our devout Muslim families being close to each other at different stages of our lives. Thus, his home, presided over by his mother, was almost like our second home in Ottawa, a real blessing when our children were so young. During Hari Raya and other religious celebrations, male members from our two families would pray together at the Civic Centre in Lansdowne Park. Such occasions would bring Muslims of many cultural backgrounds together in makeshift facilities for prayers. The crowds were large to overflowing. In a small way, these occasions served to light up our Islamic thoughts on such important festivities.

With the family happily settled in a new life with its own tempo, I was able to devote whole-hearted attention to my career at the IDRC. Working in its head office in Ottawa allowed me to broaden my circle of friends within the organization, including several at the top. Apart from deepening my relationship with colleagues in the SSD, I made many friends in other units, including President Ivan Head, Librarian Margo Montieth, Treasurer Ray Audet, and others. Ivan Head became a good friend, especially after his retirement many years later in Vancouver, where he taught and Sze-mei studied, law at the University of British Columbia. Working in Ottawa also helped me to form professional links with a large number of international organizations, especially the World Bank, Ford Foundation, Population Council, Social Science Research Council, Agricultural Development Council, and other organizations. We worked unusually closely with the World Bank, as without support for research at that time despite its sizeable development funding, the World Bank cooperated with the IDRC in jointly publishing research findings on low-cost housing. Douglas Keare and I, for example, made a couple of reciprocal visits between Washington, D.C., and Ottawa for this purpose.

As soon as I found myself reasonably settled into the working dynamics of head office, I reworked my urban statement, initially prepared in 1980 in ASRO, with the objective of having it approved as a separate programme. It took about a year for this to reach fruition, with useful inputs from social sciences colleagues in Ottawa as well as Terry McGee from UBC. The Urban Policy Programme as it was finally approved in 1981 consisted of five components, namely urban services, urban policy and programmes, urban employment, urban land, and urban-regional relations. The establishment of this new programme was crucially assisted by my working with François Belisle, a French Canadian who had obtained his doctoral degree in Geography from an American university. Our working experience dovetailed well; I looked after Chinese and English speaking areas of the world, and François looked after French, Spanish, and Portuguese speaking areas. The global programme was soon off to a good start. In the less than three years of its existence in Ottawa under my direction, the programme supported 25 projects and 43 DAPs (Divisional Activity Projects). The former required formal approval by the Division or the Board, with project summaries needing to be written according to a certain level of detail and style, whereas the latter referred to small-scale activity requiring anything from a few hundred to 25,000 dollars. Therefore, a considerable amount of travel was needed to produce this level of research activity and support. When the Urban Policy Programme was in full swing, it had an annual budget of 1.5 million Canadian dollars, which I administered.

As before, my work calendar revolved around the two SSD staff meetings, one in the spring and one in the fall, but since our relocation to Ottawa, these meetings were home based. Field staff had to come in from various regional offices of the IDRC. I had to plan my travels around these two key meetings in Ottawa. As I was far from any of the developing regions where the projects that we funded were being implemented, when planning my long trips I made a point of packing in as many meetings and activities as possible to maximize efficiency. In between the long trips, I would undertake short trips within North America. Family travel took place in the summer.

With this pattern of travel established, over the years I undertook short trips to Kingston (Queen's), Toronto (Ryerson Polytechnical

Institute; York), Corner Brook (CAG), Edmonton (Alberta), Victoria (BC), New York (twice), Dallas, San Antonio (AAG), Denver (AAG), and Hamilton (Chinese geographers). I made a couple of trips to Washington, D.C., combining them with family travel. Trips related to attending the annual meetings of Canadian (CAG) and American (AAG) geographers highlighted the IDRC's support for staff members to attend their professional meetings to maintain and update their academic status. Great latitude was allowed for staff members to plan their own travel, an attractive aspect of the IDRC job.

Using Ottawa as the base, I made a total of twelve long official trips in four years. Most of these trips ran for three weeks or more, with six lasting four weeks or longer, and the longest eight weeks. I went twice to Africa, and once each to Latin America and the South Pacific. Two trips took me on a round-the-world route. One took place from 28 November to 23 December 1982, and covered Amsterdam (via Montreal), Delhi, Ahmedabad, Delhi, Bombay, Singapore, Bangkok, Hong Kong, Seoul, Tokyo, and Vancouver. Another, from 21 April to 18 June 1984, was the longest at eight weeks, and covered Vancouver, Tokyo, Beijing, Xi'an, Nanjing, Hangzhou, Shanghai, Hong Kong, Singapore, Kuala Lumpur, Bangkok, Delhi, Bombay, Trivandrum, London, and Montreal. The first three weeks of this trip was the IDRC's "road show" in China, to Beijing, Xi'an and Nanjing, in which I took the responsibility of introducing the Social Sciences Programmes. It seemed to me that the road show could have been better organized. The audiences that I spoke to were hardly comprised of the kinds of researchers who could effectively submit fundable research projects in the social sciences. I still remember the meeting in which I spoke in Beijing. Among those that the State Scientific Technology Commission (SSTC), the IDRC's counterpart organization in China, had gathered together to listen to my introduction on social sciences in the IDRC was Cui Zhijiu 崔之久 , a leading paleo-geographer from Peking University. He was among six scholars mostly trained in the natural sciences who had been invited to listen to my presentation. Professor Cui's research interests could not have been more remote to the social sciences projects that we could fund. In Nanjing we stayed in the city's only five-star hotel, the newly opened Jin Ling Hotel in the city centre. Every day the front door of the hotel was mobbed by hordes of curious bystanders, who wanted to peep at the luxury of the interior decorations and the strangeness of its occupants. The separation between ordinary citizens and those who came from afar was sharp in the early days of reform in China. This longest trip ever taken on IDRC assignment also produced one of the longest trip reports – at 62 pages, it equalled the length of the report written for another long trip in 1983. As mentioned earlier, all IDRC trips had to be concluded by trip reports.

We took advantage of the summer in North America to travel with the family. However, in the first summer in June 1981, Ameda travelled by herself to attend a three-week course with the American Floral School in Chicago. During that period, she stayed with our good friend Marian Ming and her family. She came back with a qualification to teach Western-style flower arrangement. However, in the next summer, our family vacation involved driving to Syracuse (John Mercer), Washington, D.C. (Ronald Ng), New York (Fu-chen Lo), Cape Cod (Salah El Shakhs), Boston, and Montreal. Most of the way, we stayed with the friends mentioned and renewed friendships. We cemented ties with good friends and their families going back many years. It was the first family trip to cover a large part of the Northeastern Seaboard, an educational experience for our children. We went to leading museums in Washington, D.C., famous tourist sites and shopping areas in Manhattan, and famous universities in Boston, with obviously in our minds only a remote possibility of the children enrolling in them in the future. Staying in El Shakhs' cottage in Cape Cod with his family added to our experience of a family summer vacation in the United States. Such a vacation was a salient aspect of American life. The speedometer showed that I drove 3,390 km on this trip.

We essentially repeated the same format of family travel in the summer of 1983. In three weeks, our destination was Orlando in Florida, with the attractions of Disney World, Epcot, and Kennedy Space Center. They were dream places to visit for our children, who had just entered their teens. They were so much looking forward to the visits that I assigned them to write an essay about their impressions of visiting these places. It was a way of training them to be observant about what they were seeing and going through. Both Tao-ming and Sze-mei rose to the challenge and wrote excellent essays. What better than to sightsee and learn at the same time, with a written record to remember it all! We went via Syracuse, Gettysburg, Washington, D.C., Florence, Charleston, Savannah, and Jacksonville before arriving in Orlando. The route was purposefully designed to retrace the highlights of the American Civil War, mostly for their educational and historical value for our children. We returned with a stop of several days in suburban New York (Shorthills), staying with Fu-chen and his family again. It being our second family visit to America's largest city, we were keen to visit more tourist attractions, museums, and Chinatown, and to do more shopping. Then we returned via Kingston, Ontario, and visited Chow Wai-yin and his family, before returning to Ottawa via Montreal. I wanted to break the news to him in person of my decision to return to Hong Kong to join the Chinese University in a few months. Little did I realize that he must have been making similar plans of his own, as Wai-yin himself also returned several years afterwards to teach in Hong Kong. I chalked up a distance on 6,300 km on this trip, the longest distance I have driven on a trip.

In the summer of 1984, we were travelling together as a family for another purpose. We travelled via Europe towards Hong Kong, as will be highlighted in what follows.

Meanwhile, a storm was brewing on the home front. My elder brother, Yue-goke, saw an advertisement in Hong Kong, which offered to facilitate the education of Hong Kong students in Ottawa. It was one of the ways for Hong Kong families to prepare themselves and their children for the 1997 handover. My nephew, Tao-shing 道成, was beginning his secondary education and ready to try a different education system. In late August 1982, Yue-goke and Tao-shing arrived in Ottawa and stayed with us. This was soon followed by the arrival of my parents, who had settled in Calgary with my youngest brother and wife since September 1981. They kindly offered to come to look after Tao-shing, whom they had essentially brought up from birth in Hong Kong many years earlier.

Tao-shing's coming ushered in a period of tension and problems for the family. Already during the month when Yue-goke was still in Ottawa, Tao-shing could not get along with our children. My parents realized this as well, and therefore rented an apartment in the Chinatown area in which to live with Tao-shing. It was also near the school that he was to attend. The generation gap between my parents and Tao-shing, notwithstanding their earlier bond and close relationship, was too large to be bridged in any way. Attempts to mediate between them also led to friction between my parents and Ameda. Relationships within the family suddenly took a turn for the worse because of Tao-shing's arrival. Most serious of all, Tao-shing's academic level was not up to par by Canadian standards. He felt disheartened and returned to Hong Kong after one year.

While that year is one we would rather forget from the viewpoint of the family, it nevertheless provided a golden opportunity for us to spend time with my parents. Indeed, during that year we met at least once a week and shared some common happy experiences. We played *mah jong* often, providing occasions for Tao-ming to learn Chinese through fun and games. The time that we spent with my parents more than made up for the strain that was brought into the family because of Tao-shing's coming. This was the longest period of time that we had spent with my parents since our marriage. They also got to know our children well. During holidays and festive occasions, we had precious moments to celebrate with my parents. I also brought them into my circuit of friends and Muslim families in Ottawa. It has left for me at least many happy memories and treasured moments.

Even before the departure of Tao-shing and my parents from Ottawa, positive developments relating to my career began to unfold. In April 1983, I was promoted to Associate Director of the SSD, a decision that was advanced by several months because of President Ivan Head's support and intervention in my favour. I breathed a sigh of relief that I had been able to prove my ability to lead an independent funding programme within the IDRC. At about the same time, my involvement in initiating research activities in China increased. Every year since I was relocated to Ottawa, I visited China, especially Beijing and Guangzhou, and tried hard to identify researchers to undertake projects. However, it was still very early days since China's opening up and Chinese researchers were simply not ready to mount the kinds of projects that the Centre was prepared to fund. Besides working on my own Chinese contacts, I cooperated with my colleague Carol Vlassoff in the Population Programme. We travelled together in June 1983 through Beijing, Chengdu, and Guangzhou to develop an In-Depth Fertility Survey (China) Project with the State Statistical Bureau (SSB). That project eventually became the first project that the Division funded in China and was an immediate success. What was to become the first phase of the project cost half a million dollars, but the additional support came from the Norwegian and Danish governments, which went towards providing two mainframe computers to the SSB to run the data analysis related to the project. These were major attractions at a time when the mainframe computer was relatively costly and personal computers were not yet on the market.

Apart from my trips and work in Asia, I devoted considerable attention and time to developing contacts and projects in Africa. While based in Ottawa, I made two long trips to Africa in February 1982 and November 1983, and had multiple stops in African countries. The IDRC's regional offices in Cairo and Nairobi provided crucial local and regional support for me on these and earlier trips. I visited Cairo, Nairobi, Lusaka, Salisbury (Southern Rhodesia), Dar es Salaam, and Arusha for project development and other purposes. The stay in Salisbury in February 1982 was timely and historical, as two months later its name would change to Harare, and the country of Southern Rhodesia would become Zimbabwe. I almost witnessed the change of regime in that country and city.

The two stopovers in Nairobi were related to a most important urban research initiative linking Anglophone and Francophone countries (Sudan, Kenya, Tanzania, Senegal, Nigeria, Zaire, and Ivory Coast) in a landmark and influential project. For the first time, researchers in these African countries, who had hitherto largely worked on their own without any interaction across the language divide, were networked in a collaborative project with common research objectives in urban management and urban reform. The final meeting of this project was held in March 1985 in Abidjan, Ivory Coast, to which I had to fly from Hong Kong to attend. By then, I had already joined The Chinese University of Hong Kong. The researchers met two more times at the University of Toronto, in September 1985 and October 1986, to refine their comparative study. The end product from the project was an important and almost classic book, *African Cities in Crisis* (1989), edited by Richard Stren and Rodney White, coordinators of the project funded by the IDRC. Both Richard and Rodney were proficient in English and French, as was my IDRC colleague, François Belisle. These language skills were of great help to the success of the project. When I left my IDRC job in August 1984, I had half a dozen projects in Africa that were close to being ready for funding.

In the morning of 2 March 1983 I received a long-distance call from Rance Lee, Dean of Social Science at The Chinese University of Hong Kong who informed me that the recent drive to recruit the Professor of Geography had entered its final phase.

"Yue-man, the university has gone through the due process of recruiting the Professor of Geography. Two final candidates have been shortlisted, one a Reader in Geography at HKU and the other an American professor. Mindful of your interest in the position to which you applied in 1978, are you still interested in it?" Dean Lee was very direct.

"Thank you for remembering me and my earlier application. But since you have already gone through the process, why have you called me?" I was frank with Dean Lee because we already knew each other quite well through an IDRC-supported project headed by him.

"To be very honest with you, Yue-man, as Dean I have high respect for the academic credentials of the two short-listed candidates. But I think you are more rounded with your administrative and other experience," Dean Lee did not hide his judgement.

"Your offer is great, but I have just been promoted within the IDRC," I replied, bringing him up-to-date on my recent promotion.

"Congratulations. To facilitate our work, can you be candid and say what is the likelihood of your taking up the professorship?" Dean Lee wanted to conclude our telephone conversation.

"Let me discuss the situation with my family. I shall send you a message tomorrow to give you a more concrete expression of my position," with that, I ended our phone conversation.

After discussing the substance of the phone call with Ameda, I sent a telex to Dean Lee to say that there was a 50:50 chance of my accepting the opportunity to return to Hong Kong.

In June of that year when I was on a long Asian trip, I took several days of personal leave during a stopover in Hong Kong to visit the university. I was put up at the Yali Guesthouse, which was the base of my activities for three days. I gave a presentation on Low-cost Housing in Asia, based on my recently released edited volume on the subject, published by the IDRC. Chaired by Dr Zhu Li 朱立, the meeting was held in United College with a large attendance, including the University Secretary and some professors. The Vice-Chancellor, senior professors, and administrators had individual and joint sessions with me to size me up thoroughly. At the end of the visit, Dean Lee brought the welcome news that the university had decided to offer me the post. Given the uncertainties surrounding the run-up to 1997 in Hong Kong, I made it clear that I would only assume that post after completing my Canadian citizenship requirements. As it turned out it, even with an accelerated process, it took another fifteen months before the process was complete. Since I travelled so much on my job I needed more time than my family members to satisfy the residential requirement of having lived in Canada for three years within four years to qualify. Given this kind of exceptional treatment and understanding on the part of the university, especially by Vice-Chancellor Ma Lin, I was prepared to serve it with all my heart and soul.

Our four years in Ottawa turned out to be fulfilling in many ways and exceeded our expectations. The family grew stronger together with many happy memories and experiences. The education was to the liking of Tao-ming and Sze-mei, who made many friends and developed good working and personal habits. Sze-mei showed high academic ability, and was streamed into the enriched class beginning in 1983. We had many occasions to travel and learn together, seeing a large part of the northeastern region of the continent. We still have fond memories of spending the day at Prod Laquian's farm in Perth, Ontario, on a cold winter's day in January 1982, tobogganing on icy slopes in the bitter cold of -18 °C. We have plenty to remember about our house, as much work was required to look after it inside and out and in all seasons. Our larger home was with Nae Ismail's big family, with whom we maintained extensive links before and after living in Ottawa.

Professionally, I could not have had a better posting than working out of Ottawa. I covered universities, professionals, and institutions coast to coast, with plenty of opportunities to work with my counterparts in New York and Washington, D.C. Partly because of my work and my Chinese background, I was close to the staff of the

Chinese Embassy in Ottawa, especially with Liu Dongsheng 劉東升, the First Secretary. I attended many functions at the embassy, including one welcoming the Chinese Premier, Zhao Ziyang 趙紫陽. My international background was greatly enriched through repeated trips to Africa, Latin America, and the South Pacific. They provided good empirical comparisons with Asia, enriching my stock of knowledge about the Third World.

We left Singapore for Ottawa in 1980 with the expectation that we would be putting down deep roots in Canada. The phone call from Dean Lee changed the original plan and expectation. Looking back, it was another God-send opportunity for me to return to academia after almost ten years of working in the international development assistance field. Returning to Hong Kong was timely because my long-term interest in research on China would have ample room to develop, especially after the recent opening up of China. Returning to academia at its peak with a professorship and to Hong Kong was a dream come true. What more could I ask for?

I left Ottawa on 17 August 1984 with my family for London via Montreal. I had IDRC matters to attend to in London, Lille, and Paris. My family also had some free time to see the highlights of London and Paris before we arrived in Hong Kong on 31 August. This was our first family trip to Europe, to be succeeded by a more extensive tour several years later. We were again ready to begin another chapter of our lives on my home turf. After being away for almost two decades, I returned to serve Hong Kong and its people. Again, the wheel of fortune had brought me back home. The motto of this professional trajectory is that a career cannot be planned; it simply unfolds according to its own logic and opportunities. In my case, I recall what my father used to say to his children many a time: we simply follow what is pre-ordained by the Almighty. Time and again, I was led in directions that I did not plan. As my career unfolded further, these unexpected turns led to greater professional achievements for me and equally satisfying developments for my family.

AS UNIVERSITY REGISTRAR, IN THE COMPANY OF SOME COMMUNITY AND
UNIVERSITY LEADERS, 1986

8 Career Peaks in Hong Kong
1984-1990

Returning to work and live in Hong Kong in 1984 was the realization of a career-long objective that had almost happened before. However, this time, at least on the surface, I appeared to almost be going against the tide. As it soon turned out, many, including some members of my family, were leaving Hong Kong in preparation for the 1997 handover. However, we returned as expatriates, so there was nothing to fear. From some perspectives, it seemed that we had the best of both worlds. It was a timely return, as the future of Hong Kong soon became clear with the formalizing in September 1984 of the draft of the Sino-British Accord relating to the 1997 handover, which happened immediately after our arrival. I also returned better prepared to meet challenges and opportunities than at any time in my life. I had travelled the world many times over and was laden with global outlooks and connections and steeped in administrative and organizational skills. Most important of all, I was eager to plunge back into academic research.

In order to capture the highlights of my career in Hong Kong, which has stretched almost a quarter of a century, I propose, for a better focus of discussion, to compartmentalize my work into three periods. This chapter covers the first period, 1984 to 1990.

On arrival in Hong Kong on 31 August 1984, we were met by Ameda's family and Dr Wong Kwan-yiu 黃鈞堯, Head of Geography at CUHK. We were settled into Residence 10 and began our new lives. A Renault car was left to us by Mrs Eunice Wong 黃林婉貞, my fond former geography classmate at HKU, who had just left for Vancouver as a landed immigrant of Canada. This facilitated our mobility a great deal until April 1989, when I returned the car following her return to work in Hong Kong after completing her citizenship requirements.

The vehicle provided an immediate convenience, as moving around the campus was not easy without a car. However, we were not pleased with Residence 10, as noise was a constant nuisance caused by its proximity to the railway tracks. My family was therefore elated when the new Residence 15 was completed in February 1985 and we were allocated, through the Vice-Chancellor's intervention, a flat on the fourth floor. It was our proud home for 15 years until we moved out of the university residence in 1999. We owed another favour to Vice-Chancellor Ma Lin 馬臨 .

Tao-ming and Sze-mei were admitted to King George V (KGV) School and had to skip a grade, as the Canadian education system started one year later than the British one. This posed some difficulties for Tao-ming, as he had to skip Form 3, a major foundation year in science subjects. Sze-mei, on the other hand, shone even after skipping one year. She, in fact, was a top student in her seven years of study at the school, topping the form thrice in that period.

Returning to Hong Kong provided the opportunity for us to be with our families. Farita, Chris, and their family soon moved to work and live in Hong Kong, following Chris's promotion to a senior position at HSBC in Hong Kong. However, Yue-goke and his family emigrated to Australia (Perth) in November 1987 and returned in January 1990 after meeting citizenship requirements. Thus, globalization and the handover jitters had their effects on our family in where we lived and worked.

As I had been away from Hong Kong for so long, re-establishing social networks with old friends was a gradual process. Wong Hui Man-kay 黃許文祺 and her extended family were close to us, marked by their attendance of my inaugural lecture delivered on 29 November 1985. Chan Kai-sui 陳啟瑞, a good friend of my brother David's, invited us often to sail on his luxurious yacht from Sai Kung in Hong Kong waters. We saw Dragon Boat races at that place a couple of times. Chow Wai-yin 周威炎 returned in 1987 from Kingston, Canada, to teach at Hong Kong Polytechnic, before being appointed Professor of Physics at HKU in late 1989. Wong Kim-kam 黃劍琴 , an old and dear friend dating back to May Hall days at HKU, was a high-ranking government official. Our families reconnected soon after our return. It was a tragedy that he cut short his life in December 1989.

During my first year with CUHK, my main academic focus was on teaching and research. As Department Chair, I had the usual administrative duties and responsibilities. In addition, I was appointed concurrently the Director of the Centre for Contemporary Asian Studies (CCAS). Teaching geography in Cantonese was a challenge to me, as I had learned the subject all those years in English. I had to learn the Chinese vocabulary and terms, getting used to it after a while. Writing research papers in Chinese was another challenge, as most of my formal writing had been in English. It was another learning dimension that I have been trying to improve all these years upon my return to Hong Kong.

My first year quickly settled into a productive pattern as I managed to write ten papers in that year, including my inaugural address and many invited papers presented in Barcelona, Honolulu, Akron, Ohio (in absentia), Guangzhou, and Nagoya. I even attended an ASAIHL (Association of Southeast Asian Institutions of Higher Learning) meeting in Yogyakarta, Indonesia, in July. I attended in the capacity of the alternate member from Hong Kong to the regular member represented by Professor Rayson Huang, HKU's Vice-Chancellor. VC Ma Lin already looked positively at my international experience.

Yet my pattern of work would change radically after one year. During a private lunch with VC Ma Lin at his lodge on a Saturday afternoon in October 1985, he broached an idea to me. The two of us sat quietly in one corner of his spacious living room, at a temporary set-up of a low table for two.

Slowly, but deliberately, VC Ma began: "Yue-man, I invited you here for a private lunch with me because our Registrarship will soon be open. The present Registrar, Dr Liu Pak-wai 廖伯偉 , will soon be leaving for Australia to get new citizenship papers. That will take at least two years. I hope you will consider stepping into his vacancy."

I was taken aback, at a loss as to what to say for a while. Then, I said, "I much appreciate your considering me for the position, but given that I have been at this university for only a short time and lack experience in university administration, I am not sure if I am up to the job."

"I am sure you can learn quickly, plus the rich administrative experience in your previous international development work would be highly relevant," VC Ma continued.

Not forgetting that my foremost interest lay in research and teaching, I brought up a possible problem, "I came back to academia and have set my heart on running the Department of Geography."

"You could hold concurrently the positions of Registrar and Chair of Geography, with probably a deputy head to look after day-to-day matters," he quickly retorted.

As I could not make an immediate decision and felt that it was inadvisable to do so, VC Ma suggested I speak to Dr Liu to gain an idea of what the Registrar job entailed and evaluate its prospects.

Although my initial reaction was somewhat negative, after in-depth discussions with Liu Pak-wai and Rance Lee 李沛良 , I took it as another challenge to my ability to take on this new assignment. My private session with Pak-wai in his residence helped to allay some of my fears. Moreover, he was persuasive in pointing to the attractions of the position and its importance in leading the growth of the university. In all, I came to see it as another opportunity to prove myself and to stand by the university at a time of tribulation. Immediately, I would be put to many tests since the university was faced with many contentious issues, and was at odds with the government as well as with some institutions and schools on account of its unique education system in Hong Kong. Almost overnight, I scaled another academic height as University Registrar. As a university officer, I had a high-level administrative position that came with demanding work and heavy responsibilities. Mindful again that I had returned to academia to pursue research and teaching, I took up the Registrarship on the condition that I would be able to maintain my links to the Department of Geography. As concurrently its Head and with a light teaching load, I wanted to still be in charge of major decisions there. As it turned out, I was on top of all major developments in the department and continued to be academically productive.

Accepting the appointment of Registrar to be held concurrently with that of the Chair of Geography, along with other commitments in Hong Kong and the international community, was a severe test of my time management skills. I found that life became hectic, with the need to meet commitments not only on campus but in other parts of Hong Kong. There were many important issues and developments that I needed to take the time to shepherd into proper form and substance. Some of the major developments included the elevation of the School of Education to a Faculty, the acceptance of student members in the Senate, the establishment of Shaw College, the establishment of the Faculty of Engineering and the Architecture Department, preparations by CUHK alumni to form Convocation and preparations of plans for expansion, especially following the Tiananmen Incident in 1989. During my term as Registrar, due to a change of systems I prepared three Triennium Plans, including the Triennium Plan for 1991-94. The projects that took the bulk of my time involved issues and discussions surrounding the Education Commission Report No. 3 (ERC 3) and on-going discussions over two years with administrators at HKU.

Meanwhile, Charles Kao 高錕 was installed in late 1987 as Vice-Chancellor of CUHK, succeeding Ma Lin. As the "father of optical fibre," he brought new energy and a vision to strengthen the research capabilities and environment of the university. VC Kao's revolutionary contribution to optical fibre research eventually won him in 2009 a Nobel Prize in Physics, after a string of distinguished awards and honours. Having established the Department of Electronics in the early 1970s and served as its founding Head, VC Kao fittingly oversaw the establishment of the Faculty of Engineering during his tenure. He also brought a new approach to bear on resolving the impasse between the university and the government on the-length-of-study issue.

Dr Q. W. Lee 利國偉, who later received a knighthood, was Chairman of the Education Commission as well as Chairman of the University Council at CUHK. He was in an unenviable position, as the main issues addressed in the ERC 3 were related to the need to settle the unique but controversial problem of requiring four years of study at the undergraduate level. Staff, students, and alumni at CUHK were adamantly against any change to this long-cherished tradition. I was in good company with Jacob Leung 梁少光, F. C. Chen 陳方正, Arthur Li 李國章 and others in defending our system. The debates in the Legislative Council and among the community on the recommendations of the ERC 3 were divided. Students and staff showed their anger by staging many gatherings, including a five-hour sit-in to 9:30 p.m. on 26 October 1988 in Chater Garden in Central, which saw a turnout of 1,000 participants. Through most of the sit-in, President Chung Chi-yung 鍾期榮, of Shue Yan College, now a university, joined forces with me to show her staunch support for the four-year system. Our morale was boosted by the brief appearance of VC Charles Kao. The issue was finally resolved by the Senate, which decided to adopt a Flexible Credit Unit System, with Professor Kao taking a non-confrontational approach. One thing I learned about the job of Registrar was that there were no regular hours. Discussions and the preparation of documents often found me and Jacob Leung, along with other members of staff, working late into the evening when major issues required an immediate response. I honestly felt that I was working around the clock. My devotion to the defense of the four-year course of study earned me strong support from the university, especially from alumni and students.

The main recommendation of the ERC 3 was for the uniform

admission of students to tertiary education at Form 7, instead of the multi-channel admission system adopted by CUHK. This meant, on the surface, that CUHK bore the brunt of the change. However, with the adoption of a Flexible Credit Unit System, the impact on the curriculum was minimized. With the notional change of the curriculum to three years as the mainstream, CUHK had to adjust to the situation of students not having enough leeway to take general education and other courses. As University Registrar, I had to spend an enormous amount of time interacting with all major stakeholders, including holding many private sessions with Dr Q. W. Lee in the office at his bank. The seven-year course of study at secondary schools was implemented in the 1950s as a result of a decision made in the UK to shorten the length of studies at universities to three from four. Speculation was even rife within the Hong Kong community that the insistence on a three-year curriculum at the university level as prescribed by the ERC 3 involved a conspiracy on the part of the colonial government to ensure the continuation in Hong Kong of the three-year university system as practised in the UK before Britain's rule over Hong Kong came to an end in 1997.

To set the record straight, not only the government but many stakeholders in the community were objecting to CUHK's popular Early Admissions System at Form 6. What is most ironic is that, after two decades, entry to university from all schools in Hong Kong will be harmonized at Form 6 beginning in 2012, followed by four years of university studies. This means that the education system in Hong Kong has gone back to the one that CUHK had been running since its establishment in 1963. After two decades of fruitless meandering, Hong Kong finally discovered the value and true worth of the 6+4 system of secondary and tertiary education.

During my term as Registrar, the two universities developed cordial and close relationships when we had to deal with many common problems. With Wang Gungwu 王賡武 as Vice-Chancellor, HKU's

Senate voted overwhelmingly to change to a four-year curriculum in November 1986. Suddenly, the two universities were on common ground on the issue. This led to the administrators of the two universities meeting regularly to discuss matters of common interest, such as terms of service, length of study, student admission, and so on. At what were known as fellowship dinners held monthly, Norman Gilanders, HKU's Registrar and I took turns playing host, with the participation of Joan Lowcock, Michael Spooner, and Henry Wei 韋永庚 from HKU and Jacob Leung, David Gilkes, and S. W. Lee 李樹榮 on our side, along with other staff. The main contribution of these meetings was that they led to the establishment of a joint admission system between the two universities, soon extended to all six institutions of higher learning at that time under the management of the Hong Kong Examination Authority (HKEA). This system, later renamed the Joint University Programmes Admissions System (JUPAS), is still in use for admitting students to tertiary institutions in Hong Kong.

Beyond HKU, I also tried to touch base with other universities to learn the latest methods of university administration. Several trips were undertaken for this purpose.

To start with, I went on a 19-day trip between 29 March and 16 April 1987 to visit UBC in Vancouver, Harvard University in Boston, and Brown University in Providence. They all had exchange agreements with CUHK. I was hosted with exceptional warmth at Brown University, where Provost and Mrs Maurice Glicksman, Sidney and Alice Goldstein, Bob Kates, and David and Judith Meyer met me formally and socially during my two-day stay. Meeting with the Meyers again after almost two decades from our graduate school days at UChicago was an added joy. After the last stop in Providence, I drove in a rented car to Trumbull in Fairfield County, Connecticut, to visit Charles and Gwen Kao at their home. The purpose was to get myself acquainted with and brief Charles, who would soon travel to assume the Vice-Chancellorship of CUHK. He needed to be apprised of the salient issues of development facing the university, especially the controversies surrounding the recommendations of the ERC 3. Then I flew from New York to San Francisco to visit the University of California at Berkeley to round off my reconnaissance trip. This survey of the some leading universities in North America was of benefit to me in showing how new information technology was being applied to facilitate university administration, student evaluation, research administration, and other issues.

In February 1988 I travelled as Registrar with Ameda, along with Charles and Gwen Kao, to Perth, Australia, to attend the 14th Congress of Commonwealth Universities, held once every four years. We were representatives of CUHK in a large congregation of universities from the British Commonwealth. I presented a paper on the university's role outside national boundaries that was published later in a Congress proceedings volume. I had a special reason to be pleased about attending the Congress, as our host, Professor Robert H. T. Smith, Vice-Chancellor of the University of Western Australia in Perth, was an old and close friend. We shared a common research interest in periodic markets, on which subject I contributed a chapter to a book that he had edited. We had been in professional contact when he was holding senior academic and administrative positions at Queen's University and UBC. As a new VC, Charles Kao made a timely appearance to meet his peers from many lands. On the return trip, we stopped over in Singapore and paid a visit to the National University of Singapore, whose VC Lin Pin we had met only a few days ago in Perth. Similarly, we paid a visit to the Nanyang Technological Institute, whose VC we had also met recently. The trip to Perth had a personal bonus for me and Ameda, as my brother Yue-goke and his family had recently emigrated there. We had a happy family reunion in a foreign land.

The third trip I made in relation to my Registrarship was taken after I had stepped down from that position in early 1990. I took my eight-month sabbatical leave immediately, essentially to allow myself to make some extensive travels, for official and academic purposes and with my family. That was the longest break from work that I have ever taken in my professional life. From 20 March 1990, I took a 40-day tour of universities in the United Kingdom and Canada to broaden my understanding of universities in those countries. I was awarded a Senior ACU (Association of Commonwealth Universities) Travelling Fellowship. The trip took me through Brighton (University of Sussex), London (SOAS, ACU), Cambridge, Oxford, Leeds, Durham, and Edinburgh in the UK. At the University of Cambridge, through a former HKU physicist friend, Ho Ping-yoke, I had a private audience with Professor Joseph Needham, a distinguished scholar on science and technology in China. Travelling by bus and train within the country deepened my understanding of the life and landscape of a large part of the British Isles, which I had covered in a more comprehensive tour in 1966. One of the special coach trips that I was on involved a six-hour transect from Oxford to Leeds via Banbury, Coventry, Leicester, Nottingham, and Sheffield. I had the good fortune of staying in historic places and soaked up some British history. In Leeds and Edinburgh, I stayed at the University Guest House, which in the former was a huge and comfortable former residence of a Nobel Laureate professor, and in the latter was the impressive Old College with a history of 200 years.

My trip then covered Canada, beginning in Halifax, where at the University of Dalhousie I was greeted by Tony Tillett, a former colleague at the IDRC in Ottawa. He was Director of the Lester Pearson Institute of International Development, harking back to my work and career with IDRC. The Halifax stop also allowed me to visit Mount Saint Vincent University, the Technical University of Nova Scotia, and St. Mary's University. The next stop was Toronto, where after my formal visit with the University of Toronto on the ACU Fellowship, I also attended the annual meeting of the Association of American Geographers. At this annual meeting, I was fortunate to hear the addresses of three celebrated scholars, namely Kenneth Hare, William Skinner, and Gilbert White, the last being my former professor at UChicago. The last stop was Saskatoon, where at the University of Saskatchewan I was hosted by top officers and by the Geography Department. I met Ka-iu Fung 馮家驍 at his home institution after many years. An ardent athIete, Ka-iu had been swimming regularly for years and proudly showed me his 40-foot swimming pool beside his house. It was the largest private swimming pool of anyone I have ever known, at least in a place where the winter is so long and severe. I was extended exceptional hospitality in many of the universities that I visited on this long but memorable trip. I have much to look back on in this visit to some of the leading universities in the United Kingdom and Canada: their tradition, history, eminent professors, campus, research strengths and, above all, friendship and hospitality.

My return to Hong Kong in 1984 coincided with a period of greater openness in China, with the opening up that year of some of the country's coastal cities. My joint appointment as Registrar and Professor of Geography enabled me to open many doors for collaborative research in China. In Beijing, I developed a productive relationship with Hu Xuwei 胡序威 at the Institute of Geography under the Chinese Academy of Sciences. I contributed a chapter to his book on China's coastal cities, and we let this collaboration expand into a different project as a full-length book in English published by the University of Hawaii Press. With Zhou Yixing 周一星 of the Department of Geography at Peking University, I developed a long-standing relationship that began with two edited journal issues introducing to the Western reader the major characteristics of Chinese cities and the changes that were taking place in those places; and an article on Human Geography in China published in *Progress in Human Geography*. These efforts were aimed at introducing Chinese cities and the human landscape to the West. Hu Zhaoliang 胡兆量 , also from the same department, and I also developed another kind of friendship and cooperation that lasted many years. Over many years he purchased and collected Chinese research materials for me. Through his extensive networks, he helped me years later to scout for suitable academics to cooperate with me in contributing to several edited volumes focusing on the changing geographies and development of China. My extensive travels through northeastern and northwestern China in later years owed much to Hu Zhaoliang's help and company. Likewise, Zhou Yixing not only arranged my trip through Tibet in 2001, but also travelled with me.

I also began to develop research networks in other regions of China. Specifically, I developed strong connections with East China Normal University (ECNU) in Shanghai, where Li Chunfen 李春芬 had been a leading scholarly figure for many years. As the first PhD graduate in geography from the University of Toronto, he maintained his links with and interest in Canada. We met initially at UBC in 1981 through an IDRC connection. Then, during a visit to Shanghai in May 1990, we met again when I was conferred the title of Advisory Professor by ECNU in a dignified ceremony followed by a lecture. Liu Junde 劉君德 and Mei Anxin 梅安新 also developed long-standing research relationships with me. In nearby Nanjing, I followed up on an earlier telephone acquaintance made in London, England, while working for the IDRC to reconnect with Shen Daoqi 沈道齊. Cui Gonghao 崔功豪 was another geographer from Nanjing University that I got to know. Within Guangdong, the focus of research collaboration was in Guangzhou. At Zhongshan University, Xu Xueqiang 許學強 and Zheng Tianxiang 鄭天祥 were identified as leaders in geographical research. Xu later spent some time at HKU to improve his understanding of Western countries and their scholarship. I was also close to Wen Chang'en 溫長思, Lin Qingxing 林青幸 and Cai Renqun 蔡人群 at the Institute of Geography in Guangzhou.

Special mention must be made of my early contact with and understanding of developments in Shenzhen through knowing Yuan Geng 袁庚 and Liang Xian 梁憲 of the China Merchants Group based both in Shenzhen and Hong Kong. Mr Yuan was a visionary leader responsible for some of the initial development of Shenzhen by establishing the first foothold for outside development via his company in Hong Kong. An eloquent speaker, he spoke as an invited guest at the CCAS at CUHK and explored collaborative research in the Special Economic Zone in Shenzhen. We met several times in 1984 and 1985, efforts that facilitated the establishment of a research unit on Special Economic Zones under Dr Wong Pui-yee's 王佩儀 direction within CCAS.

The late 1980s was a tumultuous period for both the family and Hong Kong. The family entered a new stage when Tao-ming was admitted to engineering studies at the University of Western Ontario (UWO) to begin in September 1988. We arranged to leave him in London, Ontario, during our home leave that summer. The greatest sorrow occurred on 3 September 1986 when my mother died of a heart attack in Calgary. It happened so suddenly that we were in shock for months. With her passing, my father lost the will to live and also died in November 1989. The passing away of our parents within a relatively short period has confirmed in my mind their true love for each other. When mother died in 1986, they had just celebrated the golden jubilee of their marriage. Family life has never been the same now that they are gone.

In fact, the year 1989 was a notable year for China as well. Public discontent in China swelled to a boiling point that culminated in massive and prolonged student demonstrations in Tiananmen Square in Beijing. Armed suppression on 4 June led to a loss of lives and cries of vindication even to this day in certain quarters. I resigned from my membership in the Consultative Committee of the Basic Law on 5 June as a personal gesture of disapproval of the use of armed force to disperse the students. I was one of four representatives from CUHK on that Committee, along with Arthur Li, Tso Wung Wai 曹宏威, and Agnes Ng 吳夢珍. The positive impact of the Tiananmen crackdown on Hong Kong was that higher education was greatly expanded and the replacement airport at Chek Lap Kok was speedily constructed. The Tiananmen Incident exacerbated the handover jitters, with the annual emigration of Hongkongers to largely English-speaking countries exceeding 60,000 in some years. The need to replenish our manpower due to the shortage resulting from the exodus of so many people, many with a university education, was the justification to vastly expand tertiary education. Similarly, after decades of indecision about building a new airport to replace Kai Tak Airport, the Tiananmen incident spurred a quick decision to select Chek Lap Kok as the best location from many perspectives, based on repeated and confirmed propositions by professional consultants. Hong Kong was in dire need of a state-of-the-art airport to maintain and increase its competitive advantage.

Apart from my father's passing in 1989, that year also saw the deaths of my good friend Wong Kim-kam and my librarian colleague, David Yen. These sad departures were counterbalanced by Sze-mei's scoring the most positive results at her GCSE examinations. She scored an "A" in all of the eight subjects that she took, and shared the top spot in her form with two other students at KGV School. Her excellent examination results had to have formed a critical basis on which Sze-mei was awarded an Ontario Fellowship two years later, tenable at Queen's University in Kingston, Ontario, for her four years of undergraduate education in biochemistry.

During this period of my employment with CUHK, we enjoyed our expatriate status. This included home leave to Ottawa every other year. We took full advantage of this provision and undertook home leave with extensive travel in 1986, 1988, and 1990. I shall return to family travel in Chapter 14.

In one month from 10 May 1990, I took a lecture tour through different parts of China. I started in Wuhan, where I was hosted by the Geography Department of Central China Normal University. I prepared several topics for this trip, centred on public housing in Hong Kong and Singapore, cities in developing countries, urban planning in Asia, Asian cities, and a comparison of higher education between Hong Kong and North America. I prepared transparencies and slides to accompany these lectures, but the facilities in the universities visited varied greatly. Some simply did not have overhead projectors or slide projectors, an indication of the early state of technical provision in Chinese universities at that time. I then went on to Shanghai, where my host was East China Normal University, as alluded to before. The university organized a field trip to the just announced Open Area of Pudong. What I saw on this excursion to Pudong formed a critical base for me to compare the spectacular development that took place there in later years. I was then taken by the university car to Nanjing via Suzhou accompanied by Liu Junde and Mei Anxin. In Nanjing I lectured in the Department of Geography at Nanjing University, which was in the good hands of Shen Daoqi and Cui Gonghao. Proceeding to northeastern China, a long train ride took me to Ji'nan in Shandong, where Hu Zhaoliang had made the local arrangements for my lecture visit to Shandong Normal University. Another train ride brought me to Harbin. Hu was there and again made the arrangements for me to visit Heilongjiang Normal University. From Harbin, I began my return trip. Still another long train ride brought me to Beijing, where I lectured at Peking University and met many old friends, including Hou Renzhi 候仁之, who paid me a night visit at Shao Yuan, the university guesthouse. A high point of the visit to Beijing this time was an excursion to the site of the devastated Yuan Ming Yuan (The Garden of Perfect Brightness) led by Zhou Yixing. One the most elaborate and magnificent complex of palaces ever built in China, Yuan Ming Yuan was burned down over three days by Anglo-French armed forces in a colossal and savage affront on humanity. I flew back to Hong Kong on 11 June after one month in China. The trip, through surface travel and opportunities to sample different regional lifestyles, cultures, and levels of development, greatly enriched my understanding and experience of a large part of China. Many friends, especially Hu Zhaoliang, made this trip possible and enjoyable for me.

As I was completing my term of office as Registrar, developments along several fronts appeared to be preparing me for another stage of my career and service in Hong Kong and abroad. Within the university, there had been discussions concerning the reorganization of the Institute of Social Studies, with CCAS and the Centre for Hong Kong Studies coming under it. The idea was to reorganize these units into one new Hong Kong Institute of Asia-Pacific Studies, with me as the founding Director. This new appointment would be a timely one for me to take a more proactive role in spearheading social science research at the university.

As the University Registrar, I had represented the university over the years in the many meetings of the Hong Kong Examination Authority. However, other government bodies in Hong Kong were beginning to tap my experience in a range of development issues. After serving for a period in the Rent Review Committee under the Hong Kong Housing Authority, I was invited to be a full member of the Authority in February 1990. Other invitations followed after I completed my term as Registrar.

International agencies, too, were approaching me to take on different kinds of work as I was winding down my university administrative responsibilities. The IDRC awarded me with three consultancies in 1985, 1986, and 1988. I was invited by the World Bank in June 1988 to travel business class to its headquarters in Washington, D.C., to provide inputs to its strategic plans on initiating urban research in developing countries. In June 1989, the World Bank invited me again, after a global search, to write a "think piece" on urban services in developing countries for Asia. In late 1989, I was invited to write a paper on Hong Kong and China for the Human Settlement Conference to be held in Toronto in June 1990, funded by the Ford Foundation. I was contacted to take on many consultancy activities, a topic I shall deal with in the next and later chapters.

Before concluding this phase of my work with CUHK, several important contacts should be mentioned. First, soon after I settled into the university, I received in August 1986 a personal letter from Professor Dick Hodder of SOAS, University of London, asking me to consider taking up the Chair of Geography from which he was to step down for retirement. I was led to believe that SOAS chairs were normally appointed after a head hunting process. I politely turned it down and encouraged him to advertise the position rather than identifying potential individuals. The position was later filled by Graham Chapman from Cambridge. However, Dick and I maintained contact for a few years. We had a reunion in Cambridge during my visit there in 1990, and I helped his son, Rupert, to join the staff of the Department of Geography at CUHK for a term of service.

The second contact was with the Australian National University (ANU). I was invited to conduct a PhD oral examination for Rebecca Chiu in February 1987 on her dissertation on the economic development of Shenzhen. The examination was held in my Registrar's Office, with Professor Audrey Donnithorne, a former but retired professor at ANU but serving in HKU at that time, as another examiner. In November 1988, I was invited by ANU to be one of two external members in a review panel on the Department of Human Geography. This entailed five days of intensive interviewing, reading, and writing. It was an exercise undertaken once in a decade, analogous to the external examination system prevalent in the UK and Hong Kong.

The final link was related to my continuing strong relationship with Norton Ginsburg. The Chinese Urban Conference held at HKU in June 1987 brought Norton and some of his former students, including myself, together. Wang Gungwu was another eminent scholar who spoke at the conference. Then, in January 1988, we met at CUHK during Norton's appointment as a Distinguished Visiting Scholar at United College. I played a role in nominating him and preparing the printed materials in relation to his visit. It was a pleasure to spend time with him and his wife Diana in Hong Kong and at the university for which he had a high regard. Finally, I was invited to participate in the Extended Metropolitan Region Conference held in Honolulu in September 1988, where many of Norton's former students at UChicago presented papers. Norton, the Director of the Environment and Policy Institute at the East-West Center at the time, was the organizer of the conference. I considered it a great privilege and blessing to be able to stay so close to my former professor almost two decades after I had left UChicago.

As I was leaving my Registrar's post, I felt that I had completed a major milestone of my career and reached a kind of career peak. That posting had suddenly thrust me into the high circles of social and academic life in Hong Kong, an experience that was new and precious to me. I served two vice-chancellors in my term of office and found much to look back upon in those years of excitement, challenge, and friendship. I developed a close friendship with Charles and Gwen Kao, through not only working closely with Charles on a daily basis but also regularly playing tennis at their tennis court in Han Yuen. Charles's parting letter below (Figure 8.1), personally handed to me on my last day of work as Registrar, best sums up my four years of university administration.

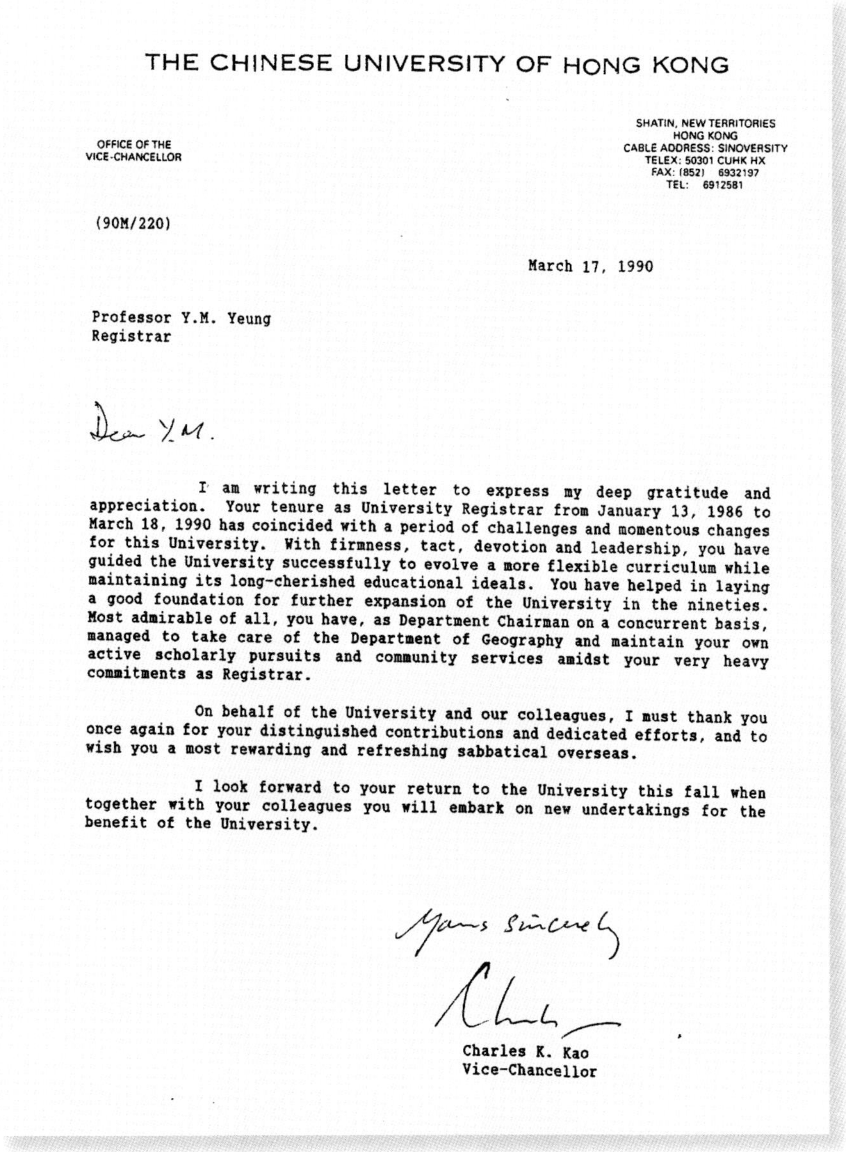

THE CHINESE UNIVERSITY OF HONG KONG

OFFICE OF THE
VICE-CHANCELLOR

SHATIN, NEW TERRITORIES
HONG KONG
CABLE ADDRESS: SINOVERSITY
TELEX: 50301 CUHK HX
FAX: (852) 6932197
TEL: 6912581

(90M/220)

March 17, 1990

Professor Y.M. Yeung
Registrar

Dear Y.M.

     I am writing this letter to express my deep gratitude and appreciation. Your tenure as University Registrar from January 13, 1986 to March 18, 1990 has coincided with a period of challenges and momentous changes for this University. With firmness, tact, devotion and leadership, you have guided the University successfully to evolve a more flexible curriculum while maintaining its long-cherished educational ideals. You have helped in laying a good foundation for further expansion of the University in the nineties. Most admirable of all, you have, as Department Chairman on a concurrent basis, managed to take care of the Department of Geography and maintain your own active scholarly pursuits and community services amidst your very heavy commitments as Registrar.

     On behalf of the University and our colleagues, I must thank you once again for your distinguished contributions and dedicated efforts, and to wish you a most rewarding and refreshing sabbatical overseas.

     I look forward to your return to the University this fall when together with your colleagues you will embark on new undertakings for the benefit of the University.

Yours sincerely

Charles K. Kao
Vice-Chancellor

FIGURE 8.1   VC CHARLES KAO'S PARTING LETTER

8 Career Peaks in Hong Kong 1984-1990 | 141

RECEIVING AN SBS MEDAL FROM MR. TUNG CHEE-HUA, 2003

9 A Long Career Climax
1990-2004

After a period of accustoming myself to the university environment and beyond in Hong Kong, I was ready to shift to high gear and embark on new undertakings, as VC Charles Kao had said. These would not only be for my own benefit, but for that of institutions and people on a wide range of scales. I was fortunate to have earned the trust and cooperation of many friends and colleagues, so that I was able to engage in multiple tasks with plentiful payoffs. Equally striking was the fact that I was able to maintain a high degree of productivity throughout this long period of my career extending for more than a decade, constituting the second period of my employment with the university, 1990-2004. It was also a period that saw our children complete their university education. They both obtained their first and advanced degrees in the 1990s. They went on to establish careers and family, happily settling down to lives in Austin and Vancouver. Indirectly, this allowed me more time to devote whole-heartedly to developing my career.

After taking a long leave of absence upon completing my term as University Registrar in January 1990, I assumed the chairmanship of the Department of Geography, later renamed Geography and Resource Management, when I resumed teaching in September of that year. I re-established myself in full-time teaching and research, supervising graduate students as well. At the same time, the newly reconstituted Hong Kong Institute of Asia-Pacific Studies (HKIAPS) was inaugurated at the same time, and I was appointed its founding director. I was also appointed Director of the Urban and Regional Development in Pacific Asia Programme within it. The Institute was set up to spearhead social science research within the Faculty of Social

Science under a more streamlined format with Hong Kong in the new regional setting of Asia-Pacific. There were high hopes of further development along both fronts, given that I had relevant academic and regional backgrounds. To be sure, there was some synergistic effect from my being the person in charge of both Geography and the HKIAPS.

As a newly established research unit within the university, created on the foundation of the Social Research Institute and its two research centres, the HKIAPS enjoyed a larger budget, with some 18 people on the payroll. Research funding would have to be provided from outside sources after the initial support of three years granted by the university. What made the HKIAPS different from other research institutes on campus at that time was that VC Charles Kao took a keen personal interest in our work. Every year a presentation was prepared and made to him, so that he could provide feedback and support for our budget. This went on for some years until the annual review was supplanted by a systematic review headed by Professor Ambrose King, with a couple of outside academics to provide an objective assessment. All of this showed how seriously and closely the Institute was supervised in its early years. Each research programme had to deliver results in order to justify its existence.

Perhaps because he thought that I should spend more time overseeing the development of the HKIAPS, the VC suggested in a friendly manner in mid-1992 that I relinquish my headship in Geography, a position that I had held for eight years. I readily accepted that suggestion, a decision that proved to be wise as it would allow me to take up the headship of Shaw College less than two years later. From about this time, encouragement was given to have the position of head of an academic department held on a rotational basis, given the increasing amount of time required to handle the personal and administrative matters relating to the post. A rotational headship had become more justified as staff and student numbers continued to grow, especially after the department moved to its present premises in the

Sino Building in 1994 following the redevelopment of the old teaching blocks in Chung Chi College.

The Department of Geography was one of the few original departments of the Faculty of Social Science when it was established in three colleges within The Chinese University of Hong Kong in 1963. The original departments were consolidated into one department with college representations but located in Chung Chi College when I joined in 1984. When I was Head, I started the PhD programme, admitting only a few students in the early years. I also started the research seminar series, so that staff members and visiting scholars would have the opportunity to present their latest research findings. The department maintained a collection of daily clippings from Hong Kong newspapers, especially on the topic of the emerging Special Economic Zones. With the later spread of digitization, this practice was discontinued. One of the unique strengths of the department was and still is its collection of maps and atlases, with facilities provided for staff and students to draw maps. Again, with computerization, this function is less in demand than before. Over the years I had been depositing into that collection many of the atlases that were gifted to me, so that they could be readily shared and used by staff and students. The department ran an Occasional Paper series, publishing a regular stream of research papers, largely by staff members and occasionally by outside scholars. I was a frequent contributor to the series, setting an example for my colleagues to follow. When I retired in 2004, I gifted some 10,000 colour slides that I had taken over the years, mainly in places that I have visited across the world. The department was a safe and proper home for them, as the equipment room, where my slides are kept, is air conditioned at all times. This slide collection has become an invaluable and permanent collection of the department.

As in any geography department, strong bonds were formed between staff and students during field trips. Over the years, my colleagues and I ran field trips in Hong Kong for students as part of their undergraduate training. Gradually, the field programme became more systematically organized as part of a required programme in the senior years. I also organized, often in cooperation with colleagues, field trips to Shanghai (with Lucy Huang 黃葉芳, December 1994), Jiangxi (with Lin Hui 林琿, December 1996), northern Xinjiang (with Leung Yee 梁怡, Chau Kwai-cheong 鄒桂昌, and Lam Kin-che 林建枝, July 2000), Guangxi (with Lucy Huang, May 2001), and Malaysia and Singapore (May 2004). There were other field trips for the staff and their families every year, such as one to Daya Bay Nuclear Plant in Shenzhen in November 2002. Reconnaissance field trips were also organized by the staff themselves, often in cooperation with our counterparts in China. Such a field trip with geography colleagues took place in the Pearl River Delta, led by Xu Xueqiang 許學強 from Zhongshan University in July 2003. In 2006 a department staff field trip was organized to study the Loess Plateau in Shanxi and Shaanxi under Cai Qiangquo 蔡強國, an expert on the subject from the Chinese Academy of Sciences.

With the high expectations that came with the establishment of the HKIAPS, I spent most of my time there to ensure that the Institute ran smoothly on a day-to-day basis and that quality research was being undertaken by my programme and the other research programmes. Only seven research programmes were chosen to operate on a longer-term basis. The main directions of the Institute were discussed and set by the Board of Management under Professor Rance Lee's 李沛良 able chairmanship. Given my extensive external links in research, the international orientation of our research was soon firmed up. In July 1991, the Institute co-hosted a Joint Seminar in Hong Kong with the East-West Center Population Field Portion, and in February 1992 we co-hosted a Megacity Workshop with the United Nations University. We also set up other collaborative relationships with the World Bank, the Asian Development Bank, the Commonwealth Geographical Bureau, and other organizations. The Institute ran an active publication programme, with a dual stream of monographs and Occasional Papers. Our goal was to publish, on average, one Occasional Paper a month, whereas monographs would be tied to programme activities. We took pride in being the most productive unit on campus in terms of published output for many years, second only to The Chinese University Press. The Urban and Regional Programme and the Social Indicators Programme were the most active in terms of publications delivered over the years.

In terms of societal impact, the most important initiative was taken in 1995 with the establishment of the Telephone Survey Laboratory. At that time, the HKIAPS was still operating from the library extension in Tin Ka Ping Building after moving there in 1993 from its original quarters in the Fung King Hey Building in 1990. In May 2001, the Institute was relocated again to the Esther Lee Building, with better facilities and a superior location for the purposes of visitors. I personally benefitted from the new location, as it is only a stone's throw away from the Geography and Resource Management Department in Sino Building. The Telephone Survey Laboratory soon became a barometer of the people's opinion on diverse public issues in Hong Kong, with Lau Siu-kai 劉兆佳 and Timothy Wong 王家英 becoming well known for their commentaries.

Support for research in each of the research programmes came in the form of a full-time research assistant. Beyond this, every programme was on its own in finding resources for undertaking research. For the Urban and Regional Programme that I was responsible for, I was able, through my friendship with Mr J. P. Lee 李澤培, to tap the resources of the Lippo Group courtesy of Dr Stephen Riady. It came in the form of an annual donation of $100,000 per year for four years from 1993. The initial focus of research was on Fujian, on which a most comprehensive and authoritative scholarly book was published in English in 2000, preceded by another book in Chinese and other research papers. This kind of funding continued for some years until a similar book on China's western region was released in 2004. This continual and reliable source of funding allowed the programme to undertake extensive field work in China, hire researchers, and embark on activities that would not otherwise have been possible. I was therefore able to focus on my research, maintaining a good pace in terms of production and quality. The reviews of some of the books arising from the China monograph series have been extremely favourable. I remain grateful to J. P. Lee and Stephen Riady for their staunch support and confidence in my work over the years.

While I was settling in to my joint appointments in Geography and the HKIAPS, still another appointment, certainly more visible and with greater university-wide impact, came my way. I was appointed Head of Shaw College in January 1994, after a due election process. I had to run a campus consisting of one-fourth of the university's staff and student numbers, with a year-round cycle of activities. I recall having to settle a minor incident, in which some students showed their displeasure in not having been involved in the selection of the new Head. I was personally not involved in the selection process, but I called an open meeting at the Lecture Theatre, to which all staff and students of the college were invited. Only moderately well attended, the gathering gave me an opportunity to say my piece and settled the student problem once and for all. My experience as a student leader myself during my undergraduate days was certainly useful. Explaining the whole process in front of students, especially a couple of vocal ones, was the only way to settle the issue. The truth I learned from this episode is simple: students want to be consulted. Since then, university and college governance has been more responsive to student needs and concerns. The issue of not extending university bus service to Shaw College was viewed by students as unjust, and the matter dragged on for some years. Only when Professor Arthur Li 李國章 became Vice-Chancellor and took a personal position on the issue was the long-standing issue finally settled.

Indeed, the College Head appointment had a high profile and involved many demands calling for a different set of skills and experience. Over the years, College staff members from different faculties would seek my help or counsel in seeking promotion, writing recommendation letters, asking for personal financial support, advice in facing litigation, settling family and personal problems, and so on. Fortunately, I was equal to the tasks that came with the Head position. I was thrice elected and served as Head for the maximum period of ten years, feeling a sense of fulfilment and mission accomplished when I completed my appointment in 2004.

This is not the place to go into detail about what I accomplished during my period as Head of Shaw College. It is sufficient to highlight some important and memorable milestones and activities during my tenure.

Soon after I took office, the initial ten-year grant from the Shaw Foundation for the founding of the College came to an end. In order to put the College on a firm financial footing, I was given the task of identifying and inviting business leaders from the Hong Kong community to join the Board of Trustees. With the introduction and assistance of friends, I succeeded in harnessing a number of able and generous Trustees who were interested in the welfare and development of the College, and willing to help financially and in other ways. Many of the improvements to the physical character of the Shaw campus in this period owed much to their generosity in supporting new building projects. Many of these Trustees are still serving on the Board, including Mr Clement Fung, the present Chairman of the Board of Trustees.

Another challenge that I soon had to face upon taking up office was to engage in the preparations involved in the building of a new student hostel for 300 that was allowed by the University Grants Committee in its triennium budget. Shaw College had to come up with half of the construction cost, which was a sizeable amount. For the good of the College, I vetoed the original design, which would have entailed building a new tall hostel block in front of Wen Lan Tang, essentially blocking off the priceless panoramic views of the Tolo

Harbour for most of the offices in that building. The eventual solution that we favoured was to add another five floors to the original Hostel 2, which would then be connected by a bridge to a low and new complex of rooms, with the newly constructed portions providing space for a total of 300 students. The space that would have been occupied by the original hostel design is now occupied in part by an outdoor multipurpose ball court, a Chinese medicinal garden accommodating a statue of Dr Sun Yat-sen, and a landscaped park. All of these facilities have greatly enhanced the landscaping and pleasant outlook of the Shaw College campus. A considerable amount of counterpart funding to build the new hostel facility needed to be raised, but eventually we managed to reach our target.

A side issue in planning and constructing the new student hostel that is not known except to a few should be mentioned here. When we had our hands full in discussing the design and location of the new hostel, Vice-Chancellor Arthur Li called me one day to request my presence in his office. He generously and surprisingly offered the ageing high-rise postgraduate hostel located in the proximity of the University Health Centre as Shaw College's new hostel facility. This was regarded as an exceptional offer, obviating the need for us to raise counterpart funding to build a new hostel on the Shaw College campus. All that was required was to resurface and refurbish the existing structure. The VC saw this as an opportunity for Shaw College to branch out to another part of the university. I, on the other hand, thought that having 300 students located outside of Shaw College would split the campus, and hence would not be conducive for the cohesiveness and overall development of the College. I shared this offer privately only with Professor Ma Lin 馬臨, Chairman of the Board of Trustees of Shaw College, who concurred with my analysis. Not having to raise counterpart funding was a near-term advantage, but splitting the campus and student body would be a long-term structural defect. I was so certain of my belief that I did not even let the issue be taken to a more collective level of discussion. The postgraduate hostel was later redeveloped by Chung Chi College, also to build a new student facility for 300. To my way of thinking, this was a much more logical choice, given the structure's proximity to and hence integration with the Chung Chi campus.

Through many activities I tried to bring staff and students together, socially and athletically. One that has been established as a unique tradition of Shaw College is the annual Cantonese Operatic Night, held since 1997. During my tenure, it was held in our Lecture Theatre. After some years, because of its growing popularity, it was moved to the Shaw Theatre. Andrew Chan 陳志輝, the present College Head and Terence Chan 陳鎮榮, University Bursar, have shown their staunch support for the event by performing regularly. Even my wife, Ameda, performed three times over the years. This annual event has become a popular event on campus, as outside professionals have also been invited, making the event an eagerly awaited annual cultural highlight with many fans on and off campus.

As College Head, I took pride and pleasure in joining student activities, especially when the students went outside Hong Kong for exchanges. Every summer, our students went for an exchange with students at the University of Victoria in Canada and at Zhejiang University of Technology in Hangzhou. I went for several years to officiate at functions at the latter university, and was eventually conferred the title of Honorary Professor with the delivery of a public lecture in 1997.

For many years, Sir Run Run Shaw 邵逸夫 had been making annual donations to Chinese educational institutions on the mainland. He began with universities, with many buildings, libraries, and other facilities bearing witness to his generosity by being named after him. After most universities had benefitted from such donations, he directed his assistance to schools and other special educational institutions. Every January, when such donations were announced, a group from the Ministry of Education in Beijing, led by a high-ranking official, would visit Hong Kong to oversee the presentation of development plans drawn up by the recipient institutions for the benefit of Sir Run

Run. Shaw College assisted, along with China's Liaison Office in Hong Kong, in organizing such a presentation session, which was routinely held at Cho Yiu Hall on campus. In January 2004, representing my last attendance at 17 of such meetings, some $200 million was again donated to Chinese educational institutions. By then, the number of institutions that had received such donations had reached a cumulative total of over 4,000. Sir Run Run's contributions were certainly a very impressive and catalytic source of funding to advance educational development on the mainland. The most special part of the visit programme for many Chinese visitors was the farewell dinner, in buffet style, held at the Shaw mansion in Clear Water Bay. Dinner was preceded by a first-run movie shown in Sir Run Run's private movie theatre with capacity for about 80 persons. In my ten years as Head, I never missed the formal presentation or the movie-dinner evening.

By virtue of my headship, I was invited in early 2002 to be the Chairman of the Preparatory Committee of the Shaw Prize. Modelled on the Nobel Prize, the Shaw Prize is viewed as the Nobel Prize of Asia. From the outset, the origin, history, purpose, structure, and organization of the world-famous Nobel Prize was an inspiration for the Shaw Prize. Ms Mona Fong 方逸華, or Mrs Shaw, was the person who could make important decisions for Sir Run Run. The other key persons were Professor Ma Lin and Professor C. N. Yang 楊振寧, Nobel Laureate in Physics and Distinguished Professor- at-Large at the university. Apart from chairing the Committee meetings, I was the go-between among all the key players. The Committee had fruitful discussions and, after several meetings, narrowed down the prizes to be awarded to candidates in only three fields from the many possible fields initially discussed. At times, I was not certain if the new prize would get off the ground, as the key personalities involved had very divergent perspectives on the subject. After several long and private face-to-face meetings with Mona Fong over lunch or tea, and two lengthy long-distance conversations with Professor Yang in New York, a deal was finally sealed. To the joy of all concerned and the Hong

Kong community, a public announcement was made on 15 November 2002 that the Shaw Prize would be launched, with the first prizes to be awarded the following year. It remains a source of great satisfaction to me to know that I have played a critical role in getting the Shaw Prize off to a flying start. Chor Koon-fai 左冠輝, an administrator of Shaw College, resigned his university position to take up the new post of setting up the Shaw Prize Secretariat in Clear Water Bay. Unfortunately, he did not stay long on the job after the first prizes were awarded.

The last activity worth mentioning during my headship was the organizing of a large-scale international conference, capitalizing on my three concurrent positions in Geography, the HKIAPS, and Shaw College. On the theme "China and the World in the Twenty-first Century", it was an ambitious project that involved playing host to 220 Chinese geographers from around the world. The conference was held over three days in August 1998 in the premises of Shaw College, where many concurrent sessions were held after the plenaries in the Lecture Theatre. All geographers coming from outside Hong Kong were accommodated in the student hostels, which had been vacated during the summer vacation. The Department of Geography played a central role in designing and running the conference and HKIAPS was responsible for publishing three books from the selected papers. It was cooperation at its best, involving three units within the university that all played crucial roles in the success of one the largest international academic gatherings held at the university.

The organization of this ambitious international conference was a reflection of my academic life for a full decade from 1994 to 2004. I had three spacious offices in each of the units and my daily routine would involve spending the most time at the HKIAPS, followed by Shaw College and Geography, with exceptions demanded by need and different daily schedules. Even returning from overseas trips, my first task often was to go to my three offices to check my mail and/or urgent messages before or after going home at our university residence.

As if three concurrent jobs were not enough, I was appointed the founding director of the newly established Shanghai-Hong Kong Development Institute in 2000, jointly set up by CUHK and Fudan University in Shanghai. This Institute was an add-on to my responsibilities at the HKIAPS, but it had its own research and publication programmes. I welcomed this additional responsibility, since it facilitated my efforts to track developments in Shanghai and collaborate with three related institutes within the university. Four research institutes within CUHK contributed to the new Institute, but all of the work involved in administration and publication was relegated to the HKIAPS. My concurrent appointments thus reached four between 2000 and 2004. I held the directorship of the Shanghai-Hong Kong Development Institute until I fully retired in 2008. In fact, I do not count the fifth appointment, as director of a research programme within HKIAPS, a position I held from 1990 to 2008. I consider the work related to directing research integral to my work at the Institute.

When I was about to complete my headship at Shaw College, Professor Ma Lin called me one morning into his office. In his usual calm way, he began:

"Yue-man, you are about to complete your long appointment as Head of Shaw College. I hope you can help the College to identify your successor because I have retired for many years and do not really know the staff."

I was slightly taken by surprise, but given the way I know Professor Ma, he was honest about needing some help. I politely replied, "Yes, so much has changed in the College in the past ten years. I surely want to have a good person to continue the work I have built up. Please give me a few days."

That was the way we concluded the short meeting. I did indeed go over the entire list of full professors, which was the place I looked. I came up with one name, that of Ching Pak-chung 程伯中, the Dean of Engineering, who had just completed his term. He was immediately available. I had worked closely with him in the Shaw Prize Preparatory Committee, the AAPC, and other committees. He had also been the warden of Hostel 1 from its inception. I could think of no better candidate. So reporting to Professor Ma accordingly was the beginning of the process to appoint Professor Ching as the Head of College after me.

Mid-way through his term as Head of Shaw College, Professor Ching was appointed to be Pro-Vice-Chancellor. The task of finding his successor again fell to me. Professor Ma Lin once again made the same request to me some time in 2007. This time, I had two medical professors in mind. Without any hesitation, I recommended Professor Joseph Sung 沈祖堯, as he had already amply demonstrated his leadership skills during the painful SARS episode in Hong Kong and thereafter. Professor Ching and I met him over lunch to sound him out and the rest is history. Professor Sung brought new vitality and a new spirit to Shaw College during his headship of only two years, followed by his installation as Vice-Chancellor of the university in 2010.

Although later chapters will deal with my consultancy work and research, it is proper at this time to highlight briefly the breadth and depth of my research, research networks, and consultancies to provide an initial idea of their scope and strength in the 1990s. Likewise, I was invited to join the editorial boards of many international learned journals. Opportunities and invitations from abroad were combined with internally driven initiatives, resulting in a sustained period of high research productivity and international visibility. My continual involvement in international research networks and activities were mutually reinforcing with the work I was leading at the HKIAPS.

The period under review marked the peak of the consultancies undertaken during my career. I have undertaken a total of over 40 consultancies in my career, with 23 international and UN consultancies carried out during the period from 1990 to 2004. The relevant international agencies that contracted me to carry out work for them included the International Development Research Centre (IDRC), United Nations Centre for Regional Development (UNCRD), United Nations University (UNU), World Bank, Asian Development Bank (ADB), United Nations Development Programme (UNDP), Ford Foundation (FF), United Nations Centre for Human Settlements (UNCHS), United Nations Educational, Scientific, and Cultural Organization (UNESCO), and United Nations Conference for Trade and Development (UNCTAD). Many of these consultancies involved the preparation of research papers and reports, whereas others required international travel providing expert advice, fact finding and analysis, and other assignments. These were valuable opportunities for me to continually update my understanding of global developments. I shall return in due course to the details of these and other consultancies that I have undertaken.

For several years after 1991, I was on the panel of advisors for two global research initiatives. One was the Global Urban Research Initiative (GURI), funded by the Ford Foundation and coordinated by Richard Stren of the University of Toronto. I was an advisor to the project and to its Asian components, against the background of twelve research teams. Meetings related to different stages of this project took me to Toronto (1991), Beijing (1991, 1992), Manali, India (1992), Jakarta (1992), Cairo (1993), and Mexico City (1995). Until 1996, The GURI network brought me together with Nazrul Islam, my former fellow graduate student at UWO in the 1960s. Despite having kept in touch for some time, this was the only period when we intersected in our work. At a meeting at the University of Toronto in 1991, we even paid a visit to James Simmons, our common supervisor at UWO, whom we met for the first time after our graduate work there. I was also on the panel of advisors for the Urban Management Programme (UMP) during its second phase, with funding provided by the UNDP. I attended meetings related to this programme in Paris (1991), New York (1991), Washington, D.C. (1994), Leipzig (1994), Kuala Lumpur (1995), and Bangkok (1999). One reason for my involvement in

UMP Phase Two was the 21-day consultancy that I undertook in July 1991 for the UNDP. This assignment took me to Pakistan, Nepal, Indonesia, and China. In August 1993, I was also appointed a senior UMP expert in a mission to visit Vietnam. The three-person mission provided expert opinions to the Vietnamese government on ways of developing its cities. I could only spare ten days to travel in that country in a three-week mission. Before I left Vietnam, I prepared a paper entitled "The Urban Condition in Vietnam". In 1995 I was invited again to lecture in Hanoi to urban planners from all major Vietnamese cities on the impact and prospects of globalization on the development of these cities.

Two other research networks occupied a great deal of my intellectual energy and efforts. One was set up by the United Nations University (UNU) on the interplay of globalization and the urban system along the western Pacific Rim in the early 1990s. Project meetings were held in Seoul (1991), Hong Kong (1992), and Tokyo (1995). However, I made additional trips to Tokyo as I played a key role in coordinating the project on world cities in Pacific Asia. I enjoyed a close working relationship with Fu-chen Lo 羅福全 of UNU. We co-edited two influential books on globalization and large cities. Another research network was put together by the US National Research Council, focusing on demographic change in the developing world. I became one of 16 members of the Panel on Urban Population Dynamics. We met in Washington, D.C. (1999), Mexico City (2000), and Woods Hole, Mass. (2000). The publication of *Cities Transformed* in 2003 rounded off the work of this panel.

On an institutional basis, the HKIAPS became part of a research network with the China Development Institute in Shenzhen, the National Institution for Research Advancement (NIRA) in Tokyo, and Taiwan's Chung-Hua Institution for Economic Research in 1995, with a common interest on research on South China. David K. Y. Chu 朱劍如 and I represented the HKIAPS by presenting research papers at the annual meetings. The four institutes established a close working relationship, but after two years we chose not to continue participating in the network due to other competing priorities. Hong Kong's place was taken up by Dr Thomas Chan 陳文鴻 of the China Business Centre of Hong Kong Polytechnic University.

In part because of my high research profile during this phase of my career, my academic productivity was at an all-time high. Between 1990 and 2004, I published 27 books, in single or joint authorship or editorship. Three books each were published in 1996 and 1998, and four in 2003. In addition, I published numerous refereed articles, book chapters, research reports, and book reviews, and delivered many keynote addresses. Many factors conspired to help me maintain a period of sustained academic productivity and activity.

Related to research and the promotion of research, I was on the editorial board of 16 international refereed journals in my career in many parts of the world. They called for different time inputs and responsibilities, but were all useful in helping me to keep up with the latest frontiers of research across many fields. The journals that I spent the most time on include: *Progress in Human Geography* (1987-99), *Third World Planning Review*, later renamed *International Development Planning Review* (1991-present), *Asian Geographer* (1991-present), *Eurasian Geography* and *Economics* (2003-present), *Geografiska Annals B* (2003-present), and *Environment and Urbanization ASIA* (2010-present).

While office administration, research and teaching, and research networks and consultancies all required my time and attention, still another dimension of my academic life during this period was serving the Hong Kong and international community. After a long period of "warming up" with the Hong Kong community and the media when I was University Registrar, I was split in many directions in public service. The decade of the 1990s was a very busy peak for me in terms of serving Hong Kong in ways related to my training and experience. I was a member of the following in the period under review: the Hong Kong Housing Authority (1990-98), Kowloon-Canton Railway

Management Board (1991-95), Town Planning Board (1991-95), Consultative Committee in the New Airport and Related Projects (1991-98), Hong Kong Pacific Economic Cooperation Council (PECC) (1990-98), and the Barrister Disciplinary Tribunal (1994-2003). In addition, I was Chairman of the Land and Building Advisory Committee (1997-2003) and of the Panel on the Pan-Pearl River Delta under the Central Policy Unit (2003-present). In order not to over-extend myself, I had to turn down other invitations to be a member or chairman of other important public committees.

Serving in such a large number of public bodies called for discipline, time management, and commitment. Serving the Hong Kong Housing Authority over a long period was compatible with my career-long research interest in low-cost housing. I spent the largest amount of time on this body since I agreed to serve as Chairman of the Ad Hoc Committee on Private Property Ownership by Public Housing Tenants – or, in short, dealing with the problem of rich tenants who were unwilling to give up their flats. My chairmanship extended from October 1994 to April 1996, and involved a total of over 20 half-day or longer sessions. Despite the hard work and commitment I put into the position, I was somewhat disillusioned, as the problem could not be effectively solved. People simply fought hard to guard their vested interests, and in this they had the support of political parties in Hong Kong's increasingly democratizing environment.

By contrast, during my involvement in the New Airport Committee, we received a great deal of feedback on development plans, although the general atmosphere related to the main development was highly politicized. Hong Kong was largely on the sidelines, as the main issues for settlement were negotiated between the governments of China and the United Kingdom. I much enjoyed and benefitted from the field trips around Hong Kong pertinent to the committee work on public housing, town planning, and the new airport. They kept me up-to-date on changes that were coming rapidly. Being a member of the HKPECC entailed a trip to Bangkok in July 1990 to lobby Dr Tanat

Kohman, a key person in the PECC movement from Thailand, for his support for Hong Kong's formal admission to PECC membership at the organization's next general meeting to be held in Singapore in May 1991. I was in the company of Joseph Wong 王永平, Matthew Cheung 張建宗, and Eleanor Ling 林李靜文 on this one-day trip. Membership of HKPECC provided my trips to Singapore (1991), San Francisco (1992), Beijing (1995), and Santiago (1997) at various PECC Congresses. The chairmanship of the Land and Building Advisory Committee over many years put me in close touch with the Hong Kong media on a regular basis.

A long period of public service through many committees greatly diminished my distance with the media. News about me and my views, especially on housing, land, town planning, airport, Hong Kong-mainland relations, and so on, appeared over time in almost every newspaper in Hong Kong. I also appeared in many radio and TV programmes, and wrote and aired many Hong Kong Letters on different subjects. Several newspapers had featured me in whole-page special reports, including Sing Pao (16 December 1995, A5), Hong Kong Economic Times (8 December 2003, A34), Wenweipo (23 November 2004, A17; 9 May 2005, C2, 10 September 2012, B10), and Takungpao (11 August 2008, A22). In June 2004, Asia TV taped a two-hour series for me on Jiangmen in the field for broadcast based on my close association with that city and a research project undertaken on the western Pearl River Delta. In recognition of my academic achievements and public service, I was conferred the honorific titles of J.P. (1995), OBE (1996), and SBS (2003).

With my many contributions to the Hong Kong community, I became a kind of local celebrity at the time of handover in 1997. I participated in the official events of the handover at the Hong Kong Convention and Exhibition Centre. On 1 July 1997 in Room 301 of the handover venue, I was introduced as one of fifteen outstanding personalities to Mr Qian Qichen 錢其琛, China's Foreign Minister, by Mr Tung Chee-hua 董建華, the newly installed Chief Executive of

Hong Kong. In that year, I also organized and attended joint academic conferences held in Zhengzhou, Henan, and Shenyang, Liaoning, under the HKIAPS and local organizations. Occasional papers were published by the HKIAPS, which focused on the interaction and implications of the handover between Hong Kong and these two provinces.

Finally, I also served the Hong Kong community in another capacity on an ad hoc basis. I was invited to chair a three-hour session one Saturday afternoon in October 2004 at the Wong Tai Sin Shopping Centre to solicit the views of the Hong Kong public with regard to Town Planning Department's plan for redeveloping the former Kai Tak Airport site. This was followed by two other similar sessions of equal duration held at the tip of the former airport runway and at the YMCA premises on Salisbury Road in the following year. Diverse opinions were collected, which were helpful in finalizing development plans.

As for serving the international community, I was appointed Director of the Commonwealth Geographical Bureau (CGB), a body that links some 250 departments of geography across the British Commonwealth through the CGB's annual newsletters and other activities. I was elected at the CGB's quadrennial general meeting during the International Geographical Union Congress held in Washington, D.C., in 1992. I completed my four-year term, and a new Director was elected at a similar meeting held in The Hague in 1996. This appointment required me to make annual summer trips to London to call on the Commonwealth Foundation to seek funding in the company of Denis Dwyer, Honorary Treasurer of the CGB. I was informally invited to continue for a second term, but I politely turned the offer down for fear of creating a political issue. The truth was that Hong Kong would be out of the British Commonwealth with its return to China in 1997. Before I left the CGB, I brought in Dr Victor Savage of the National University of Singapore, my former student there, to the body. He eventually became the Honorary Secretary and later the Director of the CGB. During my term with the CGB, I brought two of its international conferences to CUHK, in 1990 and 1994, the latter on the occasion of the silver jubilee celebration of the founding of the organization.

In 1997, in another important international appointment, I became a member of the International Scientific and Technological Advisory Board (ISTAB) of UNESCO for the purpose of helping to organize the World Conference on Science (WCS) to be held in Budapest in July 1999. Membership in the ISTAB was overwhelmingly composed of Nobel Laureates in natural science subjects, with those of us in the social sciences being a minority. With such an appointment, it was incumbent on me to attend the WCS in 1999 and to visit Hungary for the first time.

During this part of my career, two opportunities presented themselves that could have meant a career change for me. In May 1990 I received a phone call from Dean John Spence inviting me to visit UBC. I flew to Vancouver the following month as guest of the university to explore the possibility of an appointment with the Department of Geography with a concurrent appointment as Director of the Institute of Asian Research. My good and old friend, Terry McGee, was finding a way to step down from the latter after many years of distinguished service. After giving a seminar and meeting concerned academics, deans, and students, I was offered the post. However, I could not immediately leave CUHK, as a huge sum of US$6 million had just been donated by Cheng Yu-tong 鄭裕彤 and Lee Shau-kee 李兆基 to support research on South China between Yale University and CUHK through the HKIAPS. As the Director of the HKIAPS, I felt duty-bound to see through the huge donation for at least two years. Moreover, a more important reason for my reluctance to leave Asia was that my research was focused on Asia, in particular China. A move to Vancouver would have meant too much of a geographical realignment and distance from the scene of action.

Another possible career change was one not of my seeking. In 1994 there was an opening for the position of Vice-Chancellor of the City University of Hong Kong. I did not have an immediate interest in the post, but Professor Robert Steel, the former CGB Director and former Vice-Chancellor of a university in Wales, and Professor Denis Dwyer, Honorary Treasurer of the CGB, Deputy VC of the University of Keele, and my former geography teacher at HKU, insisted on nominating me for the post. They were in Hong Kong attending the Silver Jubilee Conference of the CGB. I was among the last three candidates who were interviewed in January 1996 by the Search Committee, headed by Tung Chee-hua, in his company office in Wanchai. I lost out to the candidate who eventually became the VC. I did not regret not being successful in the bid, because such a career change was not my choice. It would mean that I would have lost all opportunities to make my mark academically.

In any event, I felt that I had had a long and successful run in my career when I retired from the Chair of Geography in 2004. I was satisfied with my accomplishments in every aspect of my career, and delivered my retirement lecture and retirement dinner presentation on 3 July 2004. Both events were well attended by colleagues, students, and friends, including the newly installed Vice-Chancellor, Professor Lawrence J. Lau 劉遵義, who attended my lecture.

AFTER A PUBLIC LECTURE IN 2007

10 The Twilight of a Career
2004-2012

After retiring from the post of Chair of Geography, my regular employment with the university came to an end. However, I continued to serve in another capacity with much reduced remuneration and no regular teaching load. My main appointment as the Director of the HKIAPS (except for the academic year 2007-08) and of the Shanghai-Hong Kong Development Institute remained unchanged for the period to 2008 when I fully retired from the university. I was also appointed Research Professor, such that with a line appointment that carried emolument, I could be appointed to the two Directorships. Apart from the lack of regular teaching duties, the four years after the autumn of 2004 continued to be a very productive period, academically and in terms of public service and consultancies. My career twilight continued to be bright. This chapter covers the third period of my career with CUHK in Hong Kong from 2004 to 2012, when this memoir project was due for completion.

Directing the two research institutes became the focus of my research and related activities. There were many new research and institutional links that greatly strengthened the reputation of the university, both in Hong Kong and in the region centred on mainland China.

Worthy of special mention was CUHK's cordial and strong links with Fudan University in Shanghai in the first decade of the new century, spearheaded by the establishment of the Shanghai-Hong Kong Development Institute (SHKDI) in 2000. As Joint Director of the Institute, I oversaw its annual research activities and publication programme. During the first four years, research on either side was built on themes mutually agreed upon by the two universities, with each of the four relevant institutes at CUHK responsible for one theme each year. In 2002 I was personally responsible for the theme on China's western development, as a spinoff from a much larger and more ambitious project on that subject undertaken at the HKIAPS since 1999. The annual forum was held alternately in Hong Kong and Shanghai, but in December 2002 the forum was held in Kunming located in southwestern China. The thinking was that it made greater geographic sense to have our annual forum on the subject of western China held in the western region rather than Shanghai.

From 2005, the second cycle of research cooperation between the two universities for the Shanghai-Hong Kong Development Forum turned to current development issues of concern to policymakers and academics in both cities. Apart from occasional papers published by the SHKDI, every year a Shanghai-Hong Kong Annual was meticulously published, with photo highlights, a major events chronology, statistical abstracts, publications on the two cities, and so forth. These volumes became eagerly sought after reference materials, particularly by university libraries in Hong Kong. The annual forums lasting two to three days often produced sufficient materials for books. Just as important, they afforded opportunities for scholars and participants from both cities to take part in field trips for their benefit and to understand the latest developments in the other city. When I stepped down in 2008 from the SHKDI after leading it for eight years, I honestly felt that I had nurtured a healthy institution that had proven its worth and that had built up a momentum for sustainability.

With Fudan University, CUHK had another crucial link during this period. Among other activities, the two universities cooperated in organizing the Shanghai Forum. I was a regular participant in the Forum, held every year at Fudan University since its centennial celebration in 2005, with financial support from the Higher Education Foundation of South Korea. A similar Beijing Forum has also been held by Peking University, similarly after its centennial celebration in 1998 for the planned span of ten years, with the same source of funding. Both the Shanghai Forum and the Beijing Forum are global in orientation and grand in scale and content, with a division of labour between them with regard to subject matter. Every year they draw the best policymakers and scholars, including Nobel Laureates, from around the world. I was initially invited to attend as a scholar to present a paper at the Shanghai Forum in 2006, much like the Beijing Forum to which I was invited and attended in 2005. Given the close relationship between Fudan University and CUHK and my research experience, I was invited to be a co-organizer of a sub-forum under the Shanghai Forum on Asian cities with Professor Wang Guixin 王桂新 in 2007. For the next four years, my contribution was to help identify a theme, suggest the names of scholars outside China to be invited, and write a lead paper myself. This arrangement persisted, with close cooperation with Guixin, until 2011, when after reading my paper comparing the Chinese and Indian development models, I announced that I would conclude my contribution in favour of new blood to carry the torch forward.

During 2006 and 2007, the HKIAPS was engaged in a different kind of institutional networking effort and was reaching out to establish closer relationships with government officials and entrepreneurs within the Pearl River Delta at the city and county levels. What triggered this approach was a visit paid to me at the HKIAPS in December 2005 by Dr Chan Sai-kwong 陳世光 of Hong Kong Commercial Daily, Mr Tsang Yat-wah 曾日華 of Asia Television, and Mr Kong King-lim 鄺景廉 of Sing Tao Global Net. What followed this meeting was a high-profile two-day forum focusing on the accelerating development and growing cooperation among Hong Kong, Macao, and the western Pearl River Delta. The well-attended event was held in Yin Du Hotel in Zhuhai in January 2006. It was jointly sponsored by the three organizations mentioned above and the HKIAPS. A book published by the HKIAPS came out of the proceedings. This was the first successful attempt to bring together officials from the Hong Kong and Macao SARs with their counterparts from all major cities in the western

Pearl River Delta. Buoyed by the success of this collaborative venture, a similar forum was held in Huizhou in September 2006, at which not only the mayors of nine cities but selected county leaders in the eastern Pearl River Delta spoke about the areas under their jurisdiction and the attractions of these places. It was a grand occasion held in the largest hotel in Huizhou and attended by some 500 participants. The third and last forum in this series was held in September 2007 in Shantou, with the focus this time on the role of the eastern Pearl River Delta and the efforts being made to catch up with the other parts of the Pearl River Delta in terms of development. I was one of three main speakers, the other two being Professor Xie Baisan 謝百三 of Fudan University and Professor Lang Xianping 郎咸平 of CUHK. This series of meetings concluded on a more scholarly note in front of a large audience. These forums had the effect of encouraging different parts of the PRD to reach out to each other, with the HKIAPS playing the role of facilitator, which it had not previously attempted. It was a venture that could only succeed with the sizeable funding and other critical support offered by our partner institutions.

Another institutional link was forged in the spring of 2006, with the announcement of the findings of a study undertaken by Professor Ji Pengfei 倪鵬飛 of the Chinese Academy of Social Sciences on the competitiveness of Chinese cities. The Better Hong Kong Foundation, directed by George Yuan 袁金浩, later succeeded by Karen Tang 鄧淑德, organized the press conference to inform the Hong Kong public of the results of the study. The HKIAPS was party to the announcement, because Chinese cities have always been a focus of its enquiry. My colleague, Shen Jianfa 沈建法, and I gladly played our roles and highlighted Hong Kong's position against the background of surging Chinese cities. This pattern of cooperation among the three institutions has continued uninterrupted for seven years to 2012. It has become almost an eagerly awaited news item every year, as the competitive position of Hong Kong has become a keenly watched trend given the rapid growth of Chinese cities. Over the years, the lead that Hong Kong has enjoyed in competitiveness among Chinese cities has narrowed, but has thus far been maintained. The Chinese cities that are closing the gap in competitiveness with Hong Kong are Shenzhen, Shanghai, Beijing, Taipei, and Guangzhou, in a shifting order of importance every year.

Since opening up its casino industry to free competition in 2002, Macao has entered a period of exceptionally rapid growth. I sensed that the rapid changes taking place there would be ripe for research and investigation. I therefore organized two personal trips with Gordon Kee 紀緯紋 to Macao in March and October 2005, the latter after the historical centre of Macao was named a UNESCO Heritage Site. Sure enough, this rapidly changing SAR became the focus of a joint research project involving the Centre of Asian Studies at HKU, the HKIAPS, and the Social Sciences Faculty of the University of Macao, with funding provided by the Macao SAR government. The first phase of the study began in December 2005, focusing on the quality of life of Macao residents. There were several phases to the study, with additional aspects added to the investigation. I took on the responsibility of looking into the issue of urban planning in Macao. The project continued until 2008 and beyond, but my involvement came to an end when I fully retired from university service. This sustained involvement in research on the fast-paced changes in Macao afforded me the opportunity to learn and write about the transformation of this former Portuguese colony after its return to China. Over the period 2005 to 2008, I made more than a dozen trips to Macao to attend project and academic meetings, conduct field reconnaissance, and participate in press conferences. It was a valuable opportunity to learn and study the changes and challenges of the new Macao and to touch base with the Macao media.

From abroad, too, came a new and important institutional link. It all began in November 2005, when I was invited to join a mission to Beijing organized by the United States National Academies. It was a large delegation of 12 persons, led by Dr Larry Papay, along with Grey

Symmes, Derek Vollmer, Glen Daigger, Debra Lam, Gordon Feller, myself, and others largely from the National Academies or its guests and from the University of California at Berkeley. The purpose was to explore and enter into a dialogue with Chinese officials and researchers to determine whether a project on urban environmental sustainability in China was feasible and meaningful. After spending several days in Beijing, the visiting party was split into two. One visited Tianjin, where some novel experiments in urban sustainability were being carried out, and the other went to Nanning in Guangxi, which was to host a large UN meeting on urban sustainability in its large, new convention centre. I joined the latter group and attended the UN meeting, where I met many friends from different parts of the world. The two groups then returned and reconvened in Beijing.

Given the mix of research objectives on the part of the participants from Washington, D.C. and Berkeley, the simmering conflict came out into the open in our last group meeting before we left Beijing. The prospects for the project and further funding did not look good at this point after ten days. I was invited to another meeting held in Newport Beach near Los Angeles in February 2006, where the project was further discussed. The project was aborted because further funding beyond the initial seed money was not forthcoming from an IT company based in San Francisco with close links to UC Berkeley. I came to the realization that the success of a research project would be hampered by having excessively ambitious and diverse objectives, especially when multiple parties with their own axes to grind are involved.

Before leaving the subject of the HKIAPS and research, I should mention an opportunity that was thrust upon me. One day in November 2006, VC Larry Lau 劉遵義 called me to his office. He went straight to the point.

"The university has received a request from the government to organize an activity to mark the tenth anniversary of the founding of the HKSAR next year. I think we should do something about it"

"I agree it is an important historical landmark and we can organize an academic activity," I responded off the cuff.

"That is a good idea. I think we can organize an international conference to which experts from Hong Kong and related countries can be invited. You and I believe that the handover is a success but it needs to be critically assessed by leading scholars," he continued.

"I can organize an international conference through the HKIAPS, but with about eight months to the handover anniversary we don't have much time," I said cautiously.

VC Lau was quick to say, "Then, go ahead and do it. The university will pay for all costs involved."

I quickly set in motion what was needed and invited distinguished scholars from far and near. An international conference was held on campus in late June 2007 prior to the handover date. Much to my satisfaction, and perhaps to the surprise of some, the book bearing the title *The First Decade* was released by The Chinese University Press in September. The publication deadline I set was before the National Day of that year. All of my hard work and that of the Press, along with the cooperation and understanding of the authors from many lands, paid off. It was a job accomplished under severe time constraints.

In part because of my many research and institutional contacts, I continued to be very productive in the period 2004 to 2012. I published 15 books, singly or jointly authored or edited, as well as 40 refereed journal articles and book chapters. This level of productivity did not give any hint of my retirement.

In terms of serving the Hong Kong community, I continued to be active in many ways. After four two-year terms, my chairmanship in the Land and Building Advisory Committee came to an end in 2005. My term of eight years of service straddled the colonial and SAR administrations. This appointment had kept me close to the main issues of urban development, especially on planning, building, and land, as they evolved and as problems surfaced in Hong Kong. I learned a great deal and enriched myself in the process. More than any of my public service activities, this appointment constantly put me in the glare of media attention. I also served as a member of the Commission on Strategic Development, 2005-2009, chaired by the Chief Executive. At its meetings I would often say my piece for the good of Hong Kong. Once I argued successfully for the establishment of a Hong Kong scholarship to enable Hong Kong to attract and support promising students from outside, including those from the mainland, to study at Hong Kong universities. To my understanding, this scholarship scheme has been put into practice. Membership of this Commission put me in the company of many of the who's who in Hong Kong.

A salient point about many of my public service and related activities in this period is that they revolved around Hong Kong and its relationship with the mainland. For several years after the turn of the century, the Planning Department worked on the process of seeking closer integration between Hong Kong and its hinterland of the PRD. The process of formulating a document called Hong Kong 2030 was protracted, deliberate, and open, entailing many rounds of public consultation. From the outset, I was invited to serve as one of the expert advisors in this project. After some seven years of work, the document was finally released in December 2007. Sustainable development was a recurring theme adopted as the basis of Hong Kong's future development. This process not only paved the way for planning Hong Kong's future, but also that of Shenzhen and Zhuhai, although on a shorter time horizon. Spurred by the Hong Kong example, after a much shorter lead time in preparation, the documents Shenzhen 2020 and Zhuhai 2020 were drawn up and adopted for planning the way forward for these two cities.

In 2009 I was invited to be an advisor to the newly established Hong Kong Ideas Centre (HKIC), which has been an important forum to focus community concerns on critical development issues confronting Hong Kong. My first participation was in a seminar held in August 2009 at the Hong Kong Exhibition and Convention

Centre. The theme was Hong Kong's future against the backdrop of the rise and decline of large cities in the world. My second instance of involvement in the HKIC was in 2010, as part of a three-person team deliberating the pros and cons of building a third runway for Hong Kong Airport. Our efforts cumulated in a press conference in December of that year. Our strong endorsement of the need for a third runway came ahead of the formal release in June 2011 of the Hong Kong Airport 2030 document for consultation by the Hong Kong Airport Authority. The HKSAR government finally announced its decision in March 2012 to build the third runway. This only signals the start of a long process involving many years of preparation, further consultation and, finally, actual construction. The construction of a third runway is crucial if Hong Kong is to maintain its competitive advantage over other airports in the region.

Since 2004, the nine cities within the PRD have been engaged in a continuous process of seeking closer relationships with Hong Kong and Macao under the oversight of the central and provincial governments. Several important official documents have been released in that period. In 2004 an urban cluster cooperative development plan, 2004-2020, was released. This was followed by another planning study in 2009 on coordinating the development of townships in the greater PRD region. The latter document incorporated Hong Kong and Macao and will pave the way for closer cooperation. I was one of the consultant advisors for the study before it was finalized. I was a party to the task of reviewing of the document, which took place several times in different cities before its finalization. An even more important official document released in early 2009 laid out an outline for reforms and development in the PRD, 2008-2020. This will speed up cooperation and reform within the PRD in the years to 2020, with the role of Hong Kong and Macao clearly spelled out.

However, my greatest involvement in Hong Kong-mainland relations stemmed from my links to the Central Policy Unit (CPU), the government think tank, maintained over many years. It began with my appointment as Chairman of the Pearl River Delta Panel in 2003, changed in 2005 to the Pan-PRD Panel. The change of title came with the formation in June 2004 of the Pan-Pearl River Delta network of nine provinces led by Guangdong plus Hong Kong and Macao, hence 9+2. I have remained the Chairman of this Panel to 2012. Apart from quarterly meetings of the Panel, same day-return field trips to the PRD have been arranged to Shenzhen, Dongguan, Nansha, and the border areas between Hong Kong and Shenzhen over the years. I also travelled as Panel Chairman to attend the annual Pan-Pearl River Delta Consultative Forums held in Chengdu in 2005, Kunming in 2006, and Changsha in 2007, representing the first three years since the establishment of the regional framework. In May 2009 I also read a paper at a pre-Forum academic meeting organized and held in Nanning by the Guangxi Social Sciences Academy.

Cooperation between Hong Kong and Shenzhen entered the official track in 2006, when the CPU and the China Development Institute jointly organized the first Shenzhen-Hong Kong Cooperation Forum, held in Shenzhen, with a large audience. The annual event has since been held alternately in Shenzhen and Hong Kong, with the fourth forum held in Hong Kong in July 2010. These forums have certainly brought academics and other participants closer, along with policy measures that have facilitated the movement of people, goods, and capital across the border.

My relationship with the CPU further deepened when I was appointed Research Consultant in September 2007, an arrangement that lasted three years to 2010. This appointment, which would take half of my time, involved a wide variety of tasks from giving analysis and comments on research reports, and producing ideas papers, to attending and chairing meetings. I also travelled on trips to different parts of the mainland as a member of the CPU's official delegations. Some of these were short trips to the PRC, including Shenzhen, Zhuhai, Macao, Jiangmen, and Guangzhou, with or without the need to stay overnight. However, the longer trips to the three provinces of northeastern China in December 2007 and to Beijing in December 2009 took several days. I much appreciated the wide range of responsibilities and exposure that the consultancy provided.

Another community service I have rendered was, in fact, centred in Shaw College but its orientation was purposefully global. With generous support provided by Dr Lam Kin-chung 林健忠 and Dr Ho Hau-wong 何厚煌, as advisors and patrons, the inaugural World Youth Leader Forum was held on 20-22 July 2011 at Shaw College of The Chinese University of Hong Kong. The theme of this first Forum was "Reshaping the Post-Crisis World Order" and it attracted 71 students from 13 countries. It was an instant success. The Forum was again held on 11-13 July 2012, on the theme of "Towards a World without Poverty and Inequality", with the participation of 86 students from over 40 universities in 15 countries or administrations. Compared with the inaugural Forum, it was an improvement in every aspect, receiving overwhelmingly favourable responses from the participants. I acted as Convenor of both Forums, which were co-organized with Universiti Kabangsaan Malyasia. The Forum has been conceived as a major annual event held on campus for Hong Kong students to interact with university students from abroad. In-depth and wide-ranging discussions on selected global concerns will greatly broaden their outlook and understanding.

Although I fully retired in 2008, I continued to lecture at CUHK on an ad hoc basis. Worthy of note are the many lectures I was invited to deliver to visiting university groups from the mainland, who came with the objective of learning more about university education in Hong Kong and its characteristics. I have given countless lectures to these groups from different parts of China over the past few years. When they visited CUHK, my assigned topic was the character of The Chinese University of Hong Kong, in particular its history, college system, and general education. I almost always spoke about my experience as University Registrar and other appointments I have held at the university. Such lectures would run three hours at a stretch and, to give an idea of its frequency, I spoke about once every month in 2011 and 2012. Such lectures were arranged by the School of Continuing and Professional Studies of CUHK. In addition, Professor Tsou Jin-yeu 鄒經宇 of the School of Architecture would invite me to speak to different groups of planners and officials from Foshan and its towns on the Hong Kong experience in housing, land, and urban development, either in Hong Kong or in Foshan itself. Similarly, invitations to speak on such topics to groups from different parts of mainland China would also come from the Office of Academic Links.

My research involvement took a concrete turn when the HKIAPS was invited in 2005 by the newly established Bauhinia Research Institute to undertake a project on the role of Hong Kong in the 11th Five-year Plan, addressing the question of challenges and opportunities in the PRD. The concern over the likely marginalization of Hong Kong had attracted much attention from the community. Shen Jianfa and Zhang Li 張力 teamed up with me to work on this project, with the help of research assistants. We presented our results in a widely reported news conference in December 2006.

In fact, this study with a sharp focus on the PRD was built upon another study commissioned by Dah Chong Hong Ltd in 2002. That company was in the process of expanding its logistics business and was seriously considering acquiring a large tract of land in Xinhui within Jiangmen. Alex Chu 朱漢輝 of the company wanted an academic study to verify the worth or risk of that investment. Again, Shen Jianfa, Zhang Li, and I formed a team, with able research assistants, to investigate. That provided an opportunity for us to undertake extensive field studies to all of the major ports in the western PRD. The study we undertook in this part of the PRD formed the basis of a book on the western PRD published in 2005. The CPU also commissioned us to carry out a similar study on the western PRD immediately after our study for Dah Chong Hong.

Partly because of my working relationship with Dah Chong

Hong Ltd in the above research project, I was invited to join its Board as an independent non-executive director when the company was listed in the Hong Kong Stock Exchange in October 2007. I have continued to serve in that capacity and have learned much about the practical workings of a large and reputable business operation in Hong Kong. I consider this to be another heaven-send opportunity to broaden my work experience during my retirement. I take special pleasure in the appointment because I have long been familiar with Dah Chong Hong Ltd's business. Some of the business leaders from Hang Seng Bank and also trustees of CUHK, especially Dr Ho Tim 何添, had been associated with the company for many years. I developed a close relationship with Dr Ho when I was University Registrar. I have the greatest respect for Clement Hui 許應斌 and Alex Chu, respectively Chairman and Vice-Chairman of the group, who have risen through the ranks to become the leaders and spirit of the company. I have seen how business acumen and leadership work in a large business enterprise. The company is a success story in Hong Kong, and it has been my privilege to be associated with it.

In fact, one of the longest consultancies that I have undertaken also occurred in 2010. I was commissioned by the Hong Kong Trade and Development Council (HKTDC) to carry out a study over eight months on the exhibition industries in Germany and the United States, with one month of travel within those countries. I shall provide more details on this assignment in the next chapter on consultancies.

The year 2010 was a busy one for me. I was invited through the London Speakers Bureau to speak at a one-day logistics seminar held in Shanghai on 14 October 2010. The activity was organized by Deutsche Post AG, a reputable German firm, arguably the largest logistics firm in the world in terms of the number of employees. Again, I shall return to this activity later.

The third consultancy I undertook in 2010 was to carry out a book project for a Korean research institute. I was invited to edit a book arising from a conference held in Jeju island in June of that year on the theme of regional development in Northeast Asia. My assignment was time-specific and I was able to complete the task in good time. The book was published by The Chinese University Press in 2011.

Having dwelt with so far mostly academic and related matters in my career in Hong Kong, it is apposite to conclude this part by referring to some of my social networks. Especially during the period in the new century, I have been active in several social groups on a recurring basis.

I am a member of a group that has been meeting more or less regularly over several months at a time in relation to our common research interest and professional involvement in housing. What brought together this group of about 15 persons was the initial dinner meeting convened almost immediately after the eruption in 2003 of a scandal surrounding short piling in the construction of public housing. The then Chairman of Hong Kong Housing Authority, Dr Rosanna Wong 王䓪鳴, was under considerable pressure. Many who had served under her able chairmanship were sympathetic to her and fully believed in her integrity. We met to review the matter, which quickly turned to a discussion of other current happenings in Hong Kong. This informal, collective, and perceptive analysis of current affairs in Hong Kong has become characteristic of our irregular dinner gatherings. We have taken turns in being the host and have tried a wide range of restaurants and clubs in Hong Kong. Given the large number of people on the roster, it would take several years before one had the privilege of hosting the social event. The dinners were not so regular at one time, but since Marco Wu's retirement from the civil service, he had been lending his efficiency and time to arrange the dinners for our benefit.

For many years a group of Hong Kong academics with links to Taiwan had been meeting over dinners under the name of Lufeng Yaju, meaning literally elegant gatherings under the Victoria Peak. Given that Chinese is the language of instruction at CUHK, it was not surprising that this social group had a typical CUHK orientation.

However, as many academics of Taiwanese origin had left Hong Kong ahead of the 1997 handover, participation in Lufeng Yaju was broadened to include a large social spectrum of Hong Kong. Many guests included well-off entrepreneurs, academics at other universities and related educational institutions, government officials, and the rich and famous. The turn towards more open membership began around 1989, but became most pronounced after 2000, when China opened up more. Every year about one gathering was held per season. Such dinner gatherings were held in a range of restaurants and clubs, depending on the theme and size of the gathering. Lufeng Yaju could consist of as few as two to as many as 20 to 30 tables of guests, with a roster of well-heeled entrepreneurs footing the bill. Mr Kwok Tsun Kee 郭俊沂 , a Hong Kong academic who has attended universities in Hong Kong and Taiwan, has been tireless and good-natured about organizing and planning such social gatherings. Over the past two decades, as many as 100 gatherings have been held. Silently, but effectively, Lufeng Yaju has facilitated social networking in Hong Kong across a wide spectrum of society.

In the early 1990s Dr Chan Shui-kou 陳瑞球 organized a litchi picking tour in Dongguan, inviting academics from a few universities in Hong Kong to provide suggestions on how farming and management methods could be improved at his litchi experimental farm. The tour began on a modest scale, with two mini buses to take all of the guests and overnight accommodation provided in Dongguan. Over the years the tour expanded greatly, in terms of the number and nature of the participants. From academics, participation gradually extended to government servants, Hong Kong representatives in China's political bodies (the National People's Congress and the Chinese People's Political Consultative Conference), and the rich and famous and their families. The pattern of the annual litchi picking trip took the form of using bus transport to update participants on developments in the Pearl River Delta, with an overnight stop in Guangzhou or Dongguan. The highlight of the second day was the litchi picking activity at the farm. Guests and their families would have a memorable weekend of sightseeing, good food, and litchi picking, with gift boxes to take home. When the event concluded its fifteenth year in June 2005, as many as eight large buses were needed to ferry guests both ways. Dr Chan and Ms Leung Kwok-ching 梁國貞 were most generous hosts of the event over such a long period. It was another silent but most effective way of enabling many Hong Kong residents to keep up with developments in the rapidly changing Pearl River Delta. As one who has benefitted from such social networking, I cannot help but marvel at the extent and scope of the physical, economic, and social changes that have taken place in the delta area over the years.

AT THE FRANKFURT FAIR WITH THE LOCAL HKTDC STAFF, 2010

11 Consultancies

A prominent but hardly known dimension of my career is the fact that I have undertaken a very large number of consultancies over the years, especially in the 1990s when the demand for my services soared. A consultancy is a written invitation to provide professional or expert service or to prepare a piece of written work for an institution. This may entail travelling, meeting people, speaking to an audience or providing expert advice, and often some combination of all of these activities. Consultancy work is invariably spelled out in a formal document, a contract, with legal provisions on clearly defined time frames, deliverables, and specified payments. As the work was undertaken beyond the normal responsibilities of my regular employment, permission had to be sought from my employer, and the income shared.

Over my career I have carried out a total of 46 consultancies, with the vast majority, 36, undertaken for international agencies. The remaining 10 consultancies were undertaken for local institutions in the cities where I lived.

The first consultancy I accepted was to undertake a consultancy in 1971-72 and in collaboration with Dr Peter Weldon, a sociology lecturer at the then University of Singapore, where I taught geography. Undertaken for Design Partnership, Ltd, our task was to mount a survey of shops and shoppers in the People's Park Complex at the centre of Chinatown in Singapore. Our study of shoppers was carried out in one week, from 2 to 8 December 1971, during which 2,019 shoppers were interviewed at 10 entrances. In addition, 219 of 300 shopkeepers on three floors were interviewed. The aim of the surveys was to fathom and ascertain a variety of aspects related to the shopping complex. The shopping habits of the customers were identified from the survey results, and the good location of the complex was found to be a major reason for the presence of those shops. The study yielded 50 tables of survey data, which, with the analysis that accompanied them, should have helped with the rapid development of shopping centres in Singapore in the years that followed.

My consultancies for international bodies also began in Singapore in the 1970s. In 1970 when I was beginning my academic career. I was commissioned by Encyclopedia Britannica to write a co-authored article on Kwangtung (later Guangdong) which appeared in its 1974 edition.

As I could not readily join Canada's International Development Research Centre (IDRC) in its Asia regional office in Singapore because of my contractual agreement with the University of Singapore, the former offered me an 18-month part-time consultancy contract with the Rural-Urban Dynamics Programme of their Social Sciences Division (SSD). Within the provisions of this contract, I made two trips to Southeast Asia in relation to project development and other tasks. The first trip, taken between 17 and 29 June 1974, had two objectives. One was to gain a better understanding of universities and research institutions outside the capital city of Jakarta in Indonesia. The other was to identify individuals and institutions deemed suitable to participate in two projects on low-cost transport, and resettlement and transmigration. The trip covered Medan in northern Sumatra; Jakarta, Yogyakarta, Surabaya, and Malang on Java; and Ujung Pandang in southwestern Sulawesi. I visited a large number of Indonesian universities, many of which I did not have a chance to visit again. This trip opened my eyes to the regional diversity, cultural richness, and physical vastness of the largest and most populous country in Southeast Asia. From Yogyakarta to Surabaya I chose to travel by a hired taxi. I preferred going by taxi over flying despite holding a confirmed air ticket, because going either way would have cost approximately the same. This took six hours, giving me the rare opportunity to learn more about the human and physical landscapes of Java. This almost completed my east-west transect of Java from Surabaya to Jakarta, involving a distance of 663 km, after an earlier trip by railway and automobile in 1973 that covered the distance from Yogyakarta to Jakarta, after a housing conference held in Bali, as referred to in Chapter 5.

The second trip, to Malaysia and Thailand, was undertaken from 20 to 30 October 1974. I visited universities and government offices in Kuala Lumpur, Bangkok, Chiangmai, and Khon Kaen. The objectives of this trip were similar to those of the earlier trip to Indonesia, with a focus on finding regional universities and institutions and younger researchers to participate in the two research projects under development. Both trips greatly broadened and deepened my understanding of Southeast Asia.

Following this short-term consultancy with the IDRC, I was employed by the organization for almost ten years. Since leaving the IDRC to join CUHK in 1984, I was awarded another four consultancies by the IDRC. Two, in September 1985 and February 1988, were, respectively, to provide expert advice to the In-Depth Fertility Survey (China) Project in its second phase and manpower training for Chinese researchers in London, Ontario. This was essentially follow-up work on my supporting role in getting the project approved for funding by the IDRC before I left the organization in 1984. The consultancies entailed travel to Beijing and Shanghai. In addition, in 1986 I was invited by Vice-President Dr Joe Hulse to write a reflective and analytical piece on Social Sciences at the IDRC based on my experiences during a decade of employment there at the juncture of the second change in the directorship of the SSD. Finally, in 1993 I was invited to write a paper on urban agriculture in Asia for an international conference on that theme held in Ottawa. This was related to my earlier work at the IDRC and to a consultancy activity I had undertaken with the United Nations University.

Given its sustained interest in urban and regional development in Asia and its networking role in spearheading research on such subjects within the region, the United Nations Centre for Regional Development (UNCRD), based in Nagoya, Japan, offered me four consultancies. In 1985 and 1988, I was invited to present papers at their Expert Group Meetings on the urban poor. In the latter meeting, I was also invited to guest edit a special volume of *Regional Development Dialogue*, arising from the papers presented. In 1996 I was invited to deliver a keynote address at the International Expert Panel on Urban Infrastructure Development held in Jakarta from 21 to 22 June. A book published by the UNCRD arose from the papers that were presented there. In 1998 I was invited to present another paper on regional development policy at a meeting held at the UNCRD from 1 to 4 December.

Among the international agencies with which I have worked, the United Nations University (UNU) is the one that I had the closest and most intensive cooperation with over a long and sustained period. I was offered three consultancies. The first one, in 1985, was an invitation to prepare a research paper on urban agriculture in Asia for UNU's Food-Energy Nexus Programme. The paper essentially summed up some of the highlights of my work in developing projects on that subject at the IDRC. As work on this subject was new, over the next two decades I received invitations to contribute papers on the subject or received enquires on it. In 1992, following UNU's initiative to undertake globalization and mega-cities as a new focus of research, I was invited to act as a consultant in coordinating a multi-country project on the Asia-Pacific Urban System and to edit a book arising from it. Fu-chen Lo of UNU and I worked closely on this project, and in 1996 published *Emerging World Cities in Pacific Asia*. In yet another consultancy project in 1995, I was invited to present a paper at the Pre-Habitat II Conference held in Tokyo and to edit a book arising from the papers presented. *Globalization and the World of Large Cities* was thus published in 1998. Of the books that both Fu-chen and I have published in our careers, these two were the ones most acquired by libraries around the world. As of 2010, the 1998 book had been acquired by 1,160 libraries and the 1996 book by 779 libraries, according to www.worldcat.org/identities. To my understanding, this is one of the best publication profiles of authors whose works in historical, subject and language details are readily shown.

Soon after I had joined CUHK, I was invited by the International Social Science Council (ISSC) based in Paris to write a paper on large cities in Eastern Asia for a conference on giant cities held in Barcelona, Spain, from 25 to 30 February 1985. This consultancy was timely, as it helpfully steered my research interest to large and mega cities in Asia, a focus of enquiry that I have continued with for many years. It also provided an occasion for me to visit Spain for the first time.

Perhaps as a result of my previous frequent contacts with the organization while I worked for the IDRC in Ottawa, the World Bank has given me the largest number (six) of consultancies since I returned to work in Hong Kong, equal to those awarded by the IDRC. It all began in 1988, when I was invited to fly to Washington, D.C., to provide input on the organization's new focus on urban research and development in developing countries, to be funded by the World Bank in its strategy plans. The World Bank was to mount a fresh lending initiative on the subject. A select group of senior academics presented their ideas on 19-21 June 1988. This was followed, in 1989, by an invitation, after a global search, to prepare a "think piece" on Access by the Urban Poor to Urban Infrastructure Services in Asia. I had to go through a huge number of papers and reports that were sent to me by air mail by the World Bank, in addition to those turned up by my own bibliographic searches. My lengthy report on Asia was presented and discussed in detail, along with two other regional reports on Africa and Latin America, in a live-in expert group workshop. Invited to the workshop held at Harpers Ferry, West Virginia, from 4 to 10 February 1990 were 40-50 academics and professionals from the Third World and the World Bank. We lived and worked together in a housing/

meeting complex there during the entire period. Never in my life has a written report of mine been examined so critically and thoroughly by so many people in such an open and iterative environment as happened during that workshop. This assignment gave me an opportunity to survey urban infrastructure services across Asia in many countries and to interact with many professionals and new friends. It was such an important subject that in 1990 I was given another consultancy to modify and expand the report as the lead paper for presentation at a joint conference on the Urban Poor, held in Manila from 21 to 28 January 1991 and sponsored by the World Bank and the Asian Development Bank.

In 1991, too, the World Bank appointed me as coordinator for Hong Kong in the Extensive Housing Indicator Survey jointly funded by the World Bank and the United Nations Centre for Human Settlements (UNCHS). I recall having called on Mr Leung Chun-ying 梁振英 at his survey firm for assistance in filling in some data. He has been elected the Chief Executive of Hong Kong in the relevant election held in March 2012 and assumed office on 1 July 2012. The findings of Asian countries were presented in a workshop held in Bangkok on 21 to 23 November 1991.

Every year the World Bank publishes the *World Development Report*, which is widely welcomed for its judicious and timely focus and analytical content, along with its annual statistical profile. Companion volumes are also prepared and published to provide more regional perspectives. I was invited to prepare a paper on Urban Poverty Alleviation in 1998 for the themed report on Attacking Poverty in 2000. Similarly, in another consultancy, I, this time with Shen Jianfa as co-author, wrote a paper in 2007 on Coastal China's Urban-Rural Spatial Restructuring under Globalization. This was for a companion volume to the *World Development Report* 2009 on Reshaping Economic Geography. What is interesting in both consultancies is that they each entailed attending two academic meetings in which drafts of the paper were discussed by different discussants in two rounds. On both occasions, we stayed at the Imperial Hotel in Tokyo, accommodation provided by the Japanese government. This is a posh and semi-official hotel, almost like the Peninsula Hotel in Hong Kong in its classical and historical details. It was a show of Japanese hospitality that was much appreciated.

The next international body that commissioned my work was the United Nations Development Programme (UNDP), with which I had only one consultancy. However, the UNDP served me well in the field when I worked for other UN agencies, including the UNCHS, which will be covered below. The consultancy I undertook with the UNDP in 1991 was to be an Asian expert in the Forward-looking Assessment in the Urban Management Programme (UMP), jointly funded by the UNDP, the World Bank, and the UNCHS. I undertook to travel as a UNDP consultant to Pakistan (Islamabad, Karachi), Nepal (Kathmandu), Indonesia (Jakarta), and China (Beijing) from 23 July to 12 August 1991. This one-person mission was to cover the Asia-Pacific region as part of the global programme of the Urban Management Programme (UMP). In my trip to the first three countries, I found that the gap between planning and reality was obvious and large. The UMP as a UN agent and its work were not widely known to federal government agencies, but it had greater exposure among municipal and provincial officials. In Karachi I was delighted to visit the Orangi Pilot Project that was prominently covered in my World Bank report on the Urban Poor and Urban Infrastructure Services noted above. In my interviews with government officials and academics, I covered key urban problems, the subject of technical assistance, the impact of the UMP, assistance modalities, and recommendations. The China visit was different from the rest, since China had not previously been involved in the UMP. The emphasis therefore was on the areas in which China could be networked with other Asian cities for their mutual benefit. The UMP was seen as a purposeful vehicle for China to tackle its problems in environmental protection, urban planning, and environmental standards.

I had four consultancies in the mid-1990s with another UN agency whose work was often linked with that of the World Bank in terms of funding, the United Nations Centre for Human Settlements (UNCHS). The first was the Extensive Housing Indicator Survey, jointly funded by the UNCHS and the World Bank in 1991, already referred to above. Then, in 1993, I was invited to join a three-person mission in the capacity of Senior UMP Consultant to assist the Government of Vietnam in its urban development strategy. It was a three-week mission headed by Patrick McAuslan, with me and Terry Standley as members. I was only able to join them from 21 August to 30 August 1993. We conducted extensive interviews with government officials, academics, and other professionals in Hanoi, Haiphong, and Ho Chi Minh City. It was a timely mission to offer advice to Vietnam, which had only opened up in 1986, following China's example of economic reform. On a flight from Ho Chi Minh City to Hanoi after completing our field reconnaissance and interviews, Patrick suggested that I had to write my report before I left. I had only the next and my last day in Hanoi to write it. The report, an 11-page paper entitled, "The Urban Condition in Vietnam", was completed on my brand new laptop. It was highly appreciated by Patrick and the Vietnamese government, as I was later told. I had occasion to make further use of this report many years later, as it was one of the best snapshots of urban Vietnam soon after the country began the process of opening up the country and society, based on site interviewing and an extensive review of official reports and the literature.

With the successful completion of the UNCHS mission in 1993, I was further invited to write a keynote address for the First Urban Sector Strategy Consultation Workshop held in Hanoi on 7 to 9 August 1995. I was given to understand that urban planners in most cities in Vietnam had been invited to attend this workshop. During this and my previous consultancy trips with the UNCHS, I was served in the field by UNDP offices. In between these two activities related to Vietnam I was invited in 1994 by UNCHS to present a paper in the

Conference on the Land Market in China held in Beijing from 17 to 20 May 1994.

Also in 1995, I was invited by the UNCHS to be the coordinator and editor of a volume on Metropolitan Planning and Management in China. I was responsible for identifying researchers in China and overseeing their work, in addition to writing an overview chapter. Two cities – Shanghai and Chongqing – were initially suggested by the UNCHS. I insisted on replacing Chongqing with Guangzhou for two reasons. First, I considered that Guangzhou had more to offer in terms of its planning initiatives and its role in spearheading China's economic development. Second, and of equal importance from my viewpoint, was my familiarity with potential researchers in Guangzhou. I had my way, and worked closely with researchers from both cities. The book was successfully published by the UNCHS in 1995. I felt shortchanged in not having my name put down as editor of the volume, as I had spent a great deal of time organizing and overseeing the research and writing of the two city chapters. The other two regional volumes on Africa and Latin America carried the names of the consultants of the projects as editors.

In the 1990s one UN agency after another had embarked on programmes and activities on cities in developing countries and their relationship with globalization. The United Nations Economic, Scientific and Cultural Organization (UNESCO) gave me three consultancies to expound on the related themes. In 1994 and 1995, I was invited to write papers for special issues of the *International Social Science Journal* on Cities of the Future and The State of the Art in Geography, respectively. Likewise, in 1998, I received another invitation to write, with Fu-chen Lo as co-author, a paper on Globalization and Urbanization for the *World Culture Report 1998*.

Apart from UN agencies, private institutions were equally active in the 1990s in pursuing collaborative research on urban issues in developing countries. In 1990, through Richard Stren of the University of

Toronto, I was invited by the Ford Foundation to present a paper for the Conference on Human Settlements and Sustainable Development held in Toronto on 21 to 23 June. This proved to be the precursor to the Ford Foundation's sustained support for more than a decade of collaborative urban research on the Third World. The Global Urban Research Initiative (GURI), as it was later known, was a network of twelve teams in all major developing regions coordinated by Richard Stren for several phases of funding by the Ford Foundation. I was invited in 1991 to join the panel of advisors, for the Asian components of the project and beyond. I wrote several papers and attended meetings in different parts of the world over the next few years.

Within Asia I was invited by the Asian Development Bank (ADB) in 1993 to prepare a paper on the Southern China Growth Triangle for the Conference on Growth Triangles in Asia and the Pacific held in Manila on 24 to 26 February. Cross-border economic development had attracted attention for the considerable potential it provided for collaborative regional development. The ADB offered me another consultancy in 2000, as consultant for Hong Kong in the preparation of the *Cities Data Book*.

In 1999 the Beijing Municipal Government sent a letter to the United Nations Conference on Trade and Development (UNCTAD) in Geneva, requesting a mission to prepare guidelines for the design of a framework for the promotion of trade in services in Beijing and to look into the process of the globalization and internationalization of trade in goods and services, with particular emphasis on the characteristics of the world's large cities. The person in charge in UNCTAD happened to have access to our newly published book, *Globalization and the World of Large Cities*. Hence, I was invited to join the UNCTAD mission of four, of whom I was the only outsider. Our mission took place on 12 to 16 December 1999. I took on a major role in speaking on the subject and met government officials in three separate half-day sessions. Our mission was prominently reported in the local newspapers. It was somewhat ironic that my expert service to the Beijing government had to go through a UN agency in Geneva.

A recent international consultancy that I undertook was in October 2010. The London Speakers Bureau gave my name to Deutsche Post AG, a prominent German firm, as a consultant to speak in its one-day seminar, held in the Hyatt on the Bund in Shanghai, on the theme Logistics Development in the Next Ten Years, with particular reference to mega-cities in Asia. It was a gathering geared towards practical and futuristic issues. I very much enjoyed the different style of intellectual exchange involving fewer people but more intensive interaction with largely senior professionals. This consultancy was special in another way. I earned more in one day's work for this consultancy than for comparable time input in any other consultancy I have ever undertaken.

Similarly, in late 2010 I took on another consultancy project, with the Korea Research Institute for Human Settlements, to edit a book out of the papers presented at a large and important international conference on Collaborative Regional Development in Northeast Asia held in Jeju Island in July 2010. It grew out of my participation in the conference with the presentation of a paper. The focus of the workshop was on the interrelationship between globalization and regionalization, a focus of my previous research efforts. I had to work under tight time constraints, but the book was published on time in mid-2011.

In the new century I also took a consultancy to write an article on "Mega-cities" for *International Encyclopedia of Human Geography* (Oxford: Elsevier, 2009). Over the past decade when I was with the HKIAPS, I was the primary researcher in a number of local consultancies. These included, in 2002, a Study on the Viability of Xinhui in the Western Pearl River Delta as a Logistics Hub, funded by Dah Chong Hong Ltd and Sims Trading Company Ltd. Between 2002 and 2003, I led a consultancy to produce a commemorative volume, in English and Chinese, on *Fifty Years of Public Housing in Hong Kong*, commissioned by the Hong Kong Housing Authority. In 2003 the Central Policy Unit commissioned a study on Hong Kong and the Western Pearl River Delta: Cooperative Development from a Cross-border Perspective. In 2005 I was invited by Wheelock Properties (H.K.) Ltd to take on another consultancy, on the subject The Pearl River Delta: A Background Study for Assessing Investment Opportunities. After the establishment of the Bauhinia Foundation Research Centre, the first research consultancy went to the HKIAPS. I was invited in 2006 to undertake a study on the theme of China's 11th Five-year Plan: Opportunities and Challenges for Hong Kong.

Between 2007 and 2010, I undertook a three-year consultancy with the Central Policy Unit, which allowed half of my time to be devoted to my work as Research Consultant. There was variety in the work with an obvious policy orientation to it. I very much enjoyed the opportunity to work closely with the government think tank, and to see Hong Kong and the mainland having materially and through policy innovations drawn closer to each other. Both sides have benefitted from the closer relationships in visible and concrete ways, in the gradual substantiation of the one-country, two systems formula.

The last consultancy in Hong Kong that came my way was in 2010, when between January and August I was tasked by the Hong Kong Trade and Development Council (HKTDC) to study the exhibition industry from the viewpoint of international experience. The main body of work entailed one month of travel in Germany and the United States, which are world leaders in the exhibition industry. In Germany I travelled to Frankfurt, Hanover, and Berlin for extensive interviews and field visits. The same process was repeated in Las Vegas, New York, and Chicago. Working closely with the staff of the HKTDC throughout the period, I produced a consultancy report in August 2010, which is available as HKTDC Trade Watch (May 2011) and on the HKTDC website in an abbreviated form.

It should be clear from the above pages that consultancies have been a salient part of my career. Through the many projects I have been invited to take on, I have been greatly enriched by the experience of doing different tasks, carrying out studies, and travelling. While providing varied services, I have learned through the process and have become a little wiser because of the people that I have met, and have benefitted from new experiences and challenges. Several observations from my years of consultancy experience can be distilled.

First, work undertaken in a consultancy has to be assessed carefully in terms of how much time is required to complete it. When I travelled on trips on a consultancy, it was my habit to complete the writing portion, as far as possible, before I returned home. In this way, I did not bring work home so as not to take time from my usual work. Adherence to this principle meant that I had to be well disciplined. If I travelled through cities and countries, I would complete my work before leaving one place. This process was helpful, as I still had instant recall immediately after doing the field work in a particular place. This also meant working in hotel rooms, airplanes, waiting rooms at airports, and other such places. My experience during the three-week UNDP mission in 1991 is still fresh in my mind. Although I stayed in one of the best hotels in the cities on that trip, lighting was invariably dim in the hotel room. I almost always had to read and write in the bathroom of my hotel suite, as the bathrooms were usually lit with fluorescent tubes. Fortunately, the washrooms were rather spacious in the hotels where I stayed. When one travels on official business, one has to improvise to be efficient. I developed the habit of working efficiently on trips when I travelled extensively on my IDRC job. Training myself to be able to dictate and to work under any circumstances was extremely helpful.

Second, I was approached again and again by international agencies to take on different consultancies. This is a reflection of the quality of the work that I had produced and the efforts that I had put in. I was able to establish a reputation for timely delivery. When undertaking consultancies for international bodies, one has to establish a reputation of producing good work on time and to the best of one's ability. When one fails once to deliver, not only will the institution involved avoid the person in the future, but the news will also travel to other similar bodies.

Third, time and project management are critical for the success of consultancies. Timely delivery of deliverables is a must. Do not agree to a timeline if you have any difficulty or even any doubt about being able to meet it. Management of the budget is something that must reflect absolute honesty. These are habits that must be formed early, and be practiced even at home and at all times.

Fourth, in order to be able to work efficiently and immediately on consultancies requiring field studies and interviews, one has to be well prepared. In particular, one has to be in a frame of mind to step right away in the field to begin work, even after an overnight flight. One needs to know what to ask, how to ask it, and under what circumstances to improvise. The control of time and the situation is essential. My prior experience with the IDRC for a decade prepared me well for the UN consultancies that I undertook during the 1990s and beyond. In interviews with government officials, senior academics, and other professional, it is preferable not to use any taping device. I took notes, jotting down only key points, which had to be embellished as soon as possible afterwards, certainly not later than at night in my hotel room. Recall has to be done within the same day to the extent possible.

The fifth and last observation is that consultancies can be viewed as new opportunities to push oneself. Many of my publications would not have come about had I not taken on the additional work that the consultancies involved. I personally have been pushed in many ways and many times. I have authored many books and scholarly papers that simply would not have been written if I had not accepted the invitation to act as a consultant. Certainly my exceptional academic productivity can be traced to many causes, with the many consultancies I have undertaken being a critical factor.

SPEAKING AT A CEREMONY AT SHEK KIP MEI, FOLLOWED BY
THE RELEASE OF A BOOK, 2003

12 Research and Publications

Since teaching and research have taken up the greater part of my career, research and publications have been an integral part of most of my working life. Research has always figured prominently in my career, as this is where I derive the greatest satisfaction, especially when research results appear as respectable publications. In my decade of work in the field of international development research assistance, it was always a struggle to find the time to read and update myself. Doing research was even more difficult, except when what was required was reading rather than data collection. When I was University Registrar, again it was almost as difficult to find the time to focus my attention on research. However, I managed to work doubly hard to keep carrying out research and publishing, after meeting the demands and obligations of the demanding post. Indeed, engaging in research and writing during my Registrarship took my mind away from the contentious issues that I often had to deal with the job. In a sense, it was my way of searching for mental comfort from the challenges and excitement of my administrative post.

During my long career spanning stints in Singapore, Ottawa, and Hong Kong and with different institutions, the focus of my research shifted with time and with the job I held. I learned most of my research skills through graduate training at UWO and the University of Chicago. James Simmons and Norton Ginsburg at the respective universities were my sources of inspiration and my models as outstanding researchers and professors. They sparked my interest in the commercial structure within cities, and in public housing and retail distribution in Singapore. After my initial exposure to these subjects, I maintained my interest in these and related subjects throughout my career.

When I began my career as a university lecturer in Singapore in 1969, the environment was vibrant, not only academically, but in a new nation as the Republic of Singapore in the midst of rapid change. I plunged right into research for my doctoral dissertation on public housing and retail distribution. I also discovered an exciting urban phenomenon in the travelling night markets, which were to fade from the scene after a few short years. They were to be absorbed into the regular commercial structure of the city. I got my students to help me carry out household surveys on public housing and to record operating details of the night markets. I took a keen interest in the subject and, in the company of my wife, visited quite a number of the night markets myself. In my early years in Singapore I was in the company of Stephen (Steve) H. K. Yeh 葉華國 , a sociologist with the Economic Research Centre at the university. We collaborated on many articles related to public housing in Singapore.

I was fortunate to have completed my doctoral dissertation in 1972, soon after the establishment of Canada's International Development Research Centre (IDRC). Steve Yeh was to become the coordinator of an eight-country study on low-cost housing in Southeast Asia. Similarly, Terry McGee, then of the University of Hong Kong, was the coordinator of a hawkers and vendors project in Southeast Asia. Both Yeh and McGee invited me to play a role in their projects funded by the IDRC. This was my first exposure to multi-country research on the same subjects that I had chosen for my dissertation. It was fortuitous that I was available at the time to join these pioneering projects supported by an innovative funding agency. It was an excellent opportunity to broaden my understanding of the region and to cement my network with its professionals. With Terry McGee, it was the beginning of career-long friendship and collaboration in research.

When I left academia to work in the field of international development assistance in 1975, I was prepared to meet new challenges and opportunities. In terms of research, I was at best able to carry on some of the work that I had started earlier at the university. In later years I succeeded in latching onto the multi-country projects funded by the IDRC for which I was able to put together networks. Two edited books were published arising from projects in urban services and low-cost housing in Asia. After almost a decade of work in this field, I began to feel more keenly than ever that I should disengage myself from this career trajectory if I were to make a mark in research. This is why I welcomed with open arms the opportunity to return to academia in 1984, to The Chinese University of Hong Kong (CUHK).

Almost immediately after re-entering academia, I was able to plunge back into research with renewed vigour and energy. Especially during the decade of the 1990s after completing my term as University Registrar, I was holding multiple concurrent appointments and invited to undertake a large number of international consultancies. My research was hence externally driven as well as internally generated. As a result, I generated a very large number of publications, and broadened the focus of my research at the same time. I was able to take advantage of multiple concurrent appointments to maximize my research efficiency. Over time, my research has covered the following major broad but interconnected categories:

1. Public and low-cost housing in Asia, especially Hong Kong and Singapore
2. Retail distribution in Asian cities, periodic markets, hawkers and vendors
3. The urban poor, basic infrastructure services in Asia, urban services, low-cost transport, urban agriculture
4. Asian cities and urbanization, Pacific Asia, Southeast Asia, China and Hong Kong
5. Globalization and urbanization, mega-cities, world cities, transportation and logistics
6. Globalization and regionalization, trans-border collaborative development, growth triangles, resettlement and transmigration
7. China's openness and economic reforms, regional studies, regional cooperation, Hong Kong-mainland interactions

Since my return to Hong Kong, I have collaborated with many colleagues, friends, and institutions on numerous book projects and other research projects, with the following worthy of note. In the 1990s, I worked closely over several years with Fu-chen Lo 羅福全 of the United Nations University in Tokyo on projects on globalization and world cities involving multiple institutions and researchers in Pacific Asia and other parts of the world. The result was the publication of *Emerging World Cities in Pacific Asia* (1996) and *Globalization and the World of Large Cities* (1998). As noted before, these books have been exceptionally well received, as seen by the number of libraries in the world that have acquired them. The former book consumed perhaps more of my time and energy than any of my other edited volumes because of the large number of contributors and the diversity of approaches contained in the book.

For two four-year terms until 1996, I was East Asia representative and Director, respectively, of the Commonwealth Geographical Bureau (CGB), the only networking body of geography departments in universities within the British Commonwealth. I brought two of its major meetings, including the Silver Jubilee Celebration of the founding of the CGB in 1994, as well as another meeting earlier in 1990, to CUHK. These were some of the notable academic events hosted in Hong Kong before Hong Kong left the British Commonwealth in 1997 with its handover to China. *Pacific Asia in the 21st Century* (1993) and *Global Change and the Commonwealth* (1996) were publications arising from the proceedings.

Towards the latter part of the 1990s, I established a fruitful working relationship with Li Xiaojian 李小建, a brilliant geographer from Henan University. During the time that he was attached for several months to CUHK on a term research appointment, we worked on a project on transnational corporations in China. Four respectable journal articles stemmed from this collaboration. Li returned to Hong Kong in the new century to work briefly with me on China's western region, with the publication of another joint research paper. Since then, Li Xiaojian has been appointed President of Henan University of Economics and Law in Zhengzhou.

Within CUHK, I developed sustained and close working relationships with several geography colleagues. In the Urban and Regional Development in Pacific Asia Programme within the HKIAPS, research attention began to be devoted to an assessment of the rapid development that had transformed China's coastal areas by the early 1990s. With David K. Y. Chu 朱劍如, we systematically examined the transformation of Guangdong and Fujian, the first two provinces chosen to experiment on open policies in China. Several books in this series were published by The Chinese University Press over a sustained period of more than a decade. The first book on Guangdong was released in 1994, with a second revised edition in 1998. The Fujian book was released in 2000.

The Fujian book is arguably the most authoritative book on the transition and transformation of the province in the reform period ever published in the English language. Murray A. Rubinstein wrote a 19-page book review on the book that appeared in *China Review International*, Spring 2003, pp. 59-77, an unusually lengthy article for the review of a single book. Below is an excerpt from Rubinstein's review:

The publication of this collaborative volume comes at a timely moment in the evolution of Fujian – and of the scholarship on this province – as it reaches new heights of influence in a rapidly developing China.... The essays that make up this 572-page volume are of such a high level of scholarship, and yet so accessible, that "Fujian hands" and many other students of China, Taiwan and East and Southeast Asia as well as the educated layperson will find it both extremely useful and quite fascinating. If Fujian can be seen as a "gateway" – or better, an entrance arch – to China, then this collaborative volume, with its rich and varied set of essays, is the textual door to that geographic gateway.

The regional China review series ran to five or six volumes between 1994 and 2008. Of these, I worked in the new century with Shen Jianfa 沈建法 on *Developing China's West and The Pan-Pearl River Delta*. Editing such comprehensive regional reviews and assessments of development called for considerable preparation and collaboration with many authors, including those from the mainland. Mainland authors were not used to writing in English; thus I and Shen had to rewrite and polish chapters repeatedly to bring them to a level compatible with the standards of CU Press. The whole manuscript had to meet required standards and an external review process before it could be accepted for publication. To give the reader an idea of what the process involved, the following preliminary materials were prepared and provided at the outset to the authors of the Developing China's West book for their information. Only the guidelines for the initial chapters of the book, the first part, involving overviews of the western region, are included below for illustrative purposes.

This book is the fourth in the regional studies on China to be published by The Chinese University Press in Hong Kong. The previous volumes published are Guangdong (1994, 1998 2nd edition), Shanghai (1996) and Fujian (2000). As reference to these volumes will make clear, each book has attempted to present the most up-to-date and analytical material to the reader in as comprehensive a manner as possible. Each book runs over 500 pages and represents the best reference volume in English. The new book on China's western development is intended to serve the same purpose.

As the new book will involve the participation of many scholars on the mainland who may not be familiar with a collaborative venture of this nature, we try to be explicit in spelling out the detailed conceptual framework and chapter arrangements, so that maximum efficiency is achieved and overlap minimized. We aim at presenting the best available material, both of a statistical and analytical nature, employing Western social science techniques and approaches. This explains the suggestion of joint authorships for some chapters.

The following is an attempt to describe the basic approach to the new volume in two major parts and by chapters.

1. The introductory chapter, providing a simple factual and statistical background, will develop the theme of the book on why China has formulated the policy of developing the west as a major development platform of the 21st century. One primary objective is to promote balanced economic development, a policy goal that is all the more imperative, given two decades of rapid economic development under open policies and the resultant enlarged gap between the coastal and interior provinces. This chapter will integrate the materials from different chapters and develop its own focus. It will give a commanding and comprehensive lead-in to the subject and the book.

Part I Macro Regional Perspectives

This part in 8 chapters will introduce the main cross-cutting themes of western development. Each chapter will focus on a major subject of importance to the present and future efforts to develop the west.

2. Historical Legacy and Future Challenges

This is a critical chapter that sets out the background of China's policy of developing the west in historical and contemporary terms. It outlines, in broad sweeps, the early flourishing cultures and economic development of this extensive part of China, initially contending for power and authority with the nomadic peoples there. Its early geographical and strategic importance was assured in the establishment of the Silk Road over many centuries. However, centuries of misuse of the land have resulted in vast ecological problems which present administrators and developers have to contend with.

The central government's new policy to develop the west presents the sprawling region with new opportunities and challenges. There are many positive aspects of economic development which must be balanced against the need to preserve a sound ecological balance. Developing the west is a long-term process and goal. This chapter should briefly refer to the experience of such large-scale frontier development in North America, Asiatic Russia and Brazil and examine what possible lessons can be learned.

3. Geographical Background and Sustainable Development
This chapter provides the basic geographical background of the western region, going much beyond Chapter 1. It will emphasize the immensity of its size, diversity, richness in natural resources, strategic location vis-à-vis Central Asia and South Asia, political sensitivity because of the presence of large and numerous ethnic minorities, etc.

In view of its physical setting and past misdirected development, the ecological balance of the region is precarious. Any development plan of the future in accelerating economic growth must take as its highest priority sustainable development of both economic and environmental change.

Of the many books I have edited or co-edited during my tenure at CUHK, the studies on China's regions rank among the most important and sustained over a decade of my internally generated research. With regard to outside invitations, *Fifty Years of Public Housing in Hong Kong*, arising from an invitation from the Hong Kong Housing Authority, is the one that proved to be the most challenging in terms of both time constraints and the coverage of the subject. In twenty months two books in English and Chinese had to be prepared on a wide range of topics relating to public housing over half a century. Timothy K. Y. Wong 王家英, my co-editor, and I were essentially in charge of the Chinese and English editions, respectively, with the English edition prepared first. The book project involved many challenges, but three episodes are still fresh in my mind.

One concerned a chapter in its first proof from the publisher, which the Housing Department disapproved of. I was asked to drop the chapter, as the Housing Department considered to it problematic in that they thought the author had been unduly and unfairly critical on six points. I took it upon myself to rewrite those sentences without consulting the author. Sometimes an editor has to make difficult but discreet decisions. The truth is, I did not change the substance of the work, but only chose different wordings and presented the facts in a more objective way. Another chapter contained 35 photographs, when I had suggested the inclusion of not more than five. It was not an easy task for me to discard so many good photographs. A third chapter presented a similar problem, although here the author had gone overboard and delivered a much delayed but overly long chapter of 75 pages, when my recommended length per chapter was 30 to 35. It was a big struggle to prune so much, but it had to be done. Much of this kind of work was onerous and sensitive, known only between the editor and the author and sometimes even not known to the author, as in the first case cited.

The public housing book as well as two others entitled *The First Decade* and *The Pan-Pearl River Delta* were preceded in the preparatory stage by the same kind of introductory materials as briefly introduced earlier for *Developing China's West*. Here the time constraints were just as tight, as *The First Decade* and the public housing book were tailored to certain time-specific events. For these books to meet the time target,

I had to rely on the capable assistance of colleagues from the units of which I was in charge and from other concerned departments within the university.

Throughout most of the 1990s, I edited at least two books a year. The greatest number that I had in progress simultaneously was four books, in 1996. When that situation arose, the amount of correspondence that needed to be handled exceeded the capacity of the HKIAPS. In my experience of editing books, in the usual run of the editing process I needed to write to every author three to five times, sometimes quite a lot more. Three books at a time constituted the maximum number that my secretary at the HKIAPS could handle, without becoming confused about which authors were writing for which books. The fourth book had to be handled by my secretary at Shaw College. This task certainly went beyond her normal responsibilities. She loved, however, meeting this new challenge. My ability to edit so many books owed much to the fact that I had two senior personal secretaries in the guise of Janet Wong 汪唐鳳萍 at the HKIAPS and Daisy Chung 鍾秀群 at Shaw College. They were both trained stenographers, proficient in taking dictation. I only had one book that elicited Daisy Chung's secretarial skills. It resulted in *Globalization and the World of Large Cities*, which is the most acquired book by libraries in the world among those that I have published, in this case with Fu-chen Lo as co-editor. Besides harnessing secretarial expertise in the HKIAPS and Shaw College for my research, I was further assisted by being able to draw on the cartographical expertise of S. L. Too 杜士流, of the then Department of Geography, for maps and illustrations. Concurrent appointments greatly helped me to edit many books over the years, as they meant more resources were available at my disposal.

My sustained and multi-facetted research during my career has yielded a bountiful harvest of publications. By 2012, I had published as sole author or editor, or with others, a total of 50 books, 45 refereed journal articles, 102 book chapters, 112 research or occasional papers and others, and 41 book reviews. In addition, I have been invited to deliver 37 keynote addresses, with 10 delivered outside of Hong Kong. Delivered largely during and since the 1990s, many of these addresses have been turned into publications.

An approximate indication of the status of my publications can in part be revealed by the holdings in different kinds of libraries. A cursory survey of university libraries has revealed that many have sizeable holdings of my publications, mostly books and other titles, such as UWO (12), Toronto (41), Leeds (14), the University of Chicago (27), Harvard (43), Stanford (60), the National University of Singapore (39), Australian National University (68), CUHK (143), and HKU (146). At 546 titles, UBC in Vancouver had the largest holding of my publications, including books, book chapters, articles, book reviews, and others. Even public libraries in Hong Kong (60), Singapore (29), Toronto (12), and New York (14) had stocked my books and other titles. One can get an idea of my personal publication profile by entering the site www.worldcat.org/identities. As I indicated before, this source showed that I had two books published by UNU Press in 1996 and 1998 that were acquired, respectively, by 779 and 1,160 libraries in the world.

Concluding this chapter is a list of my publications in the form of books, journal articles, and book chapters, given below.

Books/Monographs

1. 1973   Yue-man Yeung, *National Development Policy and Urban Transformation in Singapore: A Study of Public Housing and the Marketing System.* Research Paper No. 149, Department of Geography, University of Chicago, 204 pp.
2. 1976 R   Y. M. Yeung and C. P. Lo (eds.), *Changing Southeast Asian Cities: Readings on Urbanization.* Singapore: Oxford

University Press, 245 pp. With Introduction, pp. xiv to xxiv.

3. 1977 R T. G. McGee and Y. M. Yeung, *Hawkers in Southeast Asian Cities: Planning for the Bazaar Economy*. Ottawa: International Development Research Centre, 139 pp.

4. 1983 R Y. M. Yeung (ed.), A Place to Live: *More Effective Low-Cost Housing Policies in Asia*. Ottawa: International Development Research Centre, 216 pp.

5. 1986 R Y. M. Yeung and T. G. McGee (eds.), *Community Participation in Delivering Urban Services in Asia*. Ottawa: International Development Research Centre, 279 pp. With Conclusions, pp. 255-62.

6. 1987 Y. M. Yeung and Zhou Yixing (guest eds.), *Urbanization in China: An Inside-Out Perspective. Chinese Sociology and Anthropology*, Vol. 19, No. 3-4, 1987, with Introduction, pp. 3-13.

7. R Y. M. Yeung and T. G. McGee (eds.), *Le role de la participation communautaire dans la prestation des services municipaux en Asie*. Ottawa: International Development Research Centre, 292 pp.

8. 1988 Yue-man Yeung (guest ed.), *Employment, Livelihoods for the Urban Poor: Issues and Strategies in Metropolitan Planning. Regional Development Dialogue*, Vol. 9, No. 4, Winter, 186 pp., with Introduction, pp. iii to vii.

9. 1989 Y. M. Yeung and Zhou Yixing (guest eds.), *Urbanization in China: An Inside-Out Perspective (II). Chinese Sociology and Anthropology*, Vol. 21, No. 2.

10. R Y. M. Yeung and T. G. McGee (eds.), *Partipación Comunitaria en la Prestación de Servicios Urbanos en Asia*. Ottawa: International Development Research Centre, 305 pp.

11. 1990 R Yue-man Yeung, *Changing Cities of Pacific Asia: A Scholarly Interpretation*. Hong Kong: The Chinese University

Press, 320 pp.

12. 1991　喬健 李沛良 金耀基 楊汝萬 劉兆佳 關信基編，〈中國家庭及其變遷〉。香港： 中文大學社會科學院及香港亞太研究所，382 頁。

13. 1992 R　Yue-man Yeung and Xu-wei Hu (eds.), *China's Coastal Cities: Catalysts for Modernization.* Honolulu: University of Hawaii Press, 330 pp.

14. 1993　楊汝萬編，〈中國城市與區城發展：展望廿一世紀〉。香港： 中文大學亞太研究所，515 頁。

15.　　R　Yue-man Yeung (ed.), *Pacific Asia in the 21st Century: Geographical and Developmental Perspectives.* Hong Kong: The Chinese University Press, 346 pp.

16. 1994 R　Y. M. Yeung and David K. Y. Chu (eds.), Guangdong: *Survey of a Province Undergoing Rapid Change.* Hong Kong: The Chinese University Press, 504 pp.

17. 1996 R　Fu-chen Lo and Yue-man Yeung (eds.), *Emerging World Cities in Pacific Asia.* Tokyo: United Nations University Press, 528 pp.

18.　　　Yue-man Yeung (ed.), *Global Change and the Commonwealth.* Hong Kong: Hong Kong Institute of Asia-Pacific Studies, The Chinese University of Hong Kong, 465 pp.

19.　　R　Y. M. Yeung and Sung Yun-wing (eds.), *Shanghai: Transformation and Modernization under China's Open Policy.* Hong Kong: The Chinese University Press, 583 pp.

20. 1997　Yue-man Yeung and Sun Sheng Han (eds.), *Urban Infrastructure Development.* UNCRD Proceedings Series No. 15. Nagoya: UNCRD, 174 pp.

21.　　　胡序威 陳佳源 楊汝萬編，〈閩東南地區經濟和人口空間集聚與擴散研究〉。香港：中文大學香港亞太研究所，214 頁。

22. 1998 R　Y. M. Yeung and David K. Y. Chu (eds.), *Guangdong: Survey of a Province Undergoing Rapid Change.* Hong

Kong: The Chinese University Press, 2nd edition, 536 pp.

23.   Yue-man Yeung (ed.), *Urban Development in Asia: Retrospect and Prospect*. Hong Kong Institute of Asia-Pacific Studies, The Chinese University of Hong Kong, 453 pp., with Introduction, pp. xvii-xxvi.

24. R   Fu-chen Lo and Yue-man Yeung (eds.), Globalization and the World of Large Cities. Tokyo: United Nations University Press, 530 pp.

25. 1999   楊汝萬 陸大道 沈建法編，〈邁向廿一世紀的中國〉。香港：中文大學亞太研究所，553 頁。

26. 2000 R   Y. M. Yeung and David K. Y. Chu (eds.), Fujian: *A Coastal Province in Transition and Transformation*. Hong Kong: The Chinese University Press, 556 pp.

27.   R   Yue-man Yeung, *Globalization and Networked Societies: Urban-Regional Change in Pacific Asia*. Honolulu: University of Hawaii Press, 289 pp.

28. 2001   承繼成 林琿 楊汝萬著，〈面向信息社會的區域可持續發展導論〉。北京：商務印書館，270 頁。

29.   陳述彭 楊汝萬 林琿編，〈新經濟與中國西部開發〉。香港：中文大學亞太研究所，243 頁。

30. 2002 R   Yue-man Yeung (ed.), *New Challenges for Development and Modernization: Hong Kong and the Asia-Pacific Region in the New Millennium*. Hong Kong: The Chinese University Press, 334 pp.

31.   段樵 陸德明 楊汝萬編，〈入世後中華經濟圈的機遇與挑戰〉。香港：中文大學滬港發展聯合研究所，280 頁。

32. 2003   Yue-man Yeung, *Housing in Hong Kong: A Golden Jubilee Bibliography*. Research Monograph No. 57, Hong Kong Institute of Asia-Pacific Studies, The Chinese University of Hong Kong, 301 pp.

33.   R   Y. M. Yeung and Timothy K. Y. Wong

(eds.), *Fifty Years of Public Housing in Hong Kong: A Golden Jubilee Review and Appraisal.* Hong Kong: The Chinese University Press, 487 pp.

34.　　　R　楊汝萬 王家英編，〈香港公營房屋五十年： 金禧回顧與前瞻〉。香港： 中文大學出版社，454 頁。

35.　　　　伏潤民 陳志龍 楊汝萬編，〈中國西部開發與周邊國家〉。昆明： 雲南大學出版社，328 頁。

36. 2004 R　Y. M. Yeung and Shen Jianfa (eds.), *Developing China's West: A Critical Path to Balanced National Development.* Hong Kong: The Chinese University Press, 604 pp.

37.　　　　楊汝萬著，〈全球化背景下的亞太城市〉。北京：科學出版社，241 頁。

38. 2005　　Y. M. Yeung, Shen Jianfa, and Zhang Li, *The Western Pearl River Delta: Growth and Opportunities for Cooperative Development with Hong Kong.* Research Monograph No. 62, Hong Kong Institute of Asia-Pacific Studies, The Chinese University of Hong Kong, 160 pp.

39.　　　　楊汝萬 沈建法編，〈泛珠三角與香港互動發展〉。香港： 中文大學亞太研究所，370 頁。

40. 2006　　楊汝萬 黃揚略 余統浩 酈景廉編，〈港澳與珠三角西部發展： 掌握發展新機遇〉。香港： 中文大學香港亞太研究所， 155 頁。

41. 2007　　楊汝萬 紀緯紋著，〈網絡縱橫：泛珠三角區域基礎設施的發展〉。香港： 中文大學香港亞太研究所，272 頁。

42.　　　　黃紹倫 楊汝萬 尹寶珊 鄭宏泰編，〈澳門社會實錄： 從指標研究看生活素質〉。香港：中文大學香港亞太研究所，358 頁。

43.　　　　Yue-man Yeung (ed.), The First Decade: *The Hong Kong SAR in Retrospective and Introspective Perspectives.* Hong Kong: The Chinese University Press, 422 pp.

44. 2008 R   Y. M. Yeung and Shen Jianfa (eds.), *The Pan-Pearl River Delta: An Emerging Regional Economy in a Globalizing China*. Hong Kong: The Chinese University Press, 595 pp.

45. 2009   王桂新 楊汝萬編，〈全球化背景下亞洲城市的戰略性選擇〉。上港：上海人民出版社，309 頁。

46. 2010   王桂新 楊汝萬編，〈巨變中的城：危機與發展〉。上海：上海人民出版社，398 頁。

47.   楊汝萬 沈建法 紀緯紋著，〈泛珠三角與香港："十一五"下泛珠三角九省和澳門與香港的發展〉。香港：中文大學香港亞太研究所，440 頁。

48. 2011   Won Bae Kim, Yue-man Yeung, and Sang-Chuel Choe (eds.), *Collaborative Regional Development in Northeast Asia: Towards a Sustainable Regional and Sub-regional Future*. Hong Kong: The Chinese University Press, 378 pp.

49. 2012   Yeung Yue-man, Freedom Y. K. Leung, and Patrick P. C. Choi (eds.), *Reshaping the Post-crisis World Order: World Youth Leaders Forum*. Hong Kong: Infolink Publishing Ltd., 175 pp.

50.   Yue-man Yeung, *From Local to Global and Back: Memoir of a Hongkonger*. Hong Kong: The Commercial Press.

R = refereed

Refereed Articles

1. 1971   Yue-man Yeung and Stephen H. K. Yeh, "Commercial Patterns in Singapore's Public Housing Estates," *Journal of Tropical Geography*, Vol. 33, pp. 73-86.

2. 1972   Yue-man Yeung and Stephen H. K. Yeh, "A Shop Census in Singapore's Public Housing Estates," *Town Planning Review*, Vol. 43, No. 1, pp. 166-84.

3. 1974   "Periodic Markets: Comments on Spatial-Temporal Relationship," *Professional Geographer*, Vol. 16, No. 2, pp. 147-51.

4.   Yue-man Yeung and D. W. Drakakis-Smith, "Comparative Perspectives on Public Housing in Singapore and Hong Kong," *Asian Survey*, Vol. 14, No. 8, pp. 763-75.

5. 1975   "Activity Systems as an Urban Research Method," *Southeast Asian Journal of Social Sciences*, Vol. 3, No. 2, pp. 1-8; tables in Vol. 4, No. 1, 1976.

6. 1976   Yue-man Yeung and Stephen H. H. Yeh, "Time Budgets: *Extended Methodology and Application*," *Environment and Planning A*, Vol. 8, pp. 93-107.

7. 1977   "Hawkers and Vendors: Dualism in Southeast Asia," *Journal of Tropical Geography*, Vol. 44, pp. 81-86.

8.   "High-Rise, High-Density Housing: Myths and Reality," *Habitat International*, Vol. 2, Nos. 5 and 6, pp. 587-94.

9. 1982   "Economic Inequality and Social Injustice: Development Issues in Malaysia," *Pacific Affairs*, Vol. 55, No. 1 (Spring), pp. 94-101.

10. 1985   "Provision of Urban Services in Asia: The Role of People-Based Mechanisms," *Regional Development Dialogue*, Vol. 6, No. 2, pp. 148-63.

11. 1986   "China After Mao: Modernization and Integration with the World Order," *Canadian Journal of Development Studies*, Vol. 7, No. 1, pp. 127-31.

12.   "Controlling Metropolitan Growth in Eastern Asia," *The Geographical Review*, Vol. 76, No. 2, pp. 125-37.

13. 1987   "Geography and the Developing World," Asian Geographer, Vol. 6, No. 1, pp. 43-53; also in *Professorial Inaugural Lecture Series* 10, *Chinese University Bulletin*, 17, pp. 1-12.

14. 1988 "Agricultural Land Use in Asian Cities," *Land Use Policy*, Vol. 5, No. 1, January, pp. 79-82.

15. "Livelihoods for the Urban Poor: Case for a Greater Role by Metropolitan Governments," *Regional Development Dialogue*, Vol. 9, No. 4, pp. 40-54.

16. 1991 Y. M. Yeung and Yixing Zhou, "Human Geography in China: Evolution, Rejuvenation and Prospect," *Progress in Human Geography*, Volume 15, No. 4, pp. 373-94.

17. 1995 "Urbanization and the NPE: An Asia-Pacific Perspective," *Cities*, Vol. 12, No. 6, pp. 409-11.

18. 1996 "An Asian Perspective on the Global City," *International Social Science Journal*, No. 147, March, pp. 25-31 (in 6 languages).

19. 1997 "Geography in the Age of Mega-cities," *International Social Science Journal*, No. 151, March, pp. 91-104 (in 6 languages).

20. "香港'九七'回歸的地理意義，"〈地理學報〉，第 52 卷，8-15 頁。

21. "Planning for Pearl City: Hong Kong's Future, 1997 and Beyond," *Cities*, Vol. 14, No. 5 (October), pp. 249-56.

22. 1998 "The Promise and Peril of Globalization," *Progress in Human Geography*, Vol. 22, No. 4, pp. 475-77.

23. Xiaojian Li and Yue-man Yeung, "Transnational Corporations and Their Impact on Regional Economic Imbalance: Evidence from China," *Third World Planning Review*, Vol. 20, No. 4 (November 1998), pp. 351-73.

24. 1999 Yue-man Yeung and Xiaojian Li, "Bargaining with Transnational Corporations: The Case of Shanghai," *International Journal of Urban and Regional Research*, Vol. 23, No. 3, pp. 513-33.

25. Xiaojian Li and Yue-man Yeung, "Inter-firm Linkages and Regional Impact of Transnational Corporations:

Company Case Studies from Shanghai, China," *Geografiska Annaler*, 81B, Vol. 2, pp. 61-72.

26. 2000 Yue-man Yeung and Xiaojian Li, "Transnational Corporations and Local Embeddedness: Company Case Studies from Shanghai, China," *Professional Geographer*, Vol. 52, No. 4, pp. 624-35.

27. 2001 "Coastal Mega-cities in Asia: Transformation, Sustainability and Management," *Ocean and Coastal Management*, Vol. 44, Nos. 5 and 6, pp. 319-33.

28. 2002 "Globalization and Southeast Asian Urbanism," *Asian Geographer*, Vol. 21, Nos. 1 and 2, pp. 171-86.

29. 2003 "Integration of the Pearl River Delta," *International Development Planning Review*, Vol. 25, No. 3, pp. iii-viii.

30. 2004 汪一鳴 楊汝萬 吳永輝，〝蘭州 -- 西寧 -- 銀川城市帶與西部開發。〞〈地理學報〉，第 59 卷，第 2 期，213-22 頁。

31. Jianfa Shen and Yue-man Yeung, "Development and Transformation of the Free Port of Hong Kong," *Korea International Commerce Review*, Vol. 19, No. 1, pp. 47-68.

32. 2005 "Emergence of the Pan-Pearl River Delta," *Geografiska Annaler*, Vol. 87B, No. 1, pp. 75-79.

33. 2006 "An Emerging Development Focus from the Pearl River Delta West to Western Guangdong: A Research Report," *Eurasian Geography and Economics*, Vol. 47, No. 2, pp. 243-50.

34. "Three Chinese Cities and Their Pathways to Globalization," *Town Planning Review*, Vol. 77, No. 3, pp. 345-51.

35. 2007 "Vietnam: Two Decades of Urban Development," *Eurasian Geography and Economics*, Vol. 48, No. 3, pp. 269-88.

36. "World Cities and Mega-Urban Regions in Pacific Asia: Recent Trends and Future Outlook," *Fudan Journal of*

the Humanities and Social Sciences, Vol. 4, No. 4, pp. 1-15.

37. 2008 Yue-man Yeung, Joanna Lee, and Gordon Kee, "Hong Kong and Macao under Chinese Sovereignty," *Eurasian Geography and Economics*, Vol. 49, No. 3, pp. 304-25.

38. 2009 Yue-man Yeung, Joanna Lee, and Gordon Kee, "China's Special Economic Zones at 30," *Eurasian Geography and Economics*, Vol. 50, No. 2, pp. 222-40.

39. "China's Openness and Reform at 30: Retrospect and Prospect," *The China Review*, Vol. 9, No. 2, pp. 175-67.

40. 2010 The Further Integration of the Pearl River Delta: A New Beginning of Reform," *Environment and Urbanization ASIA*, Vol. 1, No. 1, pp. 13-26.

41. Yue-man Yeung, Joanna Lee, and Gordon Kee, "Macao in a Globalizing World: The Challenges Ahead," *Asian Geographer*, Vol. 27, Nos. 1 and 2, pp. 75-92.

42. "Financial Centres in Pacific Asia after the Global Financial Crises: Challenges and Opportunities." In Yuen Zhigong (ed.), *Shanghai Forum 2010*, pp. 254-72.

43. 2011 "Hong Kong and Shanghai as International Financial Centres: Present Assessment and Future Prospect," *Hong Kong International Relations Review*, Vol. 1, pp. 11-22.

44. "Rethinking Asian Cities and Urbanization: Four Transformations in Four Decades," *Asian Geographer*, Vol. 28, No. 1, pp. 65-83.

45. 楊汝萬 紀緯紋，"澳門城市管治對城市發展和規劃劃的影響"。〈城市與區域規計劃研究〉，第 4 卷，第 3 期，100-18 頁。

Book Chapters

1. 1971 "Singapore." *Focus* (American Geographical Society), Vol. 21, No. 8, 12 pp. Reprinted in *Focus on Southeast*

Asia, ed. Alice Taylor. New York: Praeger Publications, 1972, pp. 166-84.

2. 1974   Yue-man Yeung and C. T. Chang, "Kwangtung." *Encyclopaedia Britannica*, 15th Edition, Vol. 10, pp. 554-58.

3. 1975   Y. M. Yeung and Stephen H. K. Yeh, "A Review of Neighbourhoods and Neighbouring Practices." In *Public Housing in Singapore: A Multidisciplinary Study*, ed. Stephen H. K. Yeh. Singapore: Singapore University Press, pp. 262-80.

4.   Y. M. Yeung and Stephen H. K. Yeh, "Life Styles Compared: Squatters and Public Housing Residents." In *Public Housing in Singapore*, ed. Stephen H.K. Yeh, pp. 302-24.

5. 1976   "The Marketing System in Singapore." In *Changing Southeast Asian Cities*, ed. Y. M. Yeung and C. P. Lo. Singapore: Oxford University Press, pp. 153-64.

6.   "Southeast Asian Cities: Patterns of Growth and Transformation." In *Urbanization and Counterurbanization*, ed. Brian J. L. Berry. Beverly Hills: Sage Publications, pp. 285-309.

7. 1978   "Travelling Night Markets in Singapore." In *Periodic Markets, Hawkers, and Traders in Africa, Asia and Latin America*, ed. Robert H. T. Smith. Vancouver: Centre for Transportation Studies, University of British Columbia, pp. 142-54.

8.   "The Urban Environment in Southeast Asia: Change and Opportunity." In *Geography and the Environment in Southeast Asia*, ed. R. D. Hill and J. M. Bray. Hong Kong University Press, pp. 17-33.

9. 1979   "Locational Planning." In *Housing Asia's Millions*, ed. Stephen H. K. Yeh and Aprodicio A. Laquian. Ottawa: International Development Research Centre, pp. 115-25.

10. 1980   Yue-man Yeung and D. W. Drakakis-Smith, "Planning for High-Density Urban Centres: Lessons from Hong Kong and Singapore." In *Hong Kong: Dilemmas of Growth*, ed. Leung Chi-keung, J. W. Cushman, and Wang Gungwu. Canberra: Australian National University, pp. 455-69.

11. 1982   Yue-man Yeung and D. W. Drakakis-Smith, "Public Housing in the City States of Hong Kong and Singapore." In John L. Taylor and David G. Williams (eds.), *Urban Planning Practice in Developing Countries*. Oxford: Pergamon Press, pp. 217-38.

12. 1985   "The Housing Problem in Urbanizing Southeast Asia." In *Urban Society in Southeast Asia*, ed. Gerald H. Krausse. Hong Kong: Asian Research Service, pp. 43-66.

13. 1986   Y. M. Yeung and T. G. McGee, "Participatory Urban Services in Asia." In *Community Participation in Delivering Urban Services in Asia*, ed. Y. M. Yeung and T. G. McGee. Ottawa: IDRC, pp. 9-27.

14.   Yue-man Yeung and François Belisle, "Third World Urban Development: Agency Responses with Particular Reference to IDRC." In *Urbanization in the Developing World*, ed. David Drakakis-Smith. London: Croom Helm, pp. 99-120.

15. 1987   "Cities That Work: Hong Kong and Singapore." In *Urbanization and Urban Policies in Pacific Asia*, ed. Roland J. Fuchs, Gavin W. Jones and Ernesto M. Pernia. Boulder and London: Westview Press, pp. 257-74.

16. 1988   "Great Cities of Eastern Asia." In *The Metropolis Era: A World of Giant Cites*, ed. Mattei Dogan and John D. Kasarda. Newbury Park: Sage Publications, pp. 155-86.

17.   "The University's Role Outside National Boundaries: Reflections on the Southeast Asian Experience." *CUHK Education Journal*, Vol. 16, No. 2, pp. 159-

64. Also in *What Can We Do For Our Universities? The Contribution of Universities in National Development* (Proceedings of the 14th Congress of the Universities of the Commonwealth) London: Association of Commonwealth Universities, pp. 87-93.

18. 1989　"Bursting at the Seams: Strategies for Controlling Metropolitan Growth in Asia." In *Urbanization in Asia: Spatial Dimensions and Policy Issues*, ed. Frank J. Costa, Ashok K. Dutt, Laurence J. C. Ma, and Allen G. Noble. Honolulu: University of Hawaii Press, pp. 311-32.

19.　　　朱劍如 楊汝萬 林健枝，"穗港都會帶的地理基礎和展望。" In Leung Chi-keung, Jim Chi-yung, and Zuo Dakang (eds.), *Resources, Environment and Regional Development*. Hong Kong: Centre of Asian Studies, University of Hong Kong, pp. 375-84.

20. 1990　"Introduction: Urbanization and Development" to Norton Ginsburg, *The Urban Transition: Reflections on the American and Asian Experience*. Hong Kong: The Chinese University Press, pp. ix-xvi.

21.　　　朱劍如 楊汝萬，"台灣省中部的經濟文化中心 -- 台中。" 胡序威 楊冠雄編，〈中國沿海港口城市〉。北京：科學出版社，218-26 頁。

22. 1991　"The Urban Poor and Urban Basic Infrastructure Services in Asia: Past Approaches and Emerging Challenges," *Occasional Paper No. 7*, Hong Kong Institute of Asia-Pacific Studies, Chinese University of Hong Kong, 57 pp. Also in ADB, The Urban Poor and Basic *Infrastructure Services in Asia and the Pacific* (A seminar report), pp. 27-81.

23. 1992　Yue-man Yeung and Xu-wei Hu, "China's Coastal Cities as Development and Modernization Agents: An Overview." In Yeung and Hu (eds.), *China's Coastal Cities*, pp. 1-24.

24.　　　Yue-man Yeung, Yu-you Deng, and Han-xin Chen,

"Guangzhou: The Southern Metropolis in Transition." In Yeung and Hu (eds.), *China's Coastal Cities*, pp. 240-63.

25.   Yue-man Yeung and David K. Y. Chu, "Taizhong: A Geographical and Developmental Appraisal." In Yeung and Hu (eds.), *China's Coastal Cities*, pp. 291-306.

26.   Yue-man Yeung and Xu-wei Hu, "Conclusion and Synthesis." In Yeung and Hu (eds.), *China's Coastal Cities*, pp. 307-22.

27.   "China and Hong Kong." In Richard Stren, Rodney White, and Joseph Whitney (eds.), *Sustainable Cities: Urbanization and the Environment in International Perspective.* Boulder: Westview Press, pp. 259-80.

28. 1993 "Physical and Economic Transformation of Pacific Asia." In Yue-man Yeung (ed.), *Pacific Asia in the 21st Century*, Hong Kong: The Chinese University Press, pp. 3-22.

29.   T. G. McGee and Yue-man Yeung, "Urban Futures for Pacific Asia: Towards the 21st Century." In Yue-man Yeung (ed.), *Pacific Asia in the 21st Century*, pp. 47-67.

30.   "Urban Agriculture: East and Southeast Asia." In Luc J.A. Mougeot and Denis Masse (eds.), *Urban Environment Management: Developing a Global Research Agenda*, Vol. 1, pp. 136-49. Ottawa: IDRC.

31.   "The Urban Poor and Urban Basic Infrastructure Services in Asia: Past Approaches and Emerging Challenges." In Michael Bamberger and Abdul Aziz (eds.), *The Design and Management of Sustainable Projects to Alleviate Poverty in South Asia.* EDI Seminar Series. Washington, D.C.: The World Bank, pp. 77-101.

32. 1994 "Infrastructure Development in the Southern China Growth Triangle." In Myo Thant, Min Tang, and Hiroshi Kakazu (eds.), *Growth Triangles in Asia: A*

New Approach to Regional Approach to Regional Economic Cooperation. Hong Kong: Oxford University Press, pp. 114-50.

33.   "Emerging National Economic Areas Surrounding China and Their Implications for the Asia-Pacific Region." In Jaymin Lee and Yeung Sun Lee (eds.), *Economic Cooperation in the Asia-Pacific Community*. East and West Studies Series 33, Institute of East and West Studies, Yonsei University, Seoul, pp. 117-39.

34.   "Introduction." In Y. M. Yeung and David K. Y. Chu (eds.), Guangdong: *Survey of a Province Undergoing Rapid Change*, pp. 1-17.

35.   "Urban Research in Asia: Problems, Priorities, and Prospects." In Richard Stren (ed.), *Urban Research in the Developing World*, Volume One: Asia. Toronto: Centre for Urban and Community Studies, University of Toronto, pp. 17-45.

36. 1995   "Growth Triangles in Pacific Asia: A Comparative Perspective." In Lew Seok-Jin (compiler), *Tumen River Area Development Project: The Political Economy of Cooperation in Northeast Asia*. Seoul: The Sejong Institute, pp. 57-80.

37.   朱劍如 楊汝萬，"面臨1997年回歸中國的香港的地位與作用。" 馬洪 星野進保編，〈華南地區經濟發展方向及與香港、台灣、日本經濟關係展望〉。深圳：海天出版社，206-34頁。

38.   "香港與新加坡發展對廣東工業化、城市化的啟示。" 盧瑞華編，〈建構工業城市社會的智慧〉。廣州：花域出版社，70-74頁。

39.   "Pacific Asia's World Cities in the New Global Economy." In *Cities and the New Global Economy Conference Proceedings*, Vol. 3. Canberra: Australian Government Publishing Service, 1995, pp. 974-85.

		Also in Polis (The International Journal on Urbanism, Australia), No. 3, pp. 34-41.
40.		"Globalization and World Cities in Developing Countries." In Richard Stren and Judith K. Bell (eds.), *Urban Research in the Developing World: Perspectives on the City* Vol. 4. Toronto: Centre for Urban and Community Studies, University of Toronto, pp. 189-226.
41.		"Survey of Research Institutions in Hong Kong." In Yodashi Yamamoto (ed.), *Emerging Civil Society in the Asia Pacific Community*. Singapore: Institute of Southeast Asian Studies, pp. 366-70.
42.		"Metropolitan Planning and Management in China: An Overview." In UNCHS, *Metropolitan Planning and Management in the Developing World: Shanghai and Guangzhou*. Nairobi: UNCHS, pp. 3-25.
43.	1996	Fu-chen Lo and Yue-man Yeung, "Introduction." In Lo and Yeung (eds.), *Emerging World Cities in Pacific Asia*, pp. 1-13.
44.		Yue-man Yeung and Fu-chen Lo, "Global Restructuring and Emerging Urban Corridors in Pacific Asia." In Lo and Yeung (eds.), *Emerging World Cities in Pacific Asia*, pp. 17-47.
45.		"Global Change: Challenges for the Commonwealth." In Yeung (ed.), *Global Change and the Commonwealth*, pp. 25-42.
46.		"Introduction." In Yeung and Sung (eds.), *Shanghai*, pp. 1-23.
47.		"Hong Kong's Hub Functions." In Anthony Gar-on Yeh (ed.), *Planning Hong Kong for the 21st Century*. Centre of Urban Planning and Environmental Management, The University of Hong Kong, pp. 143-61.
48.	1997	"Urban Infrastructure in Pacific Asia: Profile, Priorities and Prospects." In Yue-man Yeung and Sun Sheng

		Han (eds.), *Urban Infrastructure Development* (Nagoya: UNCRD), pp. 15-31.
49.	1998	"Introduction." In Y. M. Yeung and David K. Y. Chu (eds.), *Guangdong: Survey of a Province Undergoing Rapid Change*, 2nd edition, pp. 1-21.
50.		"Infrastructure Development in the Southern China Growth Triangle." In Myo Thant, Min Tang and Hiroshi Kakazu (eds.), *Growth Triangles in Asia: A New Approach to Regional Economic Cooperation*. Hong Kong: Oxford University Press, 2nd edition, pp. 123-62.
51.		Fu-chen Lo and Yue-man Yeung, "Urbanization and Globalization." In UNESCO, *World Culture Report 1998*. Paris: UNESCO, pp. 108-9.
52.		Fu-chen Lo and Yue-man Yeung, "Introduction." In Lo and Yeung (eds.), *Globalization and the World of Large Cities*, pp. 1-13.
53.		Yue-man Yeung and Fu-chen Lo, "Globalization and World City Formation in Pacific Asia." In Lo and Yeung (eds.), *Globalization and the World of Large Cities*, pp. 132-54.
54.		朱劍如 楊汝萬，"在亞太區際脈終中嵌驗香港的主權回歸。" 馬洪 星野進保編，〈香港回歸後的華南經濟發展與東亞經濟關係〉。香港：西迪商務出版公司，169-87 頁。
55.	1999	"亞洲沿海特大域市 --- 自然與經濟轉化、可持續發展及綜合管理。" 〈城市地理信息系統學術論壇〉。香港：中文大學地球信息科學聯合實驗室，1-8 頁。
56.		楊汝萬 胡天新，"邊界效應的轉變和邊境域市化。" 葉舜贊 願朝林 牛亞菲編，〈一國兩制模式的區域一体化研究〉。北京：科學出版社，104-11 頁。
57.		胡天新 楊汝萬，"西方城市內部空間結構研究的理論進展。" 楊汝萬 陸大道 沈建法編，〈邁向廿一世紀的中國：城鄉與區域發展〉。香港：中文大學香港

亞太研究所，125-38 頁。

58.　　　　　"亞太地區的全球化和區域轉型。" 河南大學環境與
　　　　　　規劃學院編，〈區城發展新透視〉。開封：河南大學
　　　　　　出版社，314-23 頁。

59.　2000　　"香港房屋發展的機遇。" 藍鴻震 王䓪鳴編，〈挑戰
　　　　　　與應變：我看廿一世紀〉。香港：香滬青年協會，
　　　　　　155-56 頁。

60.　　　　　"房屋政策。" 劉兆佳編，〈香港 21 世紀藍圖〉。香港：
　　　　　　中文大學出版社，195-205 頁。

61.　　　　　"Introduction." In Y. M. Yeung and David K. Y. Chu
　　　　　　(eds.), *Fujian: A Coastal Province in Transition and
　　　　　　Transformation*, pp. 1-24.

62.　　　　　David K. Y. Chu and Y. M. Yeung, "Developing the
　　　　　　'Development Corridor'." In Yeung and Chu (eds.),
　　　　　　Fujian, pp. 305-26.

63.　　　　　"Meizhou Bay as a Growth Centre." In Yeung and Chu
　　　　　　(eds.), *Fujian*, pp. 353-74.

64.　2001　　"Globalization and Regional Transformation in Pacific
　　　　　　Asia." In Asfaw Kumssa and Terry G. McGee (eds.),
　　　　　　New Regional Development Paradigms. Westport and
　　　　　　London: Greenwood Press, pp. 215-27.

65.　　　　　"Urban Poverty Alleviation in the Age of Globalization
　　　　　　in Pacific Asia." In Shahid Yusuf, Simon Evenett and
　　　　　　Weiping Wu (eds.), *Facets of Globalization: International
　　　　　　and Local Dimensions of Development*. Washington, D.C.:
　　　　　　The World Bank, pp. 221-36.

66.　　　　　"City Profile – Hong Kong." In Matthew S. Westfall and
　　　　　　Victoria A. de Villa (eds.), *Urban Indicators for Managing
　　　　　　Cities*. Manila: Asian Development Bank, pp. 185-90, 293-
　　　　　　302.

67.　　　　　陳述彭 楊汝萬 林琿，"導論。" 陳述彭 楊汝萬 林
　　　　　　琿編，〈新經濟與中國西部開發〉。香港：中文大學
　　　　　　香港亞太研究所，1-14 頁。

68. 2002 "Millennial Changes and Challenges for Pacific Asia." In Yeung (ed.), *New Challenges for Development and Modernization*, pp. 1-13.

69. "Asia-Pacific Urbanism under Globalization." In Yeung (ed.), *New Challenges for Development and Modernization*, pp. 275-93.

70. "三城故事：全球化下香港、上海和新加坡的競爭力問題。"〈城市地理信息系統學術論壇〉。香港：地球信息科學聯合實驗室，1-15 頁。

71. 2003 M. Montgomery, H. Reed, D. Satterthwaite, M. White, M. Cohen, T. McGee, and Y. Yeung, "Why Location Matters." In Mark R. Montgomery, Richard Stren, Barney Cohen, and Holly E. Reed (eds.), *Cities Transformed: Demographic Change and Its Implications in the Developing World*. Washington D.C.: The National Academies Press, pp. 29-74.

72. B. Cohen, M. White, M. Montgomery, T. McGee, and Y. Yeung, "Urban Population Change: A Sketch." In Montgomery et al., *Cities Transformed*, pp. 75-107.

73. R. Stren, T. McGee, C. Moser, and Y. Yeung, "The Challenge of Urban Governance." In Montgomery et al., *Cities Transformed*, pp. 355-409.

74. Y. M. Yeung and Marco Wu, "Introduction." In Y. M. Yeung and Timothy K. Y. Wong (eds.), *Fifty Years of Public Housing in Hong Kong*. Hong Kong: The Chinese University Press, pp. 1-16.

75. "Milestones in Development." In Yeung and Wong (eds.), *Fifty Years of Public Housing in Hong Kong*, pp. 19-43.

76. "Conclusion." In Yeung and Wong (eds.), *Fifty Years of Public Housing in Hong Kong*, pp. 431-39.

77. 沈建法 楊汝萬，"論中國西部邊境城市的發展：理論、現狀與對策。" 伏潤民 陳志龍 楊汝萬編，〈中國西部開發與周邊國家〉。昆明：雲南大學出版社，54-74頁。

78.   "發展中國家的城市管治及其對中國的含義。" 顧朝林 沈建法等編著，〈城市管治：慨港、理論、方法、實証〉。南京：東南大學出版社，59-67頁。

79. 2004   "Introduction." In Yeung and Shen (eds.), *Developing China's West*, pp. 1-25.

80.   Li Xiaojian, Y. M. Yeung, and Qiao Jiajun, "Historical Legacy and Future Challenges." In Yeung and Shen (eds.), *Developing China's West*, pp. 27-49.

81.   Y. M. Yeung, Jin Fengjun, and Zeng Guang, "Infrastructure and the New Economy." In Yeung and Shen (eds.), *Developing China's West*, pp. 107-31.

82.   "Globalization and the New Urban Challenge." In Mila Freire and Belinda Yuen (eds.), *Enhancing Urban Management in East Asia*. Aldershot: Ashgate, 2004, pp. 13-22.

83.   "世紀之交國外地理學的發展取向和特色。" 中國地理學會編，〈地理學發展方略和理論建設 -- 世紀之初的回顧與展望〉。北京：商務印書館，41-44頁。

84. 2005   楊汝萬 沈建法，"從泛珠三角的誕生看香港的契機。" 楊汝萬 沈建法編，〈泛珠三角與香港互動發展〉。香港：中文大學香港亞太研究所，243-70頁。

85.   "The Rise and Rise of the Pearl River Delta." In Luisa Tam (ed.), *The Confluence of Affluence: The Pearl River Delta Story*. Hong Kong: SCMP Books, pp. 48-51.

86.   楊汝萬，"雙龍吐艷：從城市本位到區城帶動競爭的上海與香港。"梁元生 王宏志編，〈雙龍吐艷：滬港之文化交流與互動〉。香港中文大學滬香發展聯合研究所，3-27頁。

87. 2007   楊汝萬，"房屋發展與生活環境。"黃紹倫 楊汝萬 尹寶珊 鄭宏泰編，〈澳門社會實錄：從指標研究看生活素質〉。香港：中文大學香港亞太研究所，99-110頁。

88.   Yue-man Yeung and Jianfa Shen, "Cross-boundary Integration." In Yeung (ed.), *The First Decade*, pp. 273-95.

89.   "Summary and Conclusions: From the First Decade to the Next." In Yeung (ed.), *The First Decade*, pp. 375-98.

90.   "何物〈八萬五〉?"。趙潔儀編,〈香港家書 --- 如得真情〉。香港:明報出版社,193-98 頁。

91.   "1997-2007 年間香港與中國內地一體化進程。" 江潭瑜編,〈香港回歸十年的回顧與展望〉,深圳:中圓評論學術出版社,2007,30-34 頁。

92.   Y. M. Yeung and Shen Jianfa, "Socialist Economies in Transition: Urban Policy in China and Vietnam." In H. S. Geyer (ed.), *International Handbook of Urban Policy*, Vol. 1: Contentious Global Issues. Cheltenham, U.K.: Edward Elgar, pp. 59-76.

93. 2008   "Introduction." In Yeung and Shen (eds.), *The Pan-Pearl River Delta*, pp. 1-21.

94.   Y. M. Yeung and Gordon Kee, "Infrastructure and Economic Development." In Yeung and Shen (eds.), *The Pan-Pearl River Delta*, pp. 115-42.

95.   Y. M. Yeung and Shen Jianfa, "Hong Kong." In Yeung and Shen (eds.), *The Pan-Pearl River Delta*, pp. 513-48.

96. 2009   Yue-man Yeung and Jianfa Shen, "Coastal China's Urban-rural Spatial Restructuring under Globalization." In Yukon Huang and Alessandro Magnole Bocchi (eds.), *Reshaping Economic Geography in East Asia*. Washington, D.C.: World Bank, pp. 294-319.

97.   Mega-cities." In R. Kithin and N. Thrift (eds.), *International Encyclopaedia of Human Geography*, Vol. 7, pp. 40-47. Oxford: Elsevier.

98 2010   "The Social Sustainability of Asian Cities in the Age of Globalization." In Wang and Yeung (eds.), *Challenges of Development*, pp. 213-36.

99. 2011   Yue-man Yeung and Gordon Kee, "Infrastructure

Development in the Pan-Pearl River Delta: Opportunities and Challenges." In Anthony G. O. Yeh and Jiang Xu (eds.), *China's Pan-Pearl River Delta: Regional Cooperation and Development*. Hong Kong: Hong Kong University Press, pp. 159-79.

100.   "Financial Centres in Pacific Asia after the Global Financial Crisis: Challenges and Opportunities." In Yuan Zhigang (ed.), Shanghai Forum 2010 Highlights: Keynote *Speeches and Selected Papers*. Shanghai: Shanghai Renmin Chubanshi, pp. 254-72.

101.   Yue-man Yeung and Sang-Chuel Choe, "Introduction: Challenges and Prospects of Cross-border Cooperation in Northeast Asia." In Kim, Yeung and Choe (eds.), *Collaborative Regional Development in Northeast Asia*, pp. 1-19.

102.   "The Pearl River Delta: Governance Issues and Implications." In Kim, Yeung and Choe (eds.), *Collaborative Regional Development in Northeast Asia*, pp. 309-28.

RECEIVING A DISTINGUISHED PROFESSIONAL AWARD FROM UWO, 2010

13 Recognitions and Awards

Recognitions and awards come as a person achieves a degree of success – in academic standing and public service in my case. Such things indicate that one has made a level of contribution to academia or society that is noteworthy. In addition, if a person has come from a certain background, one's life history is of interest to a certain segment of the population.

In my career, fifteen years since I left graduate school at UChicago, my first professional recognition came in the form of listing through the strength of my publications, as shown below in items listed in 1984 and 1996. Then, my high-profile appointment as University Registrar in CUHK in 1986 attracted local recognition in Hong Kong. It began with a listing in Hong Kong's Who's Who in 1988 and later in Who's Who in the World in 1995. Recognition would later also come in specialist listings in educational, professional bodies, and other handbooks, dictionaries, and directories. An idea of the recognition I had gained may be had from a chronological listing of some of the reference volumes in which my name appears, as shown below:

Contemporary Authors (1984), Vol. 110, pp. 534-35
Who's Who in Hong Kong (1988), pp. 441-42
The Elites of Hong Kong and Macau (1989), p. 203
港澳大百科全書 (1993), 561 頁
Who's Who in the World (1995), p. 1544
Reference Asia (1995), Vol. IX, p. 870
1995 Who's Who in Hong Kong (1995), p. 504
International Authors and Writers Who's Who (1996), p. 788
香港名人錄 (1997, 長沙海南出版社), 808 頁

世界名人錄 -- 中國卷 (1998), 1031 頁
Asia-Pacific Who's Who (1998), Vol. 1, p. 670
Who's Who in the World – China (1998, 中國長沙出版), p. 1031
Who's Who in the HKSAR (2001), pp. 447-48
Asian/America – Who's Who (2006), Vol. VI, p. 602

Many of these entries have been updated, but only the first issue in which the entry appeared is shown above. I have also been invited to contribute to listing in many handbooks and dictionaries, but where there was a corresponding need to purchase any of the printed product, I did not accept any such offers as a matter of principle.

From another angle, I have been the object of several bibliographic essays of substantial length that probed my professional background and contributions, and my religious background. The first essay, written in 1984 soon after my return to Hong Kong to teach at CUHK, centred on my efforts to assist the internationalization of Chinese geography. It highlighted the international dimension of my career, and the modest efforts I had made in helping Chinese geography to re-enter the international arena in the early 1980s immediately after China's opening up. I was in a position to make a small contribution because of my work in international development with Canada's IDRC. The interview piece arose out of a meeting arranged in Shenzhen in the summer of 1988. I made a special trip to meet the interviewer/writer who had come all the way from Beijing to conduct the interview. As she could not easily visit Hong Kong at that time without some travel document, I offered to make a trip to Shenzhen for the interview. The interview piece may be found in:

姜素清，"願為中國地理學的國際化作貢献。"地理知識，1988年，第一期，26-28 頁。

Another piece was published on more or less the same theme, as one of three essays written by a reporter from *Wen Wei Po* for a book published in Beijing on the occasion of the 60th anniversary of the founding of the PRC in 2009. The three pieces resulted from extensive interviewing in Hong Kong of three representative Hongkongers who had assisted China in "going out" in the early 1980s. The piece on me came after the one on Leung Chun-ying 梁振英, who was elected Chief Executive of the HKSAR in 2012. The piece on me went into some depth on my interest in China and its cities, and on how I helped to solicit votes for China at the IGU Congress held in Paris in 1984 when China applied to become a member. The Chinese delegation was headed by Professor Wu Chuanjun 吳傳鈞, whom I met and hosted in Ottawa in 1981, during the visit of China's first delegation of geographers to Canada, as guests of the IDRC. It also covered my activities in the 1980s and 1990s, in both academic efforts with a professor friend from Peking University to introduce rapidly changing Chinese cities to the Western reader. I also successfully helped Jiangmen to be picked by the RISE (Regional Integration for Sustainable Economies) project under APEC and PECC, during the latter's joint symposium held in October 1999 in Manila. I flew specifically to Manila with Clement Fung, a Trustee of Shaw College at CUHK, to make a presentation for Jiangmen (China). I won the award for Jiangmen as country representative over two other countries. More about this can be read in:

熊君慧，" 初始的陽光。" 黎晶編，〈中國陽光〉北京同心出版社 (2009)，253-63 頁。

My Muslim family background attracted some scholarly attention in mainland China. The first piece was written to mark Hong Kong's handover in 1997, carefully prepared by Liu Shuying 劉淑英, a retired headmistress of a Muslim primary school in Guangzhou. In an extensive article, she covered my educational and family backgrounds, paying heed to my working experience and international outlook. The religious influence on my drive to excel and to serve social and religious causes was noted. Another piece by Professor Hu Zhenhua 胡振華, a senior faculty member at the Central University for

Nationalities in Beijing, was written in the wake of his lecture visit to CUHK in 2002. He dwelled on his Hong Kong experience and briefly introduced my educational background, together with my career and religious highlights. The articles referred to are listed below:

劉淑英，" 在學術研究與社會奉獻之間。" 回族研究，1997，第 3 期，78-82 頁。
胡振華，" 香港穆斯林知名學者楊汝萬教授。" 中國穆斯林，138 期，2002，34-35 頁。

Still another more detailed and recent article that combined many of the themes touched upon earlier is a piece written by a former colleague in history at CUHK who had collaborated with me in research and publications for many years. Dr Lau Yee-cheung 劉義章 took early retirement from CUHK to work for the cause of furthering the dialogue between Christians and Muslims. His piece, in part directed to his larger professional objective, was devoted to me and my religious and educational backgrounds. He traced in some detail my life and career through intensive interviewing over several meetings. It covered my career to 2008, when I fully retired from university service. The citation of this piece is shown below:

劉義章，" 兼備中國情懷和世界視野 -- 記香港一位回族學者。" 劉義章 黃玉明編，〈不同而和〉，香港：建道神學院，2010，163-78 頁。

As noted earlier, the conclusion of my term as University Registrar in the 1990s ushered in a period of active research and community/public service on my part. I had served in a large number of public bodies in Hong Kong on a wide range of subjects ranging from public housing, land, town planning, railways, airport, education, regional cooperation, and the barristers disciplinary tribunal, to the Basic Law. By the mid-1990s, my sustained and multi-faced contributions to public and community service were duly recognized. In 1995, I was made a Justice of the Peace (JP) and in 1996, was conferred the title of Officer in the Most Excellent Order of the British Empire (OBE). With regard to the latter, the honour was bestowed on account of my service to the community and to CUHK, particularly in the fields of urban planning and regional development. Continuing my public service efforts to the next decade earned me in 2003 the award of the Silver Bauhinia Star (SBS), for my valuable advice to the government in the fields of housing, planning, and land policies.

Beginning in the 1990s, as my interaction with Chinese universities intensified, I became appointed to professorships at many Chinese universities, as follows:

East China Normal University, 1990, Advisory Professor
Peking University, 1995, Guest Professor
Fujian Normal University, 1996, Guest Professor
Nanchang University, 1996, Distinguished Visiting Professor
Henan University, 1996, Honorary Professor
Zhejiang University of Technology, 1997, Honorary Professor
Shenzhen Social Science Academy, 1998-2002, Honorary Researcher; 2002, Consultant
Nanjing University, 2000, Advisory Professor
Ningxia University, 2002, Guest Professor

At another level, I was conferred the title of Academician by the International Eurasian Academy of Sciences (IEAS) in 1998. I took an active part in its work when Professor Chen Shupeng 陳述彭 was leading the Academy as Vice-President of the Beijing Centre of the IEAS. I attended the IEAS meeting held at the Hong Kong Convention and Exhibition Centre in 1999. Professor Chen chaired the IEAS meeting. In fact, I was approached in 2000 to be a candidate for election as an Academician of the Chinese Academy of Sciences in 2001, through a feeler by the Geographical Society of China under the

China Association for Science and Technology. The condition was that I had to forfeit my Canadian citizenship. I was not willing to comply with this condition, as Canada is a country that I love and have pledged loyalty to. In addition, it is convenient for me and my wife to travel on a Canadian passport to visit our children and grandchildren in North America every year.

As I was to retire in 2004 and fully retired in 2008, other honours came my way. In 2004 I was bestowed the title of Honorary Member by the Hong Kong Institute of Planners at its annual dinner. In 2005, CUHK conferred on me the title of Emeritus Professor of Geography.

There were other awards of more recent vintage. In 2008 CUHK conferred on me the title of Honorary Fellow. The following is a quotation of the citation read at the conferment ceremony:

In the 21st century, leaders in every profession and industry must be endowed with an international perspective. To the average person, however, an international perspective is often spoken of but seldom sustained. Professor Yeung Yue Man is one of the rare species who commands such a perspective.

Also in 2008, Shaw College, CUHK, conferred on me the title of Honorary Fellow. This was followed by the latest offer of a similar title, Honorary University Fellow, by The Open University of Hong Kong in 2012.

Of all of the awards that were bestowed upon me, the one offered by the University of Western Ontario in 2010 is one that is most special and most memorable to me. It was a Distinguished Professional Award that was announced prominently in a local newspaper (Fig. 13.1). The ceremony of conferment took place at an annual dinner of the Richard Ivey School of Business of UWO held at the Hong Kong Convention and Exhibition Centre. In my acceptance speech, I attempted to put my time at UWO in perspective and in relation to my later graduate studies and career. This is what I said that night:

I am profoundly touched and truly thankful for the honour that has been bestowed on me this evening by The University of Western Ontario. Within reasonable time, I hope to be able to weave a story of thankfulness to highlight how special a candidate you have chosen me for this award.

To begin with, strange as it may sound, I was a student at Western almost by accident. The truth of the matter is, in the mid-1960s, I was one of two Commonwealth Scholars from Hong Kong at Western. Not being too familiar with Canadian universities, I did not put Western as one of three universities I wished to be enrolled in. Thanks to the university and perhaps equally, if not more, to the Canadian government, I was assigned to Western. At first, ignorance gave me some unease but as soon as I arrived in London and the campus, it was love at first encounter. I realized how fortunate I was to have been assigned to a first-rate university, with arguably the most beautiful campus in Canada, a truly diversified international student body, a country of exceptional natural beauty, and a superior quality of life. All this would later greatly influence my career, family and choices in life.

The second reason for me to be thankful for attending Western is that I could not have asked academically for more. I learned to work with methodical efficiency, which was the reason for my later academic prolificness. I was able to write my Master's thesis in two months and left Western after 20 months. Most important for my study and later doctoral studies, my supervisor at Western was Professor James Simmons, a promising young Canadian who had just returned with a Ph.D. from the University of Chicago – the hottest Geography Department in North America at that time. He somehow took a strong liking to me and encouraged me to proceed to Chicago to study under his teacher. I did not immediately go, because with a Commonwealth Scholarship

I had to return to my place of origin first. In any case, my straight A transcript in every subject at Western helped me to go to Chicago with a full scholarship a year later.

A third reason I need to be thankful for is that the Western experience has helped my career. To be specific, after Chicago and Singapore, I worked for almost a decade for Canada's International Development Research Centre (IDRC), initially as its Social Science representative in Asia based in Singapore and later at its head office in Ottawa directing a global programme on urban policy. My tenure at Western greatly helped me to work for a Canadian crown corporation and to hone my global views of development. It was a kind of professional work outside but revolving around academia, allowing me the opportunity to gain international experience but within hailing distance from universities. True enough, I received a signal from The Chinese University of Hong Kong which I joined in 1984. It was home coming for me after 19 years abroad with considerable administrative and academic experience and global networks, a combination that has enabled me to scale my professional ladder and served Hong Kong well. This blossoming of my career could not have been achieved without my Western background.

Finally, my family has likewise been influenced by my Western experience. In 1980 I took a momentous but not too difficult decision to uproot my family from Singapore to settle down in Ottawa, ahead of the 1997 jitters in Hong Kong. This time, it was Canadian life we had to plunge wholeheartedly into. The family confronted the harsh Ottawa winter head on by learning how to skate as a family project. Later on we skated along the Rideau Canal after we mastered the basic skills. The children liked schooling and made many friends. When I decided to return to Hong Kong in 1984 to work, they almost did not want to move. In any event, we all became Canadians and the children returned to take their university education. Our son, Tào-ming, was so influenced by my persuasion that he attended Engineering at Western, and obtained his degree in the 1990s. Consequently, the award you have honoured me tonight is a family event.

In accepting the honour this evening, I wish to pay tribute to three persons going back to the days I was at Western. First is Professor James Simmons, for without his guidance and encouragement, I would not have gone beyond the Master's degree and certainly would not have attended the University of Chicago. Second is Professor Ho Hon-hing, still an active Professor of Botany at the State University of New York in New Paltz. He was the other Commonwealth Scholar from Hong Kong on campus at Western and helped me in many ways. Finally, I must say that I was engaged when I studied at Western. My fiancée, my present wife Ameda, was a source of emotional support at long distance. (Ask Ameda to stand) In the days without the internet or even long distance phone calls, the old-fashioned letter writing was the only way to keep connected. Thanks Ameda for your patience and support in those early days.

Finally, thanks for your patience in hearing me out and renewed appreciation to my alma mater for recognizing my career.

15 May 2010

Throughout my career and life, sport has occupied an important place in providing recreation, good health, and peace of mind. It has been an important complement to the mostly sedentary work I have been engaged in, namely reading, research, and writing. There is also a secondary benefit to pursuing physical recreation, as friendships can be solidified and expanded in the sports field, whatever the chosen sport.

In my early days at school up to the period of my university

FIGURE 13.1 UWO NOTICE 2010
Reprinted with permission from SCMP.

teaching and my work for the IDRC in Singapore and Ottawa, my major preoccupation was playing ping pong (table tennis). It was an interest that united many of my colleagues at the ASRO (Asia Singapore Regional Office) of the IDRC. I won a large number of prizes over the years. Ping pong continued to be my major focus of recreation even after we moved to Ottawa to live. To me, it was an opportunity to make new friends and deepen friendships.

However, after beginning to work in Hong Kong in 1984, I switched almost entirely to playing tennis. I seriously learned the game through private couching in Singapore and continued casually in Ottawa. With initially about half a dozen colleagues at CUHK, we began to play as a group regularly on Sunday afternoons. This group was started in 1986, when I was new to my position as University Registrar. I found the game to be not only a refreshing change from my busy and highly focused job, but an opportunity to exchange views on many topics with tennis mates. We have kept this group essentially intact to this day with a few core members, but many others have come and gone. We still have about 10 active members.

As Head of Shaw College, I managed to arrange for the resources to build two tennis courts of our own at the end of the coastal road near the staff residences in 1998. We played there in private for many years until 2011, when we surrendered our courts to a new college that will be constructed there. Shaw College has been compensated with two of the three university courts nearby. Our tennis group was back to the same courts where we started playing in the late 1980s.

For the past quarter century, our tennis group, dubbed the Haoqiu Group, has become a strong gathering of like-minded individuals, socially and with regard to physical exercise, primarily from the faculties. We also had occasional social get-togethers at which our spouses would be present. In late 2010, largely through Fernand Lai's initiative but with contributions from each member, a 42-page album of photographs and other highlights of the group, entitled "Haoqiu Fellowship on Sunday Island", was published. It is a treasured memento of activities over the years that have culminated at the exclusive Shaw College courts. At its height at the end of 2010, the membership of the Haoqiu Group included the following people apart from myself: Augustine Cheng 鄭勳斌, Fernand Lai 黎永祥 , Lim Pak Leong 林伯良, Wong Kin-yuen　王 建 元 , Qin Ling 秦嶺，Dennis Yang 楊濤 , Margaret Wong 王韻娜，Archie Lee 李熾昌，Lee Sik-yum 李錫欽，and Carmen Chan 陳茄好 .

Throughout all of these years, tennis has been our Sunday priority. It has always been an important social commitment of ours, and we always play unless we travel or are hampered by rain. We have persisted in our weekend tennis activities, and have benefitted much physically as well as socially. A side benefit for me is that I have been able to garner a large number of prizes by winning in the Doubles Tennis Tournaments at Shaw College. I have teamed up with different colleagues over the years and we have won championships twice (2009, 2012), been named first runners-up five times (1999, 2001, 2004, 2010, 2011), and second runners-up once (2000). Some of these honours were won after I fully retired!

GOING UP THE NEW PARLIAMENT BUILDING IN BERLIN, 2010

14 Travels

Prompted by my interest in geography and photography, having lived in different cities and countries, required as part of my job, and with my extended and immediate families living in different parts of the world, travelling has been an essential part of my career, family, and life in general. Family travel involving Ameda, Tao-ming, Sze-mei, and me began early when we lived in Singapore and largely terminated in 1990 with a last grand tour of Europe. By an approximate reckoning, as a foursome we have travelled to some 100 cities. I would add another 250 cities that and Ameda I visited in many countries for different reasons and with various types of tours, mostly guided tours. In addition, I covered still another 250 cities in duty, work and research-oriented, and other types of trips. I myself have been to some 80 countries, many of which I visited many times over, with quite a few entailing extensive coverage on land. Some of the trips and special encounters that were alluded to in previous chapters are highlighted in this chapter. I shall also add other exceptional experience and observations to make this chapter a focus of interest.

Before I got married in 1967, I already had considerable travel experience. In 1962, I spent five weeks in Japan to attend the Ninth International Student Conference held for ten days in Tokyo, followed by extensive reconnaissance visits to other parts of Japan. That provided me with an early positive view of Japan, with its efficient ways of running its society and life. Equally, it led to an amelioration of my negative feeling of Japan derived from my childhood experiences of the Japanese occupation of Hong Kong during the Second World War. That trip was extended by a week-long visit to Taiwan. A round-the-island tour gave me good exposure to the way of life there and an early understanding of the beautiful island.

As mentioned previously, my graduate studies in London, Ontario, in 1964-66 opened my mind to the diversity of landscapes, socio-economic achievements, and life in North America. I travelled almost from coast to coast over the short period that I was a graduate student. The initial stopover in Vancouver, especially at UBC, left me with a very favourable impression of BC hospitality and its pleasant way of life. Visits to Canadian and American cities deepened my understanding of regional diversity in the continent and of life there arguably at its best. The visit to New York's World Fair in 1965 has left me many memories that have remained vivid after such a long time.

After North America, my next target was to visit Europe. I prepared myself in many ways, and as soon as I completed Master's studies at UWO I left from Montreal for London, England, in May 1966. I had a round-the-island tour of the British Isles with Trafalgar Tours. This first visit and the guided tour of the British Isles provided me with an overview of England, Wales, and Scotland. It was truly educational to me, as someone who was schooled in the British Crown Colony of Hong Kong. There was a certain sense of exhilaration and unreality when I was able to use the pound, shilling and pence in daily transactions, after having had them so often used as examples in my arithmetic class in school when growing up. Visiting the famous landmarks in London was like rediscovering them after learning about them in books or through the media in Hong Kong. Riding the Tube (underground) in London was another new experience, despite having used the subway in Tokyo many times before. My first experience of riding the Tube is still fresh in my mind because of the test of strength. After arriving at Heathrow Airport, the way to my booked residence in town necessitated the changing of subway lines. From what appeared to be never-ending walking to get to the right connections, I was feeling the weight of my suitcase, which at that time did not have wheels to roll it along. The weight of my suitcase, laden with travel literature, plus the long walks to change lines, marked my early unforgettable encounter with London.

After the British Isles, filled with energy and curiosity I travelled the length and breadth of Europe. *Europe on $5 a Day* was my guide, not only in terms of spending advice but of where to go and how to get about. I stayed mostly in youth hostels and pensions near railway stations in city centres. I walked on average at least six hours a day, including time spent in museums. Indeed, museums were my biggest preoccupation, as were famous city sights. The best photographs of European cities that I have taken were from their high points, which for that purpose I always tried to ascend. I climbed every observation tower, cathedral, hill, and tall building to get the best views. I was overwhelmed by the treasures held in the British Museum in London and the Louvre in Paris. However, when I examined the exquisite and unparalleled national treasures from China, I could not help feeling a strong sense of anger and injustice. Many of these most beautiful Chinese treasures were looted from Yuan Ming Yuan, the Summer Palace in Beijing, during the Second Opium War in 1860. The Franco-British army committed a crime against humanity by burning down the palace and plundering Chinese treasures to take home.

I used a one-month Eurail Pass, purchased in Canada, to cover most countries in Western Europe and very much enjoyed its convenience and comfort. I planned my itinerary in such a way that on long journeys I slept overnight in first-class train cabins. The Pass provided comfort and convenience, plus free boat rides and some other advantages. I rode the trains so often that I was able to remember which stretches of landscape were the most outstanding and picturesque. That between Munich and Salzburg, and between Bern and Milan would rank among the most scenic in my mind. Before and after the Pass period, I used my plane ticket to visit other large cities in Europe. In fully two months, my solo trip around most parts of Western Europe gave me a first-hand familiarity with the continent that did much to satisfy my curiosity and desire to learn. This carefully planned and smoothly executed trip taken before my marriage, further studies, and career marked an exposure to and an immersion in foreign lands and cultures that have figured prominently in my life.

Indeed, Europe became such an important part of my stock of travel experiences that I wanted to introduce it to my family. The second grand tour of Europe took place in April - May 1972, when I rendezvoused with my wife in London, England. I had come from North America after successfully defending my doctoral dissertation at UChicago, whereas Ameda had flown in from Hong Kong. We joined the Global Tour of Western Europe in two weeks that began in London, England. Of the 42 tour members there was only one other couple from Asia – from Hong Kong. They were Dennis Lau 劉榮廣 and his wife Eliza, both architecture graduates from HKU. Many years later, after I returned to work in Hong Kong in 1984, we reconnected due to our urban interests and work, becoming good friends in the process. In two weeks, the tour covered most of the must-see places in Western Europe. These included the breath-taking scenery of the Alps in Austria and northern Italy, the Black Forest in Germany, Innsbruck, Mount Titlis in Switzerland, the Roman Forum and Coliseum in Rome, a glass factory in Venice, the Eiffel Tower, Versailles in the suburbs of Paris, and so on. We left the tour in Paris and continued with a tour of Holland on our own. There, a visit to the cheese market in Alkmaar was something that particularly impressed us, as it was something completely new to us. We returned to London on 20 May 1972 and stayed for a few days with Ronald and Vera Ng in their Highgate apartment before returning to Hong Kong.

The third grand tour that I took of Western Europe began on 26 July 1990, as part of a long family tour of 40 days. I was still on long leave after completing my term as University Registrar at CUHK. It was our last family tour together before the children went for their university education. The basis of our self-guided European tour was the purchase of a 15-day Eurail Pass. I was the guide, as I wanted to show my family some of the best sights and experiences from my previous trips. We started in Rome, but the initial encounter was somewhat shocking, even for a seasoned traveller like me. People were trying to cheat tourists at every turn and in every way. We had never encountered more tricks in one day than we did on our first day in Rome. Taxi drivers blatantly overcharged, hotel staff opened and searched our handbags, pickpockets encroached on us on a city bus, a self-help restaurant overcharged us for everything, and so on. We were forced to keep on the alert. Compared with my previous visits to Rome, conditions for visitors had markedly worsened. Nonetheless, we still enjoyed its sights and artistic legacies. Venice was a complete change for the better. We visited a glassblowing factory in Morano Island after absorbing the sights and flavours of a car-free city. Milan was a refreshing change, but I was disappointed that due to an oversight of mine my family missed going to the rooftop platform of the Duomo (cathedral) at the city centre. We arrived in time at the cathedral, but stayed too long before going up to the roof. Opening hours terminated at 5.30 p.m., just about the time that we presented ourselves at the ticket counter. We then proceeded northward to Bern, Lucerne, and Basel in Switzerland. The train trip up the Jungfrau from Interlaken was a re-enactment of my previous trip in 1966. It is a fantastic way to enjoy the enchanting Swiss landscape. In Amsterdam we had a little difficulty in finding accommodation, as our arrival on 6 August coincided with the Big Ship Festival. The highlight of the stop was a visit to the van Gogh Museum, which houses many of the artist's outstanding works. Years later, I came to be acquainted with and still love Don Mclean's Starry Starry Night, which is a masterful rendition in song of Vincent van Gogh's paintings and his tragic life. That song greatly helped me to understand the wide range of objects and people in the artist's eyes in the Europe of his day. Our trip was rounded off by visits to Vienna and Munich. After we flew to Toronto, Ottawa, Calgary, and Vancouver to take care of matters related to getting Tao-ming settled into his studies and to meet friends and relatives, our family tour came to an end.

Family trips involving the four of us started when we lived in

Singapore. We had many occasions to visit Hong Kong from Singapore. After I joined the IDRC in 1975, there was provision for annual home leave with my family to my choice of destinations. Thus, we visited Bali, Yogyakarta, and Jakarta in May 1977, and the children had a taste of a different culture. In May 1978, the family visited Penang and Phuket on the way to Hong Kong. We, along with my mother who was visiting Singapore, also visited the Genting Highlands in Malaysia in November. In June 1979, we visited Manila and Baguio, with an excursion to the Pagsanjan Falls and Rapids in the Philippines. These family trips to different parts of Southeast Asia did not mean a great deal to Tao-ming and Sze-mei, they told me afterwards, as they were too young and did not remember much. Nevertheless, they provided opportunities for the family to be together and to be exposed to different cultural and economic landscapes. These were some of the less obvious benefits of family vacations that, over time, strengthened the family.

When we lived in Ottawa, we made many family trips around the Ottawa area during the summer. Reference has been made to these and other trips made to the northeastern seaboard area in 1982 and 1983. In 1984, the family took advantage of my last IDRC duty trip in London and Paris/Lille to visit some of the famous sights in these two cities, which are also my favourite cities. The visit to Versailles (Chateau de Versailles) in suburban Paris was especially memorable. It has always been one of my favourite places to visit and to show my family. Apart from the spacious and well-designed garden, the palace buildings boast lavish and ornate decorations that reflected a great historical heritage. I always impress on myself and my children that this is the place where the Treaty of Versailles concluding World War I was signed in 1919. The terms of that Treaty were widely interpreted by the Chinese as an affront to China's national dignity. China had no say in the terms. The specific article of the Treaty that caused an uproar in China related to Jiaozhou Bay in Qingdao, Germany's concession in China, which was transferred to Japan rather than returned to China. The terms were so blatantly unfair that the May Fourth Movement erupted as a spontaneous protest by university students in Beijing, spearheaded by students of Peking University. Therefore, for the Chinese, there is a historical meaning to visiting Versailles.

Two other family trips taken from Hong Kong are well worth mentioning. In June/August 1986, we spent 40 days visiting many places and achieved many purposes. We started on 29 June by visiting Seoul, where we stayed with my good Korean friend, Professor K. K. Ro, and his family. It was a most welcome exposure to family hospitality in Korea. Then, in Honolulu I picked up a rental car, which gave us mobility around the city and the island. In fact, family travel from Hong Kong took a different form from this trip onward. In most cities that we planned to visit, I would have a pre-ordered rental car waiting at the airport. After attending to business and/or vacationing in a city, I would return the car at the airport before departing for my next destination. This pattern was repeated in Los Angeles, San Francisco, and Billings, Montana. The main destination for the last-mentioned stop was Yellowstone National Park, of which we would have a comprehensive tour. We drove through the park and stayed for a few nights in the area. We also visited the cowboy country centred on Cody in Wyoming, becoming familiar with William Cody's (popularly known as Buffalo Bill) life and achievements. The next stop was Vancouver, which was hosting EXPO 86. Terry McGee was kind enough to let my family use his house while he and his family vacationed in Victoria Island. We rented cars in Vancouver, Ottawa, and Toronto, and returned to Hong Kong after completing our work and meeting friends.

The other family trip from Hong Kong occurred over a month from 30 July 1988. We started with a brief stop in Singapore to update my professional (IDRC) and family (Farita, my sister and her family) links. Then we arrived in Brisbane, with the main purpose of attending EXPO 88 hosted by Brisbane. After spending three days there, we proceeded to Sydney. We rented cars in Brisbane, Sydney, and Calgary, our next stop. This stop allowed us to drive to see Banff and Lake Louise again at a more leisurely pace. In our next two stops in Ottawa and Toronto, we mainly renewed friendships. We then drove from Toronto to London, Ontario, to get Tao-ming settled at UWO, where he had been admitted to study Engineering. It was an almost tearful good-bye we bade him before I drove back to Toronto and returned to Hong Kong from there.

Before Tao-ming and Sze-mei were born and after they left for university education, Ameda and I made many trips together, often in guided tours. The first trip we made together was a landmark journey, involving driving to Peninsular Malaysia on 20-30 March 1970. It was a most memorable trip because I was driving my newly acquired Volkswagen Beetle and Ameda was heavily pregnant with our first baby. I drove slowly and carefully, stopping in every city and town of importance. Urban Malaysia was my major interest, but the rubber and palm oil plantations were overwhelming by their presence. There were no expressways at that time, but driving could be treacherous. I saw several live accidents along the road that we took. To the extent possible, we stopped in any city and town of repute and interest. I drove all the way north to Alor Setar before backtracking to visit George Town in Penang. Jim Osborn, my fellow graduate student at UChicago, was doing field work in that city. We had a happy reunion in a foreign land. In Kuala Lumpur we met Ibrahim Ma, a Muslim and former ambassador of the Republic of China in Malaysia through an introduction by our good friend, Marian Ming, in Chicago. We then crossed the highland from west to east, and ended up on the eastern coast at Kuantan. We returned from Kuantan to Singapore in a day, a distance of 352 km, with many breaks and interruptions in the form of rivers and streams at that time. Among the things we remember well about this trip was our pleasant surprise, as Muslims, to have seen and visited so many mosques, especially the National Mosque in Kuala Lumpur and the large and imposing mosque in Kuala Kangsar. We have never visited and seen more mosques on any trip we have taken in our lives. We completed our first and only driving trip of substance in Peninsular Malaysia with the benefit of having gained first-hand knowledge of this beautiful and resource-rich country.

The second trip I took with Ameda was in Western Europe in 1972, as described above. The third long and special trip I had with Ameda took place in June 1980, after my last duty trip to Delhi out of the IDRC ASRO. I rendezvoused with Ameda on 11 June 1980 at 3.10 a.m. at the Delhi Airport. We joined a local tour to visit major sights and places within Delhi first before joining other tours to visit Taj Mahal in Agra to begin with. We then went to Kashmir by flying to Srinagar. We first stayed at a luxurious houseboat along Nagin Lake, but later moved to another one in Dal Lake. Shopping for handicrafts, carpets, embroidered clothes, paper mache, and other items kept us busy. We were enraptured by the natural beauty of Kashmir and began to understand why India and Pakistan have been fighting hard to keep this jewel since the Indian Partition in 1947. It was also the right time to be visiting Kashmir because Delhi was consistently being hit by heat waves in the high forties Celsius. We loved the natural landscapes of Kashmir, which could be depicted as Switzerland located in Asia. The Mughal gardens are delightful creations left by the former rulers. After India, our trip took us to Kathmandu, which I had visited several times before. My friend, Vidya Kansakar, an IDRC project recipient, looked after us well. The trip was completed with an overnight stop in Bangkok before we returned to Singapore.

In August 2003 prior to Sze-mei's wedding held in Vancouver, Ameda, Tao-ming, and I took a Celebrity Infinity cruise tour to Alaska for eight days. It was Tao-ming's last opportunity to travel with us before he would become a father himself next year. We enjoyed the luxury of a modern cruise liner, with all the trappings of professional performances, shopping, served meals, excursions and tours, studio photographs, and so on. Two things I recall well from this cruise trip. After boarding the cruise liner along with some 2,000 other passengers at Pacific Place Pier in Vancouver, and leaving the city by sea via the Lions Gate Bridge, I saw something I had never seen before. The view of Vancouver from there was special and beautiful. The second unforgettable view was when the cruise ship was at only a short distance from the icy landmass in Alaska: the speed at which ice was breaking away from the landmass was frightening. I was made to appreciate the severity of global warming, which was causing the icy landmass to disintegrate so quickly. If humankind does not act with a sense of emergency to stop or ameliorate global warming, it might be too late for all of us!

In the summer of 2007, Ameda and I undertook our yearly trip to North America to visit our children and grandchildren. That year was slightly different. It began with a trip to Calgary, where Khalid Yeung, my nephew, was to marry May Lin. After joining a same day-return tour to Banff and Lake Louise again, we flew to San Francisco to join a guided tour of the northwestern coast of the United States. It was an eight-day tour, a gift from Tao-ming for the 40th anniversary of our wedding. The tour had 42 people, with a good mix of nationalities. We visited Yosemite National Park, Monterrey, Pacific Ocean Drive, and Santa Barbara, and ended up in Los Angeles. A highlight of the tour was a visit to the William Randolph Hearst Estate and Hearst Castle in San Simeon. Hearst Castle is a masterpiece well worth visiting, and the swimming pools, both indoor and outdoor, are spectacular. It was our most enjoyable exposure to the area between San Francisco and Los Angeles, which we had not travelled through before.

As it turned out, August 2007 was special for the family. Sze-mei's first daughter, Lauren, was born on 9 August. In fact, Tao-ming' second daughter, Sydney, was born on 18 August the year before. Indeed, members of my family are curiously connected in their birthdays with regard to the months. Ameda and Sze-mei were born in the same month of February, the 27th and 21st, respectively. Tao-ming and Ashley, Sze-mei's younger daughter, are similarly connected, born on the 16th and 22nd of June, respectively. Wesley, Tao-ming's son and I, too, celebrate our birthdays in the month of October, on the 7th and the 1st, respectively. Nature has therefore worked wonders in networking our three generations in four months of the year by our birthdays. Is this not magic? We have to thank the Almighty!

Beyond these special trips undertaken by me and Ameda, we have joined countless guided tours to all continents except South America. On the other hand, I have travelled to Mexico City (twice), Joao Pessoa, Rio de Janeiro, and Santiago on that continent on official trips.

In terms of extensive travel on land, I have through duty travel, vacations, and other reasons covered many countries. These trips include Peninsular Malaysia (1970, 2004 field trips with CUHK students), Eastern Malaysia (1977, Sarawak; 2011, Sabah), Java (Surabaya to Yogyakarta to Jakarta, 1973, 1977), China (all provinces, Autonomous Regions, and Special Municipalities), Japan (1962 and later), Canada (1964 and later), USA (1965 and later), Europe (1966, 1972, 1990, and later), Nigeria (Kano, Zaria to Lagos, 1978), Tanzania and Kenya (Dar es Salaam to Nairobi, crossing the land border, 1983), Nepal (1977 and later), and Taiwan (1962 and later).

My travels through China have been especially extensive. From early travels in 1978 and 1979 when I was based in Singapore to the early 1980s working out of Ottawa, my visits to China were frequent and for a purpose. Since 1984, living and working in Hong Kong has afforded me many opportunities to explore, learn, and experience different regions, cities and towns, and rural areas in China. My lecture tour in 1990 was an initial sweep largely by train through a large part of China, which broadened my understanding of its diversity and similarities. Commitments involving research and regional analyses, especially when collaboration with Chinese researchers was involved, made it necessary for me to spend more time on field studies. The Pearl River Delta and its cities and towns became the first region that I travelled through repeatedly. Then, research on Shanghai and Fujian necessitated travel to those regions as well. The 10-day reconnaissance trip that I made in December 1993 with David K. Y. Chu 朱劍如 and Tang Wing-shing 鄧永成 through Fujian from Fuzhou to Zhangzhou formed the basis of our understanding of the development problems and new opportunities that have come with openness in that coastal province.

Since 1999, a new research project to systematically review and analyze the national policy to develop the sprawling western region spurred me to visit all 12 provinces and Special Municipality. It took me four years to complete this task, with the assistance of professor friends and colleagues in China. All of these academic travels, along with other official trips, have been supplemented by guided tours to many parts of China. With China changing so rapidly over the years, the need to keep up-to-date means having to travel to its different parts whenever the opportunity presents itself.

In looking back at my inventory of travels, mention must be made of trips organized by Yip Sau-wah 葉秀華, a most able and sociable secondary school principal, for over a decade. She would rally scholars, principals, and teachers and organize trips to places far and wide as travel targets were identified and groups formed. Ameda and I always travelled together and joined various groups. The first excursion that we joined, organized in April 1999, was to Hunan's famous Zhangjiajie, a World Natural Heritage site. We warmed up quickly to the group spirit because several of my former HKU classmates were in the group. The trip involved a great deal of climbing, but most of us got help from porters. The next trip, with 41 people, took place in April 2000 and centred on Jiuzhaigou, one of the most well-known sites in Sichuan, and famed for its waters. The region, located on the upper reaches of the Yangtze River, is peopled by different ethnic groups. In December 2000, the group went beyond China and visited Myanmar, focusing on its temples and other highlights in Yangon (Rangoon) and Mandalay. In April 2001, our destination was Wuyishan in northwestern Fujian near the Jiangxi border. The mountain range here is of the Danxia formation, drawing its reputation from its red sandstone and intricate landforms. In March 2008, the group capitalized on the spring season to enjoy the sight of rapeseed flowers in the Yangtze delta area. We began in Wenzhou, visited Yandangshan, and took in an evening show on the waters of the West Lake in Hangzhou, entitled "Impressions on the West Lake". In August 2008, we travelled far, to the extreme southwestern edge of Xinjiang, and at Kashi started our tour of the southern part of that huge Autonomous Region. We arrived at a rather sensitive time, with Han-Uygur relations having boiled over immediately prior to and during our trip. We crossed the Tarim Basin from Hotan to Kurla over a period of 15 hours. Our original destination was Kugu but we had to divert eastward because new ethnic-related incidents had erupted in that city. We ended up having to add another few hours of crossing the sprawling desert. In February 2009, again on the theme of spring, we spent eight days in Yunnan in a group of 23. We were captivated by the immense, almost interminable rapeseed field in Luoping, rice terraces in Yuanyang at sunrise and sunset, and literally an endless sight of rolling hills in Wanfenglin in Guizhou. Finally, in October 2009, we made our last trip with the group and went to Inner Mongolia. We concentrated our attention in the area easily accessible from Yinchuan in Ningxia. It was the peak of the golden autumn season conducive to photography. Colourful poplars (scientifically, Populus euphratica) as well as desert scenes were our daily companions. Consequently, these eight trips with the educational groups vastly expanded my love and knowledge of a large part of China. There were also weekend social trips to the Pearl River Delta for good food and togetherness. We participated in a few of these. In all, we enjoyed the company as much as the variety of places that we visited.

Given the very rich travel experience I have gained over a long career, I would pick several trips that I still remember well for what I had gone through, for better or worse. Travel is not always a bed of roses, as a couple of my trips described below will attest. Some others have given me the feeling of being special, and I have taken pleasure in reliving them again and again. Either way, preparation, chance, friendship, and local circumstances did much to elevate a trip from ordinary to extraordinary.

First, many Asian cities that I visited in the 1970s were not convenient or functional. I have pointed to the difficulties of using telephones to reach people, long-distance flights that had to stop often for refueling, air tickets that had to be reconfirmed, and cities like Seoul and Taipei with midnight curfews. Only Tokyo had an efficient and modern subway system in the early 1960s. Other Asian cities built their subways much later. For decades, Bangkok was notorious for its traffic gridlock, which immobilized travellers in cars for hours on end. However, nothing could compare with my ordeal in the flooded streets of Bangkok.

During an IDRC duty trip to Bangkok in October 1978, I was invited on the 25th to dinner by Dr John Hugh Jones, an American professor teaching transport at the Asian Institute of Technology. Dinner was served at his home on Petchburi Road not far from Hotel Erawan where I stayed. The hotel was located at the heart of the thriving business and commercial district of Ratchaprasong and has since been rebuilt as the Grand Hyatt Erawan. Since it had rained heavily most of that day, Dr Jones deputed his student, Boonsom, to fetch me and travel with me to his house. By late afternoon most parts of Bangkok were flooded. In a hired taxi, the trip to Dr Jones' house took fully two hours over a distance of 5 km. The streets were already flooded and cars were bumper to bumper all the way. After what I remember to be a good dinner and conversation with Dr Jones and his wife, I had to think of getting back to my hotel. Dr Jones' house was already flooded up to his front door and his entire lawn was covered by water. I took another taxi by myself for the return trip at 10 p.m. The taxi driver drove through heavily flooded streets lined with shops that were mostly closed. I still remember my sinking feeling when I felt the flood waters touching the undercarriage of the taxi all the way back. I was terrified that the taxi might stall at any time. The return trip did not take as long as the trip out, probably because of the much thinner traffic. I breathed a sigh of relief when I returned to my hotel after 40 minutes in the taxi. The urge to return to my hotel was constantly on my mind after dinner, because a curfew was to be imposed at midnight in view of the flooded condition of the city. I have never forgotten this watery welcome to Bangkok and the dinner that I had there, among my many visits to the city.

Second, I made a trip to Manali in the northern mountains of India over five days from 17 June 1992 to attend a research meeting reviewing the progress of South Asian countries participating in the GURI project. Our host was Om Mathur, an economics professor and organizer of the project for South Asia. Since a meeting in Kashmir was not recommended considering the tight security situation there, Manali was chosen as the second-best solution to avoid the stifling heat in New Delhi. For overseas participants like me, the trip involved an overnight stop in New Delhi before flying off to Kullu, the nearest airport to Manali. Having arrived in Manali, we stayed at Span Resorts, about 15 km from Manali itself. The meeting went well, as did the sightseeing and shopping that we indulged ourselves in a little in Manali. When we were ready to leave and had checked in our luggage at Kullu airport at about noon on 20 June to fly off to New Delhi via Chandigarh, we were informed that the flight had been put on hold after the initial landing of the in-coming flight had been aborted because of strong winds. We waited and fiddled around for three hours before being told that the flight had been cancelled. We did not want to wait another day, as even the glorious sunshine we had had that day was no guarantee that the flight could land and take off the next day. We decided to charter two van taxis for the 531 km, nine-hour overland, overnight trip to New Delhi via Chandigarh. The trip to Chandigarh was through a mountainous region, busy with truck traffic. Before reaching that city for a very late dinner, we went through Punjab, which was very quiet despite its reputation for being infested with terrorists. We hardly slept the whole night, as the van taxis did not have air-conditioning. To add to our excitement, at the last stop before New Delhi, our taxi failed to start. The other taxi driver knew how to fix a battery problem and we were off again after 30 minutes of repair work. By the next morning at six, we arrived in Om Mathur's residence in New Delhi. An indication of the travail we went through was the fact that my white shirt had turned very grey by the time we arrived. We quickly washed and had breakfast before making arrangements to return home. All of us overseas participants had missed our connecting flights and had to arrange new flights to continue our trip. The motto of this unexpected way of experiencing northern India is that you can never be sure of where and how you will travel until you have completed your trip and returned home.

Third, in the late 1970s two quite separate trips brought me to Tahiti in the French Polynesia of the South Pacific and to Seychelles, an archipelago nation consisting of 115 islands, located 1,500 km off mainland Africa and about an equal distance from Madagascar. The fabulous experiences that I had on both islands were not planned, but were nonetheless most precious. The reason for grouping these island trips is their insular and isolated status in the middle of a vast ocean and the extraordinary encounters I had in them.

My six-day stop in Papeete on the main island of Tahiti from 17 August 1977 was largely governed by air flight schedules. I had a most desirable mix of work and play. I was well received by researchers in ORSTEM (a semi-government research organization) and government officials in the Tourist Development Board. The latter even arranged a visit for me, in the company of Tiere Sanford, to Moorea, an island off Papeete frequented by tourists. I gained an idea of upper-end tourism through visits to Club Mediterranee, more commonly known as Club Med and Moorea Lagoon Hotel. On my own I joined a round-the-island tour and found the view from Taharia Intercontinental Hotel simply breath-taking. On another day I visited Bengt Danielsson in his house in Paea, 19 km from Papeete. It was stimulating to hear the

Norwegian's tale of his bold adventures across the Pacific, as detailed in his book, a copy of which he gifted me. However, what made the trip exceptional was my association with the Tahitian Chinese, mainly from Hong Kong.

On the first day after meeting researchers as part of my work, I strolled into the Chinese Association office and asked for Mr Kwok Tzi-fai 郭子輝. Mr Kwok was the Association's past president, who was recommended to me by Professor Wang Gungwu of ANU in the earlier part of my trip. That meeting with Mr Kwok opened the door to the Chinese community. Over the next few days, I enjoyed many sumptuous meals, visits to homes, and a performance of Tahitian dances. To top it all, a farewell dinner in my honour attended by over 200 people was held in the Association's premises. For the occasion, they even roasted a cow, rather than a pig, as the latter is not suitable for me. Overall, I was overwhelmed by the hospitality shown by the Chinese community and impressed by their prominent leadership in almost every major sector of the Tahitian economy. During my stay in Papeete, I met many overseas Chinese, including Chan Chong-cheung 陳中昌, Chan Sau-san 陳秀山, Yau Hon-hing 丘漢興, Siu Shi-yung 蕭時雍, Robert Wan 温惠仁, Guy Yeung 楊偉華, Emmanuel Lou 盧法安, among others, including a Mr Fu 符 who drove me around for appointments. I was able to strike a cordial note with many of them, as they were eager to know things about Hong Kong. We had a common interest in Queen's College, where at least one of them had studied before, and in playing in a top basketball team in Hong Kong that I was familiar with. The wealth exhibited by these Chinese was almost legendary, as was hinted at during my visit to the home of one of the newly made friends. Gazing at the view from his residence on the slope of a hill, my host proudly said, "What you can see from here is owned by me!" I also came away with the idea that there was good division of labour and talent among the Chinese. Each of the main economic sectors appeared to be dominated by at least one Chinese entrepreneur. The only regret that I have about my wonderful trip to

Tahiti is that I have not been successful in maintaining contact with the friends that I made there on that visit.

Another island country stopover in Seychelles began on 5 August 1978. What was intended as a stopover of three days from Mombasa to Colombo turned into six because of a strike by the staff of British Airways. Accommodation and meals were paid for by the airline, but the challenge I faced was how to use the extra days usefully and have a holiday at the same time. In the Bel Air Hotel where I stayed, I was put at the annex with several other passengers. I became acquainted with Mike William, who taught English at the Technical College in Birmingham. We happened to have access to a car owned by another person staying at the annex. Mike and I shared the job of driving around the island for a whole day, chalking up a total of 75 miles by the time we returned to the hotel for dinner. We visited Victoria, the main town and capital of the country, but it was deserted on Sunday. We saw almost all of the major sights, mainly from the many posh hotels that were open or under construction. The next few days we took public bus to key places, such as the Botanical Gardens and Beau Vallon Bay Hotel. In the former, I saw the Coco de Mer, the largest coconut in the world, also known as the "love nut" because the "double" coconut resembles a woman's buttocks. The second striking object I saw there was the Giant Tortoise, said to be largest of its kind in the world. These are the two "firsts" of Seychelles in the world, as I recall. Apart from reading two autobiographies, by Sukarno and Jawaharlal Nehru, and catching up with my IDRC paper work, I ventured to try paragliding for the first time, from the beach at the Beau Vallon Bay Hotel. The view from the air while being dragged by a speed boat was exhilarating. I also tried to water ski, but failed at the activity. I viewed this stopover in Seychelles as an enforced holiday that added to my stock of happy memories.

Fourth, of all of the many conference trips I have made during my career, the one that took place for five days from 5 September 1978 in Manila was one of a kind. Initiated by the First Lady, Mrs Imelda

Marcos, International Conference on the Survival of Humankind: The Philippine Experiment, served multiple purposes. It was said to be the Habitat country conference for the Philippines held after the UN Habitat Conference in Vancouver in 1972. Apart from its focus on population and related problems confronting humanity, the conference was held as a trial run for the IMF-World Bank conference that the Philippines would host in the following month. Attended by 130 foreign participants from 28 countries, it was viewed as one of the most important conferences ever held in the Philippines. On arrival at the Manila airport, I was whisked to the VIP lounge. Tailors were on hand to take my measurements, as the First Lady would present to me three long-sleeved barong tagalogs, the formal Philippine dress shirt for men. There were other gifts from her awaiting me when I checked into Philippine Village Hotel. As I emerged from the airport, a driver and a security guard with an assigned car took me to the hotel. The security guard, car, and driver, would accompany me for the entire duration of my stay, truly an advance trial of arrangements for the IMF-World Bank meeting.

Apart from the academic meetings that were the main fare of the conference, some of the related activities involving the participation of the President and First Lady Marcos made the conference special and memorable. They spoke, for instance, at the inauguration of the Philippine International Convention Centre (PICC), a major facility that could seat 5,000 people. From there we went to Malacañang, the presidential palace, where red carpet, candlelight, flowers, mahogany furniture, and other features made the scene resemble a state dinner. We saw impressive performances, including that by the famous Bayanihan cultural troupe. At the end of the academic programme at lunch on 9 August, the First Lady announced that the President would invite all participants to a cruise to Corregidor Island on the presidential yacht, Ang Pangulo. We set sail at 4 in the afternoon, with a majority of the delegates. The voyage took about 2.5 hours either way, and plenty of fruits and food were served on board for the buffet dinner. Corregidor Island became famous because Philippine and American troops fought together from here against Japanese invaders during the Second War World. We toured the major exhibits after landing at 8 p.m. and left after two hours. On the way back, Carmen Patena, one the top Philippine artists, sang a series of songs in different languages while we enjoyed our late dinner. We returned to Manila at almost 1 a.m. It was a week of glamorous gatherings, the orchestration of organizational details, and soul-searching. It was a unique experience and a glittering display of royal hospitality that I have not seen equaled since.

Fifth, another international meeting was held from 26 May 2002 for five days in Seoul and I brought Ameda along for the experience. The Metropolis Congress was held with an international focus, in which I was invited to play a role. The conference itself was not particularly special, but the related programmes were exceptional. I paid a high fee to register Ameda as an accompanied person. The programme to introduce Korea to the visitors was outstanding. It included visiting the Northern Village, Folk Village, Seoul Emergency Centre, and Changdeokgung Palace 昌德宮(one of five main palaces in Korea, named a UNESCO Heritage Site in 1997; it reminded me of the Forbidden City in Beijing). President Kim Dae Chong officiated at the opening ceremony of the Congress, addressing the gathering. The dinner banquet was hosted in wonderful style by Mayor Goh Kun of Seoul at Gyeonghuigung Palace, making it grand and memorable. Dinner was served in the open court, with performances to entertain us. By previous arrangement, the Congress was concluded in an exceptional style. Participants and accompanying persons (the latter having to pay pricy tickets) were invited to watch the opening match of the World Cup held in Seoul. Ameda and I went promptly to have the standing buffet first before entering the stadium to watch the opening ceremony and shows. The opening match between the last World Cup champion France and Senegal ended in a surprise defeat of the former by 0:1. I have attended many international conferences before, but this week in Seoul stands out from others for its superb organization, the places visited, the dignitaries who played their part, and the World Cup opening and match. Altogether, it was a week of exceptional experiences that can hardly be replicated.

Sixth and last, I touch briefly on a privileged and unusual trip, as a guest of Cathay Pacific (CX) in Hong Kong to help take possession of a new airplane in Toulouse, France over three days from 19 October 2010. Twelve of us from largely political and other circles were invited to make the special trip. After using the first-class lounge at the Hong Kong International Airport, we left on a late evening flight to fly business class on a CX overnight flight to Paris. We arrived at 5.30 a.m. the next morning and, after killing some two hours at Charles de Gaulle Airport, we took a short flight of an hour to Toulouse. We were put up in the Crowne Plaza Hotel at the centre of town. We had a short tour of Toulouse, which is France's third-largest city with a population of about 1 million. The next day at the Airbus Centre we listened to some presentations about the airline business. This was followed by a visit to Carcassonne, an ancient castle town that is well preserved to this day. We very much enjoyed our lunch and the ensuing tour of the town. On the third day we visited the Airbus Centre again, and after lunch there was a ceremony to receive a brand new Airbus 330-300 plane, with speeches, cocktails, and photos. With the other staff members of Cathay Pacific who had been rewarded for their good work, about 50 of us boarded the sparkling new plane. We flew in it and touched down at Chek Lap Kok after 12 hours at 12.30 p.m. the next day Hong Kong time. It was a visit that was special and memorable. The visit to the Airbus factory and business centre added new dimensions to my understanding of the airline business and technological improvements that I would not otherwise have known.

A WATER BUCK IN NAIROBI NATIONAL PARK, 1978

15 Forty-six Magic Moments

As a theme continued from the previous chapter based on my travels, this concluding chapter presents the truly exceptional scenes that I have selected from my stock of travel experiences. I consider these to be natural and man-made wonders of outstanding value and significance. To me, they had the effect of creating magic moments that have been stored in my memory. I consider myself to have been extremely fortunate to have travelled so much and have so many possible candidates to choose from. I shall present 10 scenes in each category with some brief descriptions. Under each category I shall select another 13 scenes, with only scant comments.

Natural Wonders

1. Safari – Going on a safari was my favourite pastime in East Africa, and one that I engaged in whenever I had the time to travel to a national park to come face-to-face with animals and see them in the wild. Whether it is a Thompson gazelle, a cheetah, or a lion that one encounters, staring into each other's eyes in the open field does create a different kind of sensation in an individual than one would experience anywhere else. From my first visit and several subsequent visits to Nairobi National Park on the outskirts of the city in March 1978, with the exception of the elephant I saw all the Big Five (elephant, rhino, buffalo, leopard, and lion) and other animals. In November 1983 after a duty trip to Tanzania, I arranged a weekend trip to Namanga National Park in Amboseli near the Kenya-Tanzania border. There were many more animals in this much larger park, with elephants present in abundance. In fact, the destructive behaviour of the elephants on the vegetation was clear and widespread. This was

LAKE LOUISE, CANADIAN ROCKIES, 2007

one difference between the two national parks that I visited.

2. Banff Lake Louise – Banff and Lake Louise are often mentioned in one breath because they typify some of the most scenic landscapes in Canada. Situated a short distance north of Calgary, Banff and Lake Louise are often visited in the same day excursion. Banff National Park has the distinction of being the first national park established in Canada and has been designated by UNESCO as a World Heritage Site. Lake Louise, on the other hand, is much smaller and is an Alpine lake that is set against impressive glacier-clad peaks, even during the summer. Moraine Lake is an added attraction nearby because of its indigo blue waters. Altogether, Banff Lake and Louise offer unspoiled wilderness, modern amenities, and opportunities for hiking, cycling, and outdoor activities that rival the best of their kind. Most of my visits to the area took place during the summer.

3. Landscaped mountains in Southern Utah – If the Canadian Rockies are breath-taking in their charm and serenity, the mountains of southern Utah spread across several national parks are spectacular in a different fashion. In a region that is relatively dry, wind erosion over a long period has worked miracles and given rise to landscapes that result from aeolian processes eroding and denuding landforms. After attending the AAG annual meeting in April 1983 held in Denver, Colorado, I joined a post-conference tour to transect the American Rockies from Denver to Las Vegas in three days. Led by two physical geography professors from the University of Utah, we went through several national parks, namely Bryce, Zion, and Arches and saw dry landforms that were truly dazzling. The view from Dead Horse Point is one that I still savour. Landscape arches were very common, although the largest number was found in the Arches National Park. The landscape in this part of the American Rockies offers another type of excitement and natural wonder different from that found in Canada.

THE SUPERB NATURE-MAN SETTING IN RIO DE JANEIRO, 1982

4. Rio de Janeiro setting – The view from Corcovado Mountain and the huge Statue of Jesus Christ in the direction of the Sugar Loaf Mountain and the mixed urban forms of the city is arguably one of the most beautiful in the world. This view presents the best mixture of human settlements and natural surroundings, with bays, bodies of water, sandy beaches, and hills intermingled with human habitats to result in an exceptionally charming urban setting. It is not surprising that Rio de Janeiro has sometimes been regarded as having evolved into an outstanding city that has harnessed man and nature in a most pleasant manner. However, the law and order situation was something else. During my visit in August 1982 to that city to attend the IGU Inter-Congress, some fellow participants were confronted in a rude way through mugging and other unpleasant experiences. Nevertheless, there were other pleasant aspects to our visit that left us with many good memories of this vibrant city.

5. Hong Kong by night – If the geographical setting of Rio is exceptionally picturesque, the skyline of Hong Kong, day or night, is unparalleled in its beauty, orderliness, and density. Set against Victoria Peak and viewed from across Victoria Harbour on the Kowloon waterfront, the Hong Kong skyline as constituted by many signature high-rise buildings and civil structures, is captivating to visitors and residents alike at any time. Although building heights are subject to control for the purposes of town planning, most of the buildings along the Hong Kong waterfront have been built according to needs and taste. The end result is pleasant to look at and functionally efficient. The night scene is even more enchanting, especially at 8 p.m. every night, when A Symphony of Lights begins. This is a multi-media show of lights and sounds emanating from the most famous skyscrapers. The dazzling 10-minute show of light and sound is very much welcomed by everyone, whether tourists or Hong Kong residents. During important occasions such as Chinese New Year and National Day, fireworks over the harbour will light up the sky to the merriment and enjoyment

TURTLE LAYING EGGS, KELANTAN, MALAYSIA, 1979

of all concerned. The colourful and bustling atmosphere along the waterfront is repeated on a daily basis.

6. Turtles Laying Eggs – Sea turtles procreate by laying eggs once a year, reputedly returning to the same beach or even the same spot to do so. When I worked for the IDRC ASRO in Singapore, my colleagues and their families drove in two cars all the way up the eastern coast of Peninsular Malaysia. We arrived in the Kuala Terengganu area and went specifically to Kuala Dungun, a small place along the coast famous for its sandy beach where sea turtles habitually came to lay their eggs. We stayed in a hotel and at 2.15 a.m. on 24 August 1979, we were roused from bed. By the time we arrived at the scene, a small crowd had already gathered. My family of four saw the entire process of a sea turtle laying eggs and was thrilled. Although a turtle lays many eggs, these eggs have become commercial objects that fetch good prices. As a result, it is said that the over-commercialization of the process has led to the risk of sea turtles not being able to renew their species. Incidentally, after watching a turtle lay eggs, we drove all the way north to Kota Bharu where in a kampong we bought some real fresh durians. That was the first time that I was able to eat the "king of fruit" and appreciate its taste after 10 years of living in Singapore. Since that trip, durians have become one of my favourite fruits.

7. Ha Long Bay, Vietnam – Although I made my first trip to Vietnam in 1993 as a UN consultant, it was not until my fourth trip to that country that I finally travelled to Ha Long Bay, the most beautiful part of the country. It was in December 2009 when Ameda and I joined a tour that had a full day in Ha Long Bay as the main attraction. The way to describe the scenery in Ha Long Bay is for one to imagine oneself to be in Guilin in China, but in an open sea environment and surrounded all the time by limestone beauty. Ha Long Bay belongs to Ha Long City in Quang Ninh province, situated 170 km east of Hanoi. It boasts of scenic ocean karst topography and has become

HA LONG BAY, VIETNAM, 2008

ENDLESS RAPESEED FIELDS, LUOPING, YUNNAN, 2009

a popular travel destination because of its unspoiled natural beauty. Several islands there can be climbed to attain panoramic views. The bay, with a core area of 334 sq km, features thousands of limestone islands of varying shapes and sizes. Listed as a UNESCO Heritage Site in 1994, Ha Long Bay is the top tourist destination in Vietnam and is on lists of natural wonders of the world.

8. Guilin, China – Like Ha Long Bay in Vietnam, Guilin, located in the northeastern part of Guangxi, has drawn its fame from ancient times because of its karst topography. The most scenic part of the area is best appreciated by taking a boat ride on the Lijiang from Guilin to Yangshuo over a distance of 84 km. It has been said that, "The most scenic part of China is Guilin, and the most scenic within Guilin is Yangshuo". The exceptional beauty of the limestone landscape is derived from its "verdant hills, sparkling water, eccentric caverns, and exquisite stones," as the popular saying has it. On the boat trip from the city of Guilin to Yangshuo one passes countless amazing landscapes that lift one's spirits. The boat trip can be complemented by visits to amazing and well-lit limestone caverns with innumerable stalactites and stalagmites within the area. Not surprisingly, Guilin has been listed as the second most beautiful place in China after the Great Wall in "China's 10 Scenic Places".

9. Luoping Flower Field – Every year from early February to late March, Yunnan's Luoping draws thousands upon thousands of visitors and photographers from all over China and Japan who come for a spectacular sight. This is the sight of yellow fields that stretch almost as far as the eye can see. The fields are devoted to the growing of rapeseed plants, the flowers of which produce seeds from which edible oil is extracted. The bright yellow flowering plant is a member of the Brassicaceae family (brassica napus). The fields of flowering rape have the ability to attract crowds, and hence have become a vehicle for some communities to develop a tourist industry. Similarly extensive

and colourful fields are found in Wuyuan in Jiangxi province and Huangshan in Anhui province. The fields of yellow stem from human endeavour, but the result is a natural phenomenon of gargantuan proportions. My visit to Luoping in February 2009 is filed in my mind as one of the most splendid sights I have seen.

10. Yuanyang Rice Terraces – During the same trip to Yunnan in February 2009, another highlight was visit to the rice terraces in Yuanyang county, about 300 km south of Kunming near China's border with Vietnam. The terraced fields had been watered shortly before our arrival. Rice cultivation on the terraces has been practised for the past 2,000 years, and is a product of the successful blending of human ingenuity and natural forces. Flooded rice terraces are nuanced objects to watch and photograph, especially during the hours of sunrise and sunset when the angled and colourful light provides ideal conditions for photography. The terraced fields are magnificent and on a colossal scale, occupying as much as 2,200 sq km. They stand as a monument to the traditional ingenuity of the Hani minority, who have been living there for untold generations. The Yuanyang rice terraces are the world's largest and most spectacular example of their kind, and are a reflection of wisdom inherited from a distant past. With its age-old rice farming techniques, hilly topography, and beautiful weather, the area is truly a scenic wonder of China.

In addition to the above ten natural wonders, I would add another thirteen with briefer introductions.

1. Yellowstone National Park – This was the first national park in the world. Established by the USA in 1872, the practice of designating an area of land a national park has spread to other countries. Essentially a huge mountainous area of wild country, it has one of the best-preserved natural ecosystems in the Earth's temperate zone. It has the world's largest collection of geysers, including Old Faithful.

AT A NATIONAL PARK IN SOUTHERN UTAH, 1983

2. Huangshan, China – A UNESCO World Heritage Site, Huangshan is a mountain range in southern Anhui province in eastern China. A major tourist destination, Huangshan has been a subject of traditional Chinese paintings and literature, and is famed for its scenery, sunsets, granite peaks, pine trees, and views of the clouds from above.

3. Hailougou, China - Possibly the largest low-latitude and low-altitude glacier in the world, it is only 380 km southwest of Chengdu, Sichuan. Easily accessible on conducted tours, Hailougou boasted of a huge glacier of 31 sq km, with a tongue of 5.7 km and many hot springs. Our visit in February 2008 offered many spectacular sights after fresh snowfall and bright sunshine.

4. Kashmir, India – In weather, vegetation, and natural conditions, it is highly similar to the Alps in Europe. It is a complicated place, politically and ethnically, but it is a jewel of natural beauty, for which

reason and others it has been the subject of fighting between India and Pakistan.

5. Java's rice fields – The view from my train window on a trip from Yogyakarta to Jakarta in 1973 was unforgettable. I saw rice being harvested in the paddy fields of Java by hundreds of people at the same time. Never have I seen so many people working at the same time for a harvest. It was intensive agriculture at its height.

6. Niah Cave – On a reconnaissance trip across the Trans-Sarawak Highway in April 1976, a stopover in Niah near Miri provided me with the opportunity to visit Niah Cave. It is huge – at least the size of a football field, with wooden structures and ladders built to enable pickers to climb up to collect birds' nests, regarded as a delicacy.

7. Niagara Falls – The ferocious waterfalls between Canada and the United States are a natural wonder because of the huge volume of water that courses down and because the falls can be approached from very close up. I have seen it in both winter and summer, and from down below the falls for a special experience. The surroundings have become very commercialized over the years.

8. Jungfrau, Switzerland – In a stopover in Interlaken, Switzerland, most people take a train that climbs slowly up and down the Jungfrau, a snow-clad mountain at the top. The view from the train window was, for me, just like a lesson in physical geography. Apart from the exceptionally scenic Swiss mountain views, examples of U-shaped valleys, overhanging waterfalls, and other landscape features bearing evidence of former glacial erosion were readily visible. The trip up and down the mountain took the greater part of one day.

9. Skating on the Rideau Canal – Ice skating is a favourite and common pastime in Canada. However, skating on the Rideau Canal

along the streets and against the backdrop of downtown Ottawa is a natural wonder that can be enjoyed at no cost, and was an activity that my family would never forget.

10. Shilin in Yunnan – Situated 85 km east of Kunming, Shilin County is home to a host of strange rock formations better known as the Stone Forest. The karst geology and geomorphology have given rise to endless shapes and sizes of stone. No other natural wonder made of stone of its size and variety can be found in China or anywhere else in the world.

11. Qiantang Tidal Wave – The exceptionally strong tidal wave created by the Qiantangjiang every autumn is a tourist attraction. Tragedy sometimes occurs if people do not take sufficient safety precautions. I experienced the phenomenon after lunch on 25 September 1999 during a visit to Hangzhou, which is one of the best places to watch the yearly miracle.

12. Moguicheng, Xinjiang – In northern Xinjiang there is Moguicheng, literally meaning a city of devils because of the weird landforms that have formed due to years of wind erosion. Covering an area of 105 sq km, Moguicheng is reminiscent of the wind-eroded semi-arid landscape that I saw in southern Utah.

13. Hongshixia (Red Stone Gorge), Yuntaishan – Yuntaishan is a large and popular national park in northern Henan that has been designated a UNESCO World Heritage Site. In my visit there in April 2010, I spent three hours going through its Hongshixia. That was the amount of time that I needed to go through the route during off-peak hours, versus five hours during peak times. The route had been carved out of red sandstone to make a passageway for the multitude of visitors. A very impressive canyon that is paired with the Grand Canyon of the United States as sister canyons.

1. Egyptian Pyramids and Temples – Of the wonders of the ancient world, Egyptian pyramids and temples stand out. My first visit to the Great Pyramid of Cheops (Khufu), built in the 4th century, was made in July 1978. The pyramid, found in a cluster of three, was located 7 km away from Cairo. I climbed the inside of the Pyramid of Khufu to get a feeling of its masonry structure. I climbed 150 steps to see the Pharaoh's burial chamber, along one small low passage. There was only one small entrance, but many false ones. This cluster represented only a small proportion of the 138 pyramids found in Egypt. In April 1982 I made my first visit to Luxor and was greatly impressed by what I saw in the Valley of the Kings and of the Queens. In the former my attention was drawn to the location of the tomb of the last boy Pharaoh – Tutankhamun – discovered by British archaeologist Howard Carter in 1922. Karnak Temple and Luxor Temple astonished me with their colossal columns and animal statues. The light and sound show in the

READY TO ENTER THE PYRAMID, CAIRO, 1978

former still ranks among the best that I have ever seen. I was pleased to travel with Ameda in February 2000 to show her the antiquities in both cities. Certainly the pyramids have been ranked among the seven wonders of the ancient world.

2. Teotihuacan (Pyramid of the Sun, the Moon) – In October 1995 after attending an academic meeting in Mexico City, I stayed an extra day to make a trip to see Teotihuacan, 40 km to the northeast. At the destination I found two large structures – the Pyramid of the Sun and the Pyramid of the Moon – located at the end and along one side of a long promenade, respectively. The Pyramid of the Sun was bigger, sitting on a large base. It had about 20 storeys of steps to climb, but the view from the top was magnificent. The story has it that whole site was buried for many years after the pyramids were built. Only a chance discovery by a person led to the ancient structures seeing the light of day. These Mexican pyramids are different from Egyptian pyramids, not only in how they were constructed but in the guiding thoughts and philosophy behind their construction. Mexican pyramids can be climbed, as opposed to being off-limits to people as the ones in Egypt are. Egyptian pyramids were never meant to be climbed.

3. The Great Wall of China – This is one of the greatest engineering feats of man. Built over many centuries and for thousands of miles, the Great Wall was an effective barrier in keeping out nomadic invaders from the north. The main parts of the wall, thousands of miles of it, were constructed in the Ming dynasty between the 14th and 17th centuries. In 1987 UNESCO designated the Great Wall as a World Heritage Site. One of the best and most easily accessible places to appreciate the grandeur of the Great Wall is at Badaling near Beijing, but remnants of the wall can be seen in many parts of northern China. The Badaling section is open to the public and one can get a feeling of the reality and greatness of the Great Wall by actually climbing the steps along the wall.

THE GREAT WALL OF CHINA, BEIJING, 1979

4. The Forbidden City, Beijing – Throughout its long history China saw the rise and fall of dynasties and, with them, the construction and destruction of countless palaces. The Forbidden City at the heart of the present capital of Beijing, completed in 1420 A.D., was, in fact, the Forbidden City of the Ming and Qing dynasties. It had been the home and court of 24 emperors. In 1987 UNESCO announced the Forbidden City to be a World Heritage Site as the major gathering of conserved ancient wooden constructions in the world. The palace is exceptionally rich in what remains of the life of the emperor, his court and work, living conditions, and pleasures behind the high walls that separated imperial life from that of the rest of the country. I was so enraptured by what the palace had to reveal that during my duty visits to Beijing in the early 1980s, I made a point of visiting it every year for four years.

5. Terra Cotta Warriors, Xi'an – Discovered in 1974 by a farmer digging a well in suburban Xi'an, China, were terra cotta warriors in an entire army formation and chariots with horses in intricate detail. These were finely crafted and assembled to guard Emperor Qin Shihuang to his afterlife. The site has become a leading national icon of ancient China under the ruler that first united the country. It consists of a cavernous vault containing the artifacts in several halls. It is almost surreal to go down to the pit and stand next to a life-sized terra cotta warrior of exquisite creation. This is generally regarded as the most important archaeological find in the 20th century, not only in China but in the world.

6. Winter and Summer Palace, St Petersburg – St Petersburg in Russia is the site of the former Winter Palace of the Czar – the Hermitage – which has now become one of top four museums in the world. It occupies a considerable amount of ground in the city. Petrodvorets – the former Summer Palace of a past empire, located 70 km from the city, was razed by the Germans during the Second World War.

TEOTIHUACAN (PYRAMIDS OF SUN AND MOON), MEXICO CITY, 2005

HERMITAGE (WINTER PALACE), ST. PETERSBURG, 1996

Its biggest attraction was its elaborate system of fountains, which has been restored. It was said that Italian designers and engineers assisted with the original design and construction. Dubbed the "Capital of Fountains", the Summer Palace appealed to me during my visit in 1996 as the best of its kind that I have seen anywhere.

7. Basilica, St. Peter's, Rome – The view from the Dome of the Basilica of St Peter's Cathedral in Rome provides, in my experience, the best commanding view of St Peter's Square and beyond of the city. Getting to the Dome involves climbing up a large number of stairs, but one is more than adequately rewarded by the incomparable panoramic views of the church complex and the city. I never failed to climb the Dome to obtain the best views of Rome during my three grand tours of Europe.

8. Eiffel Tower, Paris – An engineering marvel built as the entrance to the 1889 World's Fair hosted by Paris, the Eiffel Tower is a global cultural icon of France. Reaching a height of 320 metres and at various times the highest structure in the world, it is one of the most recognized structures on earth. Named after the engineer who designed and built the tower, the views from its various levels would rank among the best in Paris. From these observation platforms, one can appreciate the evidence of sound urban planning.

9. Agra Taj Mahal, India – The Taj Mahal in Agra, north of New Delhi, is the epitome of Mughal art and is widely recognized as one of the most famous buildings in the world. It was built in 22 years in the 17th century by Shah Jahan as the tomb of his beloved wife. Intended as the home of the Queen in paradise, the building and its grounds on the banks of a river together symbolize Muslim architecture at its best. UNESCO has designated the Taj Mahal as a World Heritage Site.

10. Sydney Opera House – Built on the shore of Sydney Harbour, the Opera House is the pride and symbol of Sydney and Australia. It was

EIFFEL TOWER, 1972

based on the winning design in an international competition by Danish architect Jorn Utzon in 1957. An example of modern architecture that is as functional as it is exquisitely beautiful, construction was a long and challenging process. In 2007 it was included on the list of UNESCO World Heritage sites. I personally have visited the iconic building and seen it from both the inside and outside, near and far, many times, even from the air. It is probably the most photographed building in the city and the country, widely acclaimed for its originality and sheer beauty.

Following the pattern I have used before, I will add another thirteen man-made wonders, as follows.

1. The Butchart Gardens, Canada – In Victoria, BC, Canada, the Butchart Gardens have become a must-see place on Canada's west coast. Built in 1904 by Mrs Butchart, the garden has grown into a complex of 55 acres of stunning floral show gardens. It has become a National Historic Site of Canada, with a year-round floral show programme. A visit from Vancouver is a day-long excursion.

2. Disney World, Orlando – This is a symbol of modern America and its best example of mass entertainment. Much bigger than the original Disneyland in Anaheim near Los Angeles, Disney World consists of a complex of theme parks and water parks, offering magical trips to the Magic Kingdom, Epcot, Animal Hollywood, and so on.

3. The Strip, Las Vegas – Somewhat similar to Disney World, the Strip in Las Vegas clustering facilities and people in several blocks on the main road represents another kind of American mass entertainment and business. The Strip concentrates about a dozen leading posh hotels that feature casinos, conference facilities, and shopping and other attractions for the family and other visitors.

4. Parliament Rooftop, Berlin – Within the imposing traditional

VIEW OF ST. PETER'S SQUARE FROM BASILICA, ROME, 1966

AGRA TAJ MAHAL, 1980

parliament building (Reichstag) in Berlin, completed in 1894, the Bundestag, or the new parliament, was built to mark a Germany newly united since 1990. It is a strikingly attractive and modern glass structure, along which visitors can ascend the spiral staircase to reach the top. The large glass structure was designed by the famous British architect, Norman Foster, in 1999, and built atop the refurbished Reichstag building. At the rooftop, one can enjoy panoramic views of Berlin.

5. Harbin Ice and Snow Festival – Every January a winter festival of ice and snow is held in Harbin, Heilongjiang. It offers a range of ice-related activities, including ice lanterns, ice sculpture competitions, winter outdoor swimming, and various winter sports. Sun Island Park and Songhua River are centres of activity. One has to be prepared for very cold temperatures to enjoy the winter wonderland. In our 2004 visit, the temperature was -26 ℃.

6. Red Square, Moscow – Made famous in part by military parades, the Red Square at the heart of Moscow has many attractions. The impressive halls of the Kremlin dominate one whole side of the square. Other sides are occupied by St Basil's Cathedral, the GUM Store, and the State History Museum. On the Red Square itself is Lenin's Mausoleum.

7. Coliseum, Rome – The remains of a large Roman amphitheatre in the heart of Rome is an iconic structure that reminds us of gladiator combats of the past. It was the largest structure ever built in the Roman Empire, known as much for its beauty as for its bloody history. Very accessible to the public, the Coliseum is one the greatest works of Roman architecture and Roman engineering.

8. Mogao Caves Dunhuang 敦煌莫高窟 – Located along the Hexi Corridor in Gansu province as a major point along the Silk Road, and

SYDNEY OPERA HOUSE FROM THE HARBOUR, 1984

designated a UNESCO World Heritage Site, the Mogao Caves dwarf the three other similar caves in China. The complex of caves totals 735 caves and abounds in frescos, sculptures, and other media that depict life and people over the ages.

9. Angkor Wat, Cambodia – The largest Hindu temple complex in the world, Angkor Wat was built by King Suryavarman in the 12th century as his state temple and capital city. Situated in Angkor in Cambodia, the temple complex is still awesomely beautiful, despite being badly in need of repairs. Cambodians are heirs to the Khmer empire, which prospered in mainland Southeast Asia but declined partly as a result of excessive expenditures on the building of temples.

10. Borobudur, Indonesia – A large-scale Buddhist stupa and temple complex built in central Java from the 8th century. Easily accessible

from Yogyakarta, Borobudur is situated on the Kedu Plain against the backdrop of the volcanically active Mount Merapi, which erupted in late 2010. Declared a UNESCO World Heritage Site, it is the single largest Buddhist structure anywhere in the world, comprised as it is of three platforms with 504 Buddhist stupas.

11. Kecak (Ketjak) Dance, Bali – Originating in the 1930s in Uluwatu, Bali, it is a traditional Ramayana monkey dance performed by a circle of 150 or more performers wearing checked cloth around their waists. Normally set around a bonfire, the performers percussively chant "cak" and throw up their arms in harmony. The atmosphere was unique and exciting as judged by the four dances that I watched in the 1970s and 1980s.

12. Shwedagon Pagoda, Myanmar – Shwedagon Pagoda is a complex of temples, stupas, and statues in the heart of Rangoon (Yangon), with a history going back 1,500 years. The main stupa is mind-boggling, as it is covered with gold and encrusted with rubies, sapphires and, according to one count, 5,448 diamonds. Who would challenge the number? It must have earned the favour of rulers of the past and present in that country.

13. Central bazaar, Istanbul - Situated in the old central city area, the Central Bazaar, or the covered central market is probably the largest of its kind anywhere. With shops in the hundreds and many entrances, it had an atmosphere that is Oriental dating back to ancient times. Although dominated recently by jewellry shops, the range of goods sold was huge.

Epilogue

Individuals write their memoirs for different reasons. To me, my story of coming from a family with roots in Hong Kong for three generations and the account of my own life speaks of a time of rapid change not only in Hong Kong but the world at large. I regard myself as fortunate to have been able to survive the Second World War and to have gone through the early part of my life spatially rooted to a small part of Hong Kong Island – Wanchai – and in later years to have had the chance to roam the world. Even before the onset of rapid globalization, I pursued graduate studies in North America and spent some fifteen years working in Singapore and Ottawa. My work with Canada's International Development Research Centre effectively extended my work domain to the entire world. International agencies were our peers and constant travels took me to different parts of the world.

This story of a Hongkonger is exceptional in that it is a reflection of a native-born individual with deep roots in Hong Kong. He returned to his native land to serve its people and institutions. He has seen and experienced so much of the world that his career is worth telling to readers in Hong Kong and beyond. The essence of this story is encapsulated in the title of the book.

There are other reasons for writing this memoir. Under the impact of accelerating globalization and the shadow of the handover in Hong Kong, many Hongkongers chose to emigrate ahead of the 1997 political jitters. My family was no exception. Many in my generation and the next have settled down in Canada, the United States, Australia, China, and Singapore. Some occasionally visit Hong Kong, but their understanding of Hong Kong and the original family from which they have descended is extremely limited. To a small extent, this memoir will enable them to trace their roots.

In fact, with my family having Muslim roots in China from as far back as the late Ming dynasty, it is my belief that many of the turning points in my own life were guided by my religious convictions. Although only incidental references have been made to the Islamic teachings and their influence on my family, it is my fervent hope that through this book younger generations of my family will discover, or feel inspired to search for, at least some part of their Muslim roots. It is a challenge to carry on the Islamic faith in Western countries, but wherever our younger generations may live, I would urge them to discover this faith that has critically guided me in my journey through life.

More broadly, this memoir contains the gems of my life experiences and the turning points of a career that simply unfolded according to its own logic and to chance. The element of chance was prominent at several stages. I was able to achieve much on many fronts largely as a result of opportunities that came my way. The critical element was that I was ready for the call of duty. In my view, there is much in my life story that may be of benefit to younger readers. Do not be disheartened by what appear to be wretched disappointments at the time. They might be important turning points in your career for better things to come. If you learn from failures and prepare yourself, you may have even better opportunities at a later time. My career flourished largely as a result of several turning points that I did not plan or anticipate. As someone with deep religious beliefs, I can only thank the Almighty for where and how I was led.

I have dedicated this book to my parents and to other individuals who have helped shape my life and career. I would also dedicate this memoir to the younger generation of Hong Kong, upon which the value, competitiveness, and unique role of this geographically beautiful and strategically pivotal city will rest.